AMERICANS IN PARIS

For A. Walton Litz
with many thanks
from the grateful author

AMERICANS IN PARIS

George Wickes

GEORGE WICKES

NEW FOREWORD BY
VIRGIL THOMSON

& new indebtedness
duly acknowledged
on p. 278.

A DA CAPO PAPERBACK

Library of Congress Cataloging in Publication Data

Wickes, George.
Americans in Paris.

(A Da Capo paperback)
Reprint of the ed. published by Doubleday, Garden City, N.Y.
1. Americans in Paris. 2. Paris – Intellectual life. 3. American literature – 20th century – History and criticism. I. Title.
[DC718.A44W5 1980] 001.3'094436 80-18371
ISBN 0-306-80127-2 (pbk.)

A selection from AMERICANS IN PARIS
first appeared in
THE PARIS REVIEW

This Da Capo Press paperback edition of *Americans in Paris* is an unabridged republication of the first edition published in New York in 1969 by Doubleday and Company, Inc., supplemented with a new Foreword by Virgil Thomson. It is reprinted by arrangement with the author.

Published by Da Capo Press, Inc.
A Subsidiary of Plenum Publishing Corporation
227 West 17th Street, New York, N.Y. 10011

Manufactured in the United States of America

FOREWORD

It Was Like That

With the ending of the Franco-Prussian War in 1871, liberated Paris became almost overnight the European center of advance in painting and poetry. Even in music, never a major specialty there, and in spite of the grand finale of German music being staged in full panoply by Wagner and Brahms, new ways of writing it were popping up in France. And as always, a handful of Americans were around for picking up the new ways and depicting the new life-style. Henry James himself was among them, and all those budding Impressionist painters who would formerly have gone to Rome or Munich.

A second stage of Paris leadership began with the new century, and its American followers are the subject of this book. It describes a family from San Francisco named Stein—Michael and Sarah (espoused), Leo and Gertrude (siblings), who took residence on the Left Bank beginning in 1903. They all started right off buying pictures, pooling their funds. Gertrude and Leo were also writing books. Instinctively they all bought the newest art there was—Matisses and Picassos, which were never even shown to the public before 1905—and in 1906 a sizable Cézanne. Also new was Gertrude's writing; nothing quite like it existed anywhere. Just as Cubist painting was to burst out full-blown in 1909, Gertrude's *Tender Buttons* was to follow in 1913, a literary masterpiece still explosive and still (which was its aim) incomprehensible.

World War I and its aftermath brought to France four young, about-to-be-major American writers—e.e. cummings, John Dos

Passos, Scott Fitzgerald, and Ernest Hemingway. For all of them France was the impetus and coloration of their ripening.

In 1921 Aaron Copland and Virgil Thomson arrived, in 1923 George Antheil (by way of Berlin), in 1926 Roy Harris from California. And by 1926 Walter Piston and Roger Sessions had come under the influence. That influence, for all of these young composers, was in general Paris, France—but more specifically, except in the case of Antheil, the precepts and pedagogy of Nadia Boulanger. And it was those other five, via Paris and Boulanger, who constituted from the mid-twenties to the late thirties a sort of commando unit which invaded every domain of music and procured for us all and for our younger colleagues the recognition at home and in Europe that Americans had so long hoped for.

George Wickes's book ends in 1939 with the return to America of Henry Miller, another writer of major status and also one following predominantly European models, in his case James Joyce and Louis-Ferdinand Céline. I am glad Miller got in. Mostly Miller is either left out or considered a special case, simply because he arrived late, after 1929, when the already famous ones were leaving. But Miller is a part of the great American invasion that took place exactly as Wickes dates it, from 1903 to 1939. And he is the end of it. After the next war everything was to be different. Europe was much weaker artistically and America was stronger. Also Europe was to become more and more expensive. In the old days, when our pennies were like dollars, one could have for almost nothing the richest life an artist could imagine. Read about it and weep.

VIRGIL THOMSON
New York City
June 1980

CONTENTS

ILLUSTRATIONS

WHY PARIS

In the doubtful autumn of 1939 when Frenchmen were being mobilized and demobilized and no one knew whether this time there was going to be a war or not, Gertrude Stein had retired to the mountain village of Bilignin where for many years she had spent her summers. It was a good place to be at that uncertain time, removed from the highroad of armies and political turbulence, close to the soil, where one could be sure of finding enough to eat if the worst happened. Gertrude Stein hoped that the worst would not happen, but she thought it prudent to be prepared. She took a detached view of political events, a characteristic French view that daily life went on anyhow through wars and turmoil. After all, she had been through one war already.

So in 1939, when another war threatened, she stayed on in Bilignin after the summer was over, she and her inseparable companion of thirty-odd years, Alice Toklas. They were to weather the war in that part of France and to come through it quite well, considering that they were both Jewish and American. For even in occupied France they enjoyed a privileged status that protected them from the Germans.

It was in Bilignin some seven years before that Gertrude Stein had written her memoirs, *The Autobiography of Alice B. Toklas.* Now once again the place gave her the leisure, and the times put her in a reflective mood. By now she had spent more than half of her life in Paris, and she had childhood memories of Paris going back to the age of four. Looking back over sixty years' experience, she wrote *Paris France,* a loving tribute to the city, the country, and the people. In its unpretentious way this little book explains why a wise old American woman had made France her home for most of her life and would stay there till the end. It also explains better than anything else that has been written what Paris and France meant to American writers and artists during the first four decades of this century.

"Paris, France is exciting and peaceful," the book begins, suggesting both the stimulus of the great metropolis and the well-ordered calm of its everyday life that made Paris a good place to live. Like most Americans who stayed for any length of time, Gertrude Stein lived *bourgeoisement* in a quiet neighborhood where she did her marketing, walked her dog, and knew all sorts of ordinary citizens. This side of Paris was as important to her as any, and she found the daily life congenial, democratic, easy, and comfortable. At the same time people respected her privacy and let her live as she chose, free from the pressures for conformity that she would have felt in America. Such qualities, she felt, made the French the most civilized people on earth. For the Americans who found Paris a good environment to live and work in, French civilization did not necessarily mean the sort of thing taught in courses for foreigners at the Sorbonne—the Gothic cathedrals, the court of Louis XIV, Racine and Corneille. Gertrude Stein pays no attention to the official glories in *Paris France*. Instead she tells little anecdotes which demonstrate how civilized the ordinary Frenchman is in his daily life—how sensitive, unsentimental, polite, frank, reserved, logical, and sensible. The French, she finds, have a down-to-earth understanding of the basic facts of life and death, the family and the soil.

"But really what they do do is to respect art and letters, if you are a writer you have privileges, if you are a painter you have privileges and it is pleasant having those privileges." Underlying French civilization is a traditional respect for certain values, which Gertrude Stein illustrates through an anecdote about having her car parked in an already overcrowded garage, a homely instance of the rule that in France a woman of letters takes precedence over a millionaire or a politician. As many Americans have discovered to their surprise, the police and other authorities tend to treat artists and writers deferentially, regarding them as useful members of the commonwealth, not as oddities or parasites. The French take it for granted that the arts have a place in the national well-being. This does not mean that every Frenchman aspires to be an artist or would substitute art for plumbing, but simply that he recognizes its function and respects its practitioner. To an artist coming from a land where altogether different values exerted pressure on the arts, the French attitude was a reassuring source of self-respect.

More specifically, Gertrude Stein theorizes about the impact of Paris on the modern arts. Much of the book is devoted to the thesis that "Paris was where the twentieth century was." Civilization and the arts are governed by mysterious laws. For some undiscovered reason certain ages and certain countries are more creative than others. After speculating about the alternatives, Gertrude Stein concludes that Paris was the right place to be from 1900 to 1939. England refused to leave the nineteenth century, America was overwhelmed by the technology of the twentieth century, but France remained relatively unaffected. In an age when the new science made the world a disturbing place, Paris still gave the impression that the world was round. She was both modern and traditional, she accepted change but did not let it change her, and thus she provided a background of cultural stability conducive to the arts. "So Paris was the place that suited those of us that were to create the twentieth century art and literature, naturally enough."

Certainly Paris was where the avant-garde was, the great international center for creative experiment in all the arts. Most of the creating, according to Gertrude Stein, was done by foreign artists and writers. Paris had always been hospitable to foreign artists, and in the twentieth century the three great geniuses of Paris—Picasso in painting, Stravinsky in music, Joyce in literature—were all foreigners. There was plenty of native genius too, providing a rich humus for the cultivation of new talent.

Experiment was the keynote of the arts of Paris. All kinds of new movements and styles proliferated there, in a constant evolution from the turn of the century on—fauvism, cubism, dada, surrealism, to mention only the major developments. And all the arts worked together in Paris in a total synthesis that enriched them all. To an American working in relative isolation or at best in a Greenwich Village, such an atmosphere opened up new worlds and enlarged his sensitivity to all the arts.

Inevitably the question of expatriation arises. Why couldn't the artist stay home and be just as creative? Why must he go whoring after foreign fashions? There are several answers, the best of them provided by Gertrude Stein: "America is my country but Paris is my home town." She always remained thoroughly American and found that living in France made her more aware of her native country. She had a theory that a writer must live abroad to be fully alive to his inner feelings and able to express himself. "That is why writers have to have two countries, the one where they belong and the one in which they live really." She was not an expatriate in the sense of being an exile; she never felt alienated from her native land. She had gone to Europe in response to a deep-seated cultural instinct. The distinction is an important one, for the expatriates discussed in this book went abroad for positive rather than negative reasons. Some of them may have been at odds with their society, but the important thing is that they settled in Paris to work seriously.

This book is not about that overworked subject, the rootless expatriates of the lost generation. It is about the American writers, artists, and composers who lived and worked in Paris during the first four decades of this century. A certain amount of anecdote is part of the story, but the point is not that the protagonists were odd characters who did funny things but that they were artists who did highly original things. Bohemia is part of the setting, not because *la vie de bohème* is picturesque but because Bohemia is where the avant-garde was.

So many Americans went to Paris that it is impossible to do them all justice. This book does not even mention Alexander Calder, Glenway Wescott, Stuart Davis, Katherine Anne Porter, Peggy Guggenheim, Janet Flanner, Abraham Rattner, and a hundred others. Since the subject is inexhaustible, it seemed best to focus on a few exemplary figures who would then stand for all the others. These artists, writers, or composers all lived in Paris for an appreciable length of time—several years, a decade, half a lifetime—and produced some of their most significant work there—in most cases their best work. Individually and collectively, they present an impressive record of the impact of Paris on the American imagination.

Paris meant something different to each of them, a pleasant ambiance, a sense of freedom, a foreign temperament that challenged and complemented their own, or a way of life conducive to creation. All of them found it a good place to work. Naturally they learned about their art and craft from the artists they encountered. What they produced cannot be called French, though one or two adopted a Parisian style, and none was unaffected. Chiefly they felt the all-pervasive classical spirit of France, even in an iconoclastic age. Under this influence they became more conscious of form, style, language, or medium than any previous generation of Americans.

Each of them responded differently to the opportunities Paris offered. Before the war Gertrude Stein and her circle collected the modern art of Paris, with far-reaching consequences for American art—and perhaps literature. In her experimental writing Gertrude Stein seemed to be imitating the cubist painters. Daniel-Henry Kahnweiler, the great apostle of cubism, sees close similarities between her writing, Schoenberg's music, and the painting of Picasso and Gris. But perhaps the analogy can be pushed too far. One of the so-called cubist poets, Pierre Reverdy, rejected the whole notion: "*La poésie cubiste? Terme ridicule!*" Picasso himself, when Gertrude Stein's brother Leo asked his opinion, did not see how words could be used abstractly, apart from their meanings. In any case Gertrude Stein evolved as a writer during a period which she spent mostly in the company of painters, surrounded by French-speaking people. These circumstances may account for her idiosyncratic style. Then too, living abroad left her free from the restraints of convention, free to develop the eccentricity that was an essential part of her talent.

E. E. Cummings and John Dos Passos represent the war experience of their generation that brought them to Paris in the first place and induced them to return afterward. This is the story told by Malcolm Cowley in *Exile's Return*, the best chronicle of his generation's collective experience. The "gentlemen volunteers" he writes about were more privileged than the doughboys and their experience less typical, but they happened to be more literate, so their war record remains. Cowley lists the writers who drove ambulances and camions during the last two years of the war: Cummings, Dos Passos, Hemingway, Slater Brown, Robert Hillyer, John Howard Lawson, Julian Green, William Seabrook, Harry Crosby, Sidney Howard, Louis Bromfield, and Dashiell Hammett. Almost all of them returned to Paris during the early twenties. Cowley feels that the war uprooted his contemporaries by transporting them to a foreign land where they became mere spectators with no share in what was going on, that the armistice left them both disengaged from society and restless for further adventures. But there were plenty of good positive reasons for going to Paris after the war, beginning with the fact that many Americans had fallen in love with its charms while in uniform.

After the war American poets flocked to the city of Villon and Baudelaire. Besides Cummings, Robert Hillyer, Ezra Pound, William Carlos Williams, Archibald MacLeish, Stephen Vincent Benét, Allen Tate, and Hart Crane all gravitated to Paris, some staying four or five years. Before the war T. S. Eliot had studied philosophy at the Sorbonne for a year and even contemplated becoming a French poet like the two American-born symbolists, Stuart Merrill and Francis Vielé-Griffin. After the war Pound spent four years in Paris, where his Montparnasse studio was the scene of his multifarious activities as sculptor, composer, editor, literary dictator, and occasionally poet. Through their poetry and criticism Eliot and Pound made American writers more susceptible to French literature than ever before. Laforgue, Eliot said toward the end of his life, "was the first to teach me how to speak," and the symbolists, he added, "are now as much in our bones as Shakespeare or Donne."

Ernest Hemingway, more than any other American, epitomizes Montparnasse in its heyday, a glamorous, legendary Arcadia for postwar disillusionment. Actually Hemingway was critical of its wastrels and poseurs, as were most serious writers. Still Montparnasse was the headquarters of the American literary avant-garde in the twenties, and scornful or not, the writers congregated in its cafés. Quite a few of them were first published there in little magazines or in subsidized volumes produced by amateur publishers. Hemingway himself owed much to both and even played his part in editing Ford Madox Ford's *Transatlantic Review*. Hemingway spent his apprentice years in Paris, produced much of his best work there, and later looked back upon those years as his best.

Man Ray also lived in Montparnasse, but his orbit was less exclusively American. In fact he knew no Americans at first and was surrounded by French poets and artists from the moment of his arrival. In New York during the war he had belonged to a circle that included several Parisian refugees and with two of them had formed the nucleus that was later known as New York dada. Thus when he went to Paris a few years later, he was welcomed by the local dadaists. Of the many American artists who worked in Paris, two in particular were accepted as members of French movements, Mary Cassatt in the nineteenth century and Man Ray in the twentieth. Just as she had settled down among the impressionists, so he became identified with the dadaists and surrealists successively. During the period between the wars he played a conspicuous part on the Paris art scene as a master technician who experimented in all the visual arts.

Virgil Thomson represents the generation of composers that chose Paris as the best place to study music. Like most of his contemporaries he felt the need for a cosmopolitan setting to develop his gifts and instinctively rejected the Germanic musical tradition which prevailed in America. During the teens of this century Paris suddenly emerged as an international center of music and ballet. During the twenties many young American composers studied with Nadia Boulanger, acquiring from that great teacher a liberal education as well as a classical discipline. To American audiences French music still meant Debussy, but composers in Paris like Thomson and George Antheil felt the more modern influence of Erik Satie and the neoclassicism of Stravinsky. Antheil had a brief, precocious career in Paris in the mid-twenties. Thomson, who had to wait until the thirties for recognition, introduced America to a new concept of musical theater with *Four Saints in Three Acts,* a work that achieved a synthesis of the arts in the Parisian manner.

Henry Miller went to Paris when most of the Americans were coming home. In New York he had long felt the influence of Paris through such manifestations as the Armory Show and little magazines like *Transition.* He had been writing for years but had been completely frustrated in his efforts to express himself. Paris was the catalyst he needed. The city satisfied his emotional, intellectual, and creative needs as New York had never done. There he was able to find himself as a writer and do his best work in the dadaist and surrealist vein. There he found the material for his first published novel and the only conceivable place where it could be published. In one of the earliest reviews of *Tropic of Cancer* Edmund Wilson called the book "the epitaph for the whole generation of American writers and artists that migrated to Paris after the war." The book can also be read as a satire on that generation, exposing all the comic and sordid reality behind the romantic expatriate myth. In his cancerous view Miller best represents the period of the depression and the foreshadowing of a second world war that was to bring the era to a close.

THE MOTHER OF US ALL

CHRONOLOGY I

1903	Leo Stein rents studio at 27 rue de Fleurus, begins painting, buys his first Cézanne. In September Gertrude Stein comes to live at 27 rue de Fleurus
1904	Picasso moves to Paris
1904–06	Gertrude Stein writes *Three Lives* (published 1909)
1905	Fauves at the Autumn Salon Gertrude and Leo Stein buy their first Matisse and Picasso
1906	Picasso, *Portrait of Gertrude Stein* Matisse, *Le Bonheur de Vivre*
1906–08	Gertrude Stein writing *The Making of Americans* (published 1925)
1907	Picasso, *Les Demoiselles d'Avignon* Picasso meets Braque Alice Toklas arrives in Paris
1908	Braque paints his first cubist landscapes at l'Estaque in homage to Cézanne First cubist exhibition, paintings by Braque at Kahnweiler's gallery The Rousseau banquet Gertrude Stein begins writing portraits
1909	Kahnweiler exhibits Picasso's early cubism
1911–12	Juan Gris joins cubists Collage invented by Picasso and Braque
1912	Gertrude Stein, *The Portrait of Mabel Dodge at the Villa Curonia*
1913	Armory Show introduces the School of Paris to America, Matisse burned in Chicago
1914	Gertrude Stein, *Tender Buttons*

1.

27 rue de Fleurus

Gertrude and Leo Stein were as different as it is possible for sister and brother to be, yet remarkably close. The youngest of five children, only two years apart in age and orphaned in adolescence, they had depended on each other from childhood and had grown up with similar tastes. They developed an intimacy that persisted until both were well along in their thirties and concluded in what one writer aptly calls their "divorce." For a period of ten years before the break, however, they lived together in relative harmony and demonstrated great flair in assembling the finest collection of modern art in Paris. After they were estranged each denied the other's claims to superior judgment, but the fact is that the sureness of taste they showed in common disappeared after they separated. Kahnweiler, the art dealer who specialized in the cubist painters, remarked on the Steins' collective taste and their individual differences, describing Leo as abstract, Gertrude as concrete. Temperamentally, intellectually, and even physically, they were totally unlike. Alice Toklas was struck by the difference when she first met them. Both had the same golden coloring, both wore the same brown corduroy costumes and the Greek sandals designed by Raymond Duncan, who lived across the courtyard at 27 rue de Fleurus for a time, but otherwise she would not have recognized them as brother and sister. Leo was tall, thin, and austere, "like an

Egyptian statue of a handsome giant" to Nina de Montparnasse, the French model who fell in love with him in 1905. He had a golden beard, a swinging stride, great grace and beauty. Gertrude on the other hand was short and dumpy, with a massive figure like a block of granite.

Leo would have made a good professor or art critic if he had had to earn a living. He loved the role of cicerone and had great aptitude for it. When relatives and friends visited Europe, he guided them about, showing them the sights worth seeing and explaining everything. He was not merely a walking Baedeker, he could convey his enthusiasm and his perceptions. The young ladies found him a fascinating and inexhaustible talker. At the rue de Fleurus it was he who explained all the pictures. "People came, and so I explained, because it was my nature to explain," he writes in his book of criticism and reminiscence, *Appreciation: Painting, Poetry and Prose.* He also explains why he did not publish any criticism during his early years. "Many wanted to know why I didn't write. I said I couldn't write. This was before I knew of Freud, so I could not tell them about inhibitions. If I had been living somewhere else, I would have known about Freud before this, but he was late to arrive in France."

Some measure of his hypochondria and neurosis can be gained from his letters, of which a selection appeared posthumously in *Journey into the Self*. As the title is meant to suggest, he spent his life in self-analysis. Indeed that was his life's work. Despite his very considerable gifts he was never able to accomplish anything solid. During his years at the rue de Fleurus he fancied himself a painter, never realizing that his whole bent was critical rather than creative. Meanwhile Gertrude was working steadily away, producing a great mass of manuscript material, even if she could not get it published. No wonder Leo never appreciated her writing.

Still, those were good years for him, and his letters reflect a change when he settled in Paris. Before that they are the chatty, rather empty letters of a dilettante skimming over the surface of things. Afterward he seems busier and more purposeful, painting and visiting galleries. His letters take on substance, full of philosophy, religion, psychology, aesthetics. One letter is quite a good essay on the modern painters he has just discovered at the Autumn Salon. Just as earlier he had spent months in the Louvre and the Uffizi studying Renaissance painting, so now he showed the same tireless concentration in his search for new artists and soon became the leading connoisseur of modern French art. In the spring of 1903 he bought his first Cézanne. The following September, when Gertrude came to live with him, they decided to pool their resources and start buying together. It was he who led the way in discovering new artists, but in collecting pictures she complemented him. He had the sharper nose, but in the long run she had surer instincts, because she felt art instead of intellectualizing it as he did.

The heroic days of 27 rue de Fleurus were those before the war, from 1903 to 1914, when Leo and Gertrude Stein together made art history by collecting a group of paintings by unknown artists. Nowadays any museum would covet their collection; in those days the paintings looked very strange to the unaccustomed eye. The studio, with its walls covered with paintings, presented an astonishing sight. *The Autobiography of Alice B. Toklas* tells how it first impressed the visitor in 1907:

> It is very difficult now that everybody is accustomed to everything to give some idea of the kind of uneasiness one felt when one first looked at all these pictures on these walls. In those days there were pictures of all kinds there, the time had not yet come when there were only Cézannes, Renoirs, Matisses and Picassos, nor as it was even later only Cézannes and Picassos. At that time there was a great deal of Matisse, Picasso, Renoir, Cézanne but there were also a great many other things. There were two Gauguins, there were Manguins, there was a big nude by Valloton that felt like only it was not like the Odalisque of Manet, there was a Toulouse-Lautrec. . . . There was a portrait of Gertrude

> Stein by Valloton that might have been a David but was not, there was a Maurice Denis, a little Daumier, many Cézanne water colours, there was in short everything, there was even a little Delacroix and a moderate sized Greco. There were enormous Picassos of the Harlequin period, there were two rows of Matisses, there was a big portrait of a woman by Cézanne and some little Cézannes, all these pictures had a history and I will soon tell them. Now I was confused and I looked and I looked and I was confused.

The Steins collected painters as well as paintings. Soon after they started buying Matisses, they met the painter and his wife and quickly became friends. About the same time Leo discovered Picasso and began another friendship, one that was to mean much to Gertrude. It was at the Steins' that Matisse and Picasso first met. Other painters came: Rousseau, Derain, Braque, Vlaminck, Pascin, Delaunay, Marie Laurencin, and among the Americans, Alfred Maurer, Maurice Sterne, and Marsden Hartley. The painters in turn brought friends to see the pictures, and before long they were coming in such numbers at odd hours that the Steins decided to hold open house regularly on Saturday night. In a few years the Saturday nights became a celebrated institution, one of the sights of Montparnasse, an attraction to informed art critics, patrons, and curiosity-seekers alike. And Matisse, Picasso, and their followers began to prosper.

Leo Stein may well have seemed "the great American Maecenas" to a poor French model like Nina de Montparnasse, but as a matter of fact he and Gertrude were not rich. They were able to assemble their spectacular collection by buying carefully at a time when the painters had no reputations and almost no sales. They paid 500 francs for their first Matisse and 150 for their first Picasso ($100 and $30 respectively). When an unexpected 8000 francs came their way, they promptly spent the entire sum on paintings. They had the acquisitive instincts of the great collectors without the means, so instead of retaining a Berenson or a Duveen to find them old masters, they did their own searching in contemporary art. They learned rapidly and soon developed extraordinary discrimination. Naturally they made mistakes, but they later corrected them by selling off inferior works to buy better ones as their collection grew and evolved.

There were four Steins in Paris, for Leo and Gertrude were reinforced by their eldest brother Michael and his wife Sarah, who lived at 58 rue Madame, around the corner from 27 rue de Fleurus. Michael, who had become head of the family at his father's death, had managed the family's finances so astutely that they were all provided with adequate incomes. More interested in art than business, he was able to retire to Paris and look after his interests from a distance.

The Steins appeared at precisely the moment when the modern school of Paris was getting under way. The impressionists were slowly gaining recognition, but the great postimpressionists—Van Gogh, Gauguin, Toulouse-Lautrec, and Cézanne—were still unknown, except to the younger generation of painters. The Autumn Salon, which opened its doors in 1903, exhibited painters who were not acceptable to the official salons. Of these Cézanne was the most influential in leading the way beyond impressionism—"*le père de nous tous,*" Matisse once called him. Ambroise Vollard provides a glimpse of the Steins at the Autumn Salon of 1905 in his *Recollections of a Picture Dealer*, recalling their purchase of the portrait of Madame Cézanne. "Every time I went to the exhibition I saw the Steins, the two brothers and the sister, seated on a bench in front of the portrait. They contemplated it in silence till the day when, the *Salon* being closed, Mr. Leo Stein came to bring me the price of the painting. He was accompanied by Miss Stein. 'Now,' said she, 'the picture is ours!' They might have been ransoming someone they loved."

The Autumn Salon of 1905 was the first decisive event in the history of twentieth-century art, announcing a new movement and a new generation of painters. In addition to ten Cézannes and three Rousseaus, the exhibition included works by Matisse,

Vlaminck, Derain, van Dongen, Marquet, Friesz, and Rouault. For several years the "fauves," as they were christened, were to dominate the avant-garde. They were given their name by a scornful critic whose other claim to immortality is that a few years later he nicknamed the other major style that emerged before the war, cubism. The word *fauves* has connotations in French that do not come across in the literal translation of "wild beasts." Gertrude Stein rendered it more appropriately as "a zoo." The word calls to mind particularly *les grands fauves*, the great beasts of prey raging in their cages, where a Parisian living in a well-ordered world would normally expect them to be. Fauve is their color too—tawny—and the word suggests the rank, feral odor in the close quarters of the Paris zoo, the Jardin des Plantes.

The Autumn Salon of 1905, then, was a lions' den, and the visitor was beset from all sides. The paintings were shocking when seen for the first time, with their flat perspective, crude drawing, and lurid colors that violently misrepresented nature. Leo Stein later remembered Matisse's *Femme au Chapeau* as "the nastiest smear of paint I had ever seen." Even though he recognized it at once as something he had been waiting for, he found it too unpleasant to accept for several days. Not that this was the first Matisse he had seen; he had prepared himself during the previous year by going to the Autumn Salon, where Matisse had thirteen paintings, and in the spring to the Salon des Indépendants, where an important large Matisse was displayed, *Luxe, Calme et Volupté*. Matisse had also had a one-man show at Vollard's gallery, which the Steins frequented.

Matisse, already thirty-five, was still unrecognized and struggling to survive. Always described as bourgeois because he looked like a doctor and led a quiet married life, he had nonetheless abandoned a safe livelihood producing marketable paintings to explore new directions and at a time when he had no money had made an act of faith in art by selling his wife's brooch to buy a small Cézanne. In *The Autobiography of Alice B. Toklas* Gertrude Stein reports several anecdotes from the painter's life, notably the one about Matisse painting in his overcoat and gloves one winter in order to keep the room cold and so preserve the fruit he had bought for a still life. Her anecdotes are factually inexact, but they accurately convey the hardships that Matisse and his wife had to endure for a number of years. The two summers before the Steins met him he had spent on the Mediterranean and begun using the warm bright colors that were to become the special mark of fauvism and of his own work.

In 1905 all four Steins went to the Autumn Salon and bought Matisse's *Femme au Chapeau.* This is the only statement that can be made with any assurance, for Gertrude later claimed she was the one who decided to buy it, Leo said he was, Sarah said she and Leo had chosen it, and Matisse later gave the credit to Sarah, probably because she was his most loyal supporter. The painting ended up in the Michael Steins' collection, but only after it had belonged to Leo and Gertrude for a number of years. Who paid the money matters little. What is important is that the Steins appreciated *La Femme au Chapeau* while the general public reacted violently. Leo speaks of people howling; Gertrude says they were scratching at the painting in their fury.

Thereafter all four Steins became patrons and friends of Matisse, providing the moral and financial support he so desperately needed. For the next two years they bought almost his entire output, and the Michael Steins continued to buy his work for the thirty years they lived in Paris. They specialized in Matisse, as did their friends from Baltimore, Claribel and Etta Cone. The two sisters had been to the Autumn Salon, but had not liked the Matisses. A few months later the Michael Steins brought them to the Quai Saint-Michel to buy. Thus began a lifelong romance between the painter and the two spinsters. On that occasion they only bought a drawing and a water color for $20, but they gradually took courage and continued to buy steadily thereafter until their collection, composed predominantly of works by Matisse, was valued at $3,000,000. The figure reflects inflation in the prices paid for modern painting rather than the wealth of the Cone sisters, who had originally inherited incomes of $2400 each. In time their incomes grew, but like the Steins they had to be careful at first. Their tastes were always more cautious, and without the Steins to urge them, it is hard to believe that they would ever have started collecting Matisse.

The Steins' discovery of Matisse marked a turning point in his fortunes. But appreciation unquestionably meant more to him than a steady income. Between the painter and his patrons a genuine friendship grew, reflected in the cordial postcards to Gertrude and Leo that chart his travels to Germany, Spain, Collioure, Tangier, and Russia during the years before the war and in his devoted correspondence with Sarah thereafter. Near the end of her life and of his own he was still thanking her for the encouragement she had given him in dark days.

For three years Leo and Gertrude acquired his most important paintings: *La Femme au Chapeau* in 1905; *Le Bonheur de Vivre*, the climax of fauvism, in 1906; *The Blue Nude* in 1907. Then their interest in Matisse waned, as did fauvism itself. The Michael Steins remained faithful. When in 1908, at Sarah's suggestion, Matisse started a school, she helped organize it and took painting lessons herself. In later years Gertrude made fun of this venture and of Sarah's devotion, referring to Matisse as "*cher maître*" and creating the impression that his pupils were all amateurs. But the Académie Matisse flourished so long as Matisse could find time for it, and its many talented pupils extended the master's influence and prestige abroad. Chief among its American alumni was Max Weber, who became the leading postimpressionist in this country; following his example many American painters subsequently experimented with fauvism and cubism. Weber, incidentally, was one of the earliest admirers of Rousseau, bought as many of his works as he could afford, and back in New York in 1910, arranged Rousseau's first one-man show anywhere.

Matisse became known in America through the Steins. In 1906, when the San Francisco earthquake sent Michael Stein home to look after his interests, Sarah brought along three

Matisses, the first to cross the Atlantic, and sold one of them. Alice Toklas, who lived in San Francisco, met the Steins at this time, immediately admired the very fauve portrait of Madame Matisse with a green stripe down her nose, but put off Sarah's invitation to go to Paris until the following year. Sarah also invited Harriet Levy, another friend of the Steins who later bought Matisses, acquiring a small but respectable collection. Even Bernard Berenson bought one very early, pre-fauve Matisse, and what was more important, defended the painter in print on the occasion of his first one-man show in New York in 1908.

That modest exhibition was arranged by the photographer Edward Steichen, a friend of the Steins in Paris, and shown at the Photo-Secession Gallery of Alfred Stieglitz. It was followed by two more Matisse shows at the same gallery in 1910 and 1912 and an exhibition of the American disciples of Matisse. New York can claim not only his first one-man show abroad but the astonishing consequence that three Matisse drawings were displayed in the Metropolitan Museum at a time when the painter was still being vilified in Paris. From the impressionists on, the French were slow to appreciate their new artists. The Americans accepted them more readily—though it is true that the Armory Show aroused much hostile criticism in 1913. Matisse, who was best represented among the French artists in that exhibition, was the favorite target of criticism. When the show moved to Chicago, art students named a dummy Henri Hairmatress, conducted a mock trial, and burned two Matisses in effigy. The Steins were represented there too; they had lent three of their Matisses for the show, including one of those sentenced to burn, the curvaceous *Blue Nude.*

The Steins discovered Picasso about the same time as Matisse, but on the subject of Picasso their opinion was always divided. Gertrude said there was a camp of Matisseites and a camp of Picassoites. If so, just as surely as Sarah was the leading disciple of Matisse, Gertrude was the great champion of Picasso. As usual it was Leo who made the discovery, so that he was perfectly justified later in claiming, "I was the only person anywhere, so far as I know, who in those early days recognized Picasso *and* Matisse. Picasso had some admirers, and Matisse had some, but I was alone in recognizing these two as the two important men." He seems to have recognized Picasso at first sight. In November 1905 he wrote a letter to a friend reporting his discovery of "a young Spaniard named Picasso whom I consider a genius of very considerable magnitude and one of the most notable draughtsmen living."

At that time Picasso was even more obscure than Matisse. He had moved to Paris permanently in the spring of 1904, settling in an old wooden tenement in Montmartre that was to become famous in the history of modern art. *Le bateau lavoir*, so called because it was supposed to resemble the laundry boats on the Seine, was a warren of artists, writers, actors, and Dostoevskian characters, a number of whom appear in Picasso's early paintings. There in a few years Picasso rapidly moved through a series of styles or "periods," as they are usually called–blue, harlequin, rose, "Negro"–and then on to the great breakthrough of cubism.

He and Braque independently discovered cubism at the same time, and for several years their paintings were virtually indistinguishable as they explored cubism together through several stages. Taking Cézanne's injunction, "You must see in nature the cylinder, the sphere, the cone," they began by representing their subjects geometrically as an arrangement of three-dimensional shapes and planes. Discarding Renaissance perspective, they viewed the objects they painted from several angles simultaneously. In the process they broke down outlines and shapes, notably in the case of the musical instruments they were fond of painting, presenting them in diagrammatic form, dismantled, with parts seen from different aspects. Then they reversed the process of abstraction by introducing letters and numbers into their paintings, and finally real objects, bits of rope and newspaper, labels and calling cards, all sorts of odds and ends. "Look," they exclaimed, "we can make works of art out of the contents of our wastebaskets." Collage, which may have begun as a spoof, proved to be an important development in twentieth-century art. Since Picasso and Braque, modern artists have regarded their paintings as objects, not as representations. Cubism attracted many followers and quickly became the dominant style of the century, with Picasso its guiding genius.

Leo Stein saw his first Picassos shortly after the Autumn Salon of 1905 and soon bought one from the dealer who had advised him to look at the paintings. The dealer, Clovis Sagot, was a former clown, and the painting, appropriately enough, was a portrait of a family of saltimbanques with an ape. Leo soon bought a second Picasso from Sagot, a nude girl with a basket of flowers. This is the first Picasso that Gertrude remembers in *The Autobiography of Alice B. Toklas,* where she says she was shocked by the drawing of the legs and feet, whereupon Sagot offered to guillotine them.

Though she did not take to his paintings right away, she claims that she and Picasso understood each other from the first time they met. The meeting was important to both of them, for Picasso was to become the hero of *The Autobiography of Alice B. Toklas,* and Gertrude Stein was to be, after Guillaume Apollinaire, the greatest literary advocate of cubism. Picasso's early correspondence with Gertrude and Leo, a succession of scrawls in uninhibited French, reflects a growing friendship, first with Leo, then with Leo and Gertrude, then with Gertrude and Alice Toklas.

In the spring of 1906 Picasso began painting his portrait of Gertrude Stein, but even after eighty or ninety sittings the face remained unfinished. Like all good Parisians Picasso and the Steins always left the city during the summer months. The Steins spent their summers outside Florence, and the painters usually went south for a different light and landscape. On his return in the fall Picasso immediately finished the face without seeing the model again. The portrait of Gertrude Stein marked an important stage in Picasso's development, the transition to his "Negro" period, which in turn led on to cubism. The body and hands are those of a Renaissance portrait, but the face is stylized like a mask with blank archaic eyes. What is even more disturbing, perspective and scale are distorted, with the side of the face that should be receding brought forward and one eye distinctly smaller than the other. In this the portrait anticipates *Les Demoiselles d'Avignon*, Picasso's major work of the following year that is usually regarded as the starting point of his cubism, noteworthy among other things for its simultaneous presentation of full face and profile. The portrait of Gertrude Stein reveals the same kind of "simultanism" at a less developed stage.

While she was sitting for her portrait, Gertrude Stein brought "the Miss Etta Cones," as Picasso called them, to the rue Ravignan to buy water colors, drawings, and etchings off the floor of Picasso's notoriously messy studio, and during the same year she sold a Picasso drawing to their sister-in-law. Picasso also sketched portraits of Leo Stein, the Michael Steins' son Allan, and later of Dr. Claribel Cone. As his painting moved into cubism, however, most of the group lost all taste for it. Even Leo felt that Picasso had gone wrong when he began to have "ideas." He ridiculed analytic and synthetic cubism in a passage that parodies his sister's style: "But when the analysis is only a kind of funny business, the synthesis will be only another kind of funny business. With this kind of funny business analysis, anything can be analyzed into any elements, and with this funny business synthesis any elements can be synthesized into any form. The analysis and the synthesis alike are mere funny business, and it is absurd to take them seriously." Only Gertrude remained loyal to Picasso, increasingly so as she lost interest in Matisse. For her own reasons she later exaggerated the rivalry between the two painters and their followers, including those in her own family. In truth they all remained on good terms until separated by the war. She herself wrote "portraits" of Matisse and Picasso that served as the text for a special number of Stieglitz's *Camera Work* in 1912, designed to acquaint the American public with the two leading artists in Paris.

Picasso became the most important painter and remained the

most important man in her life. It was Picasso the man, his personal genius, his temperament, his sardonic Spanish humor, rather than his work that captivated her imagination. She never developed any interest in Braque's painting during the period when he and Picasso were experimenting so closely together; she liked Braque well enough personally, but she only acquired two of his paintings after the war. In discussing cubism she entirely ignored his contribution, having decided that "the only real cubism is that of Picasso and Juan Gris," whom she calls "her two dearest friends." It suited her to think of cubism as Spanish, and besides, Gris was her own discovery, not Leo's. She was one of the first to buy his work and one of the few in his short lifetime to encourage him. After his death she commemorated him in "The Life and Death of Juan Gris."

By the time Gris joined the cubists, their movement had already won over all the young painters and had ramified in various directions, including that which she called the "catastrophic" or "earthquake" school of Delaunay. It had also alienated all the Steins except Gertrude. Leo acquired his last Picasso in 1910, and then only because the painter wanted to pay off a debt. According to his account, Gertrude had not yet begun to collect on her own. "In 1911 or 1912," he wrote, "Gertrude bought a cubist Picasso, the first picture for which she was responsible to come to 27 Rue de Fleurus."

Early in 1914 Leo and Gertrude broke up their household and separated for good. Leo says they did not quarrel. "We simply differed and went our own ways," he wrote a few days before his death, but in the same notes he pointed out the profound differences in character that may explain why they were never reconciled. He may have been able to view these differences with intellectual detachment, but Gertrude felt them as a constant reproach. Although he made several friendly overtures in writing, they did not meet again, even when he visited Paris after the war. They saw each other once again but did not speak. Alice Toklas tells of the encounter in her memoirs. "One day, about this time, we got into a traffic jam on the boulevard Saint Germain near the church of St. Germain-des-Prés. I saw Gertrude bowing very politely to a man who had taken off his hat and had bowed to her. I had not had time to see his face. I said to her, Who was that? and Gertrude answered, Leo. She had not heard from him or of him during the war years. I said, Not possibly. And she said, Yes, it was Leo. Gertrude when we got home wrote her story, 'How She Bowed to Her Brother.' Leo still had his beautiful walk, which was not historical but mythological."

Of his departure from 27 rue de Fleurus he offers some explanation: "When my interest in Cézanne declined, when Matisse was temporarily in eclipse, when Picasso turned to foolishness, I began to withdraw from the Saturday evenings." Gertrude Stein does not discuss the matter, but Alice Toklas says that they quarreled over Picasso's painting and Gertrude's writing. In reporting Picasso's angry resentment of Leo's criticism, she suggests how Gertrude may have reacted too. Others thought Alice Toklas and Leo's mistress had come between them.

The most plausible explanation is provided by Hutchins Hapgood in his autobiography, *A Victorian in the Modern World.* Hapgood, a few years older than Leo and Gertrude, had known and liked both through the years they lived together in Paris. He first met Leo on a ship bound for Japan in 1895 and Gertrude the following year in Heidelberg. His description of Leo seems to offer the best explanation of that difficult character. "Whenever I think of Leo Stein, I like him better than when I am with him. He couldn't leave the slightest subject without critical analysis." He was capable of arguing a minor point, Hapgood says, over and over again all the way around the world. "He was almost always mentally irritated. The slightest flaw, real or imaginary, in his companion's statements, caused in him intellectual indignation of the most intense kind. And there seemed to be something in him which took it for granted that anything said by anybody except himself needed immediate denial or at least substantial modification. He seemed to need constant reinforcement of his ego."

Gertrude first impressed Hapgood as "an extraordinary person: powerful, a beautiful head, a sense of something granite . . . something wholly intense . . . a deep temperamental life-quality." But he goes on to add that "even at that moment of her youth, with a kind of almost unfeminine beauty, with a brilliant academic past behind her, the ego was apparent. She, like her brother Leo, was by an inner necessity compelled to be conscious of her essential superiority." She and Leo were not in conflict then. "At this time in Heidelberg and, for some years afterwards, Gertrude was possessed by a singular devotion to Leo; she admired and loved him in a way a man is seldom admired and loved; it was a part of her profound temperament." Over the years Hapgood saw them often, in Florence and in Paris, and found her as devoted to Leo as ever. Of the household at the rue de Fleurus, he wrote, "It was a pleasant and attractive atmosphere, simple, human, and unpretentious. Gertrude was quiet, generally silent, but with a deep warmth that expressed itself in her handclasp, her look, and her rich laughter." After the war Hapgood found himself excommunicated from the rue de Fleurus for reasons he never understood, and after the publication of *The Autobiography of Alice B. Toklas,* he wrote in his own autobiography, "No more remarkable change has probably ever taken place in a human being's personality than that which has happened in the case of Gertrude Stein. In later years, when the critical Leo could not follow the direction of her writing nor the direction of her emotional life, she seemed to feel herself spurned and insulted." Hapgood was a sane and sympathetic observer who admired the qualities of both Leo and Gertrude. He was not a partisan of either. His interpretation seems the best we are likely to get.

Whatever the reasons, Leo left 27 rue de Fleurus and went off to Florence, where he was to live for the rest of his days. They divided the collection between them, both keeping some of the Cézannes, Gertrude taking most of the Picassos, Leo most of the Matisses and the Renoirs. Gertrude kept *La Femme au Chapeau,* which she sold to Sarah Stein during the war, when she needed money. Leo had already sold *The Blue Nude* to John Quinn after the Armory Show. Both Gertrude and Leo sold off paintings at the time of their separation and thereafter, never at any great profit, to meet pressing needs.

By the time of his death Leo's share of the collection was gone. Gertrude left twenty-eight Picasso and seven Juan Gris paintings, twenty-eight Picasso drawings and one Picasso sculpture. By the terms of her will, these were to remain in the possession of Alice Toklas for her lifetime, with the provision that she could sell some to underwrite the publication of Gertrude Stein's manuscripts by Yale University; thus eight handsome volumes of Gertrude Stein's previously unpublished writings were subsidized. Picasso's portrait was left to the Metropolitan Museum, which Gertrude Stein probably regarded, reasonably enough, as America's Louvre.

Leo's departure marked the end of an era. His withdrawal to Florence seems a symbolic gesture, for he ceased to collect modern art. He visited Paris again in later years, talked with Picasso again, and thought Matisse had done more interesting work after the war. But the great days were over, for the painters as well as the collectors. Matisse had left Paris for the south of France, and the *bateau lavoir* group had been disbanded by the war. In 1914 Picasso had seen Braque and Derain off at Avignon when they took the train to go to war. Of these intimate friends he commented later, "I never found them again."

Even cubism went to war—as camouflage. Gertrude Stein tells of one cold winter evening during the first year of the war when she and Picasso were walking down the Boulevard Raspail. "All of a sudden down the street came some big cannon, the first any of us had seen painted, that is camouflaged. Pablo stopped, he was spell-bound. C'est nous qui avons fait ça, he said, it is we that have created that, he said. And he was right, he had. From Cézanne through him they had come to that."

2.

Postimpressionism in Prose

"Gertrude Stein was born at the Armory Show," according to Mabel Dodge, who had much to do with the event. She had known the Steins in Paris and Florence, where Gertrude had written the *Portrait of Mabel Dodge at the Villa Curonia.* Mabel Dodge had the *Portrait* printed and bound in eighteenth-century Florentine wallpapers, and when she established her salon in New York, left copies at the door for callers to take with them. "It was in this casual manner," Carl Van Vechten recalls, "that I and a considerable section of New York became acquainted with the prose of Gertrude Stein." For this reason perhaps, Mabel Dodge was asked to do an article on Gertrude Stein's writing for a special issue of *Arts and Decoration* devoted to the Armory Show. Her article, "Speculations, or Post-Impressions in Prose," makes the point that Gertrude Stein's experimental writing was influenced by the paintings on her walls. "In a large studio in Paris, hung with paintings by Renoir, Matisse and Picasso, Gertrude Stein is doing with words what Picasso is doing with paint. . . . She has taken the English language and, according to many people, has mis-used it, or has used it roughly, uncouthly and brutally, or madly, stupidly and hideously, but by her method she is finding the hidden and inner nature of nature."

The theory that she was writing in a postimpressionistic manner undoubtedly originated with Gertrude Stein herself. And evidently she took it literally rather than metaphorically. It is quite understandable that she should exploit the prestige of the paintings she had collected, but that belonged to her personal legend, not to her own writing. It might seem strange that a writer should ally herself to a school of painting, but she wanted to indicate that she shared the experimental spirit that prevailed among the painters of the School of Paris. Not only that, but she wanted to dissociate herself from all literary influences and precedents in order to discover twentieth-century literature all by herself. She conducted her most important literary experiments in the years before the war, at a time when she was isolated not only from the language she wrote but from the society of other creative writers who used that language.

Gertrude Stein was not exaggerating when she claimed that she was the first to write in the twentieth-century manner. *Three Lives*, written in 1904–06 and published in 1909, was the first work to announce the new age in literature. *Tender Buttons*, published in 1914, was the second, and her other writings of the prewar decade, her many short sketches and her long novel, *The Making of Americans*, though not published till much later, were radical investigations in a new method. All of these works were highly experimental as she explored the possibilities of language and syntax, sometimes beyond the bounds of intelligibility. Fifty or sixty years later her writing is still avant-garde, most of it beyond the common reader, some of it inaccessible to all but a dedicated few. Most readers find most of Gertrude Stein not only difficult but boring, but since the few are mostly writers themselves, she has had a considerable influence on the writing of the generation that followed hers.

She began writing in 1903. One short work preceded her experimental writings, a novel dated October 24, 1903, that remained in manuscript until after her death. The writing shows few signs of developing in the direction she was to take henceforth. The prose is fairly conventional, though it grows progressively flatter, as her indifference to punctuation increases, creating that illiterate run-on effect that was to become characteristic. Her personality asserts itself in down-to-earth colloquial expression and her own brand of aphorism. But otherwise her first novel is not indicative of things to come.

After moving to Paris, she began translating Flaubert's *Trois Contes.* Leo was avidly reading all of Flaubert at the time and no doubt expounding him to Gertrude. She must have wanted to improve her French, but she also regarded the translation as a literary exercise, and the immediate consequence was *Three Lives.* Flaubert, who appears so remote to us, must have seemed almost a contemporary to the Steins, the writer who presided over the period just ended. Henry James had frequented Flaubert's circle in Paris less than thirty years before, and James was still very much alive. Actually the French master was to have his greatest influence on English writing in the twentieth century.

Gertrude Stein also attached great importance to the influence of Cézanne on her writing. While she was working on *Three Lives,* she and Leo acquired the portrait of Madame Cézanne that Vollard had exhibited at the Autumn Salon of 1905. In *The Autobiography of Alice B. Toklas* Gertrude Stein wrote of herself, "She had begun not long before as an exercise in literature to translate Flaubert's Trois Contes and then she had this Cézanne and she looked at it and under its stimulus she wrote Three Lives." At the end of her life she was still saying, "Everything I have done has been influenced by Flaubert and Cézanne, and this gave me a new feeling about composition."

Cézanne may have stimulated her, but Flaubert's influence is more apparent. Of his three tales, only the first served Gertrude Stein as an example, but it gave her all the suggestions she needed. "*Un Coeur Simple*" is the story of an uneducated peasant woman who spends her entire life as a servant in the same household. Félicité is the name of this poor creature whose lot is anything but felicity. Ignorant, illiterate, scarcely better than a beast of burden, she spends herself in devoted service to an idle class that is indifferent to her feelings. Her simple-minded faith is as extravagant in color and design as the stained-glass windows that inspire it, and as she dies she is received into heaven by the Holy Ghost, whom she has long visualized, not as a dove, but in the form of a parrot, like her beloved Loulou, long since dead and stuffed. The story has moments of great pathos, but the feeling is understated, partly because Flaubert writes in an unemotional, matter-of-fact manner, partly because Félicité, whose point of view is obliquely taken into account, is incapable of self-pity or even, in her mute peasant way, of self-awareness.

Two of Gertrude Stein's three stories follow the same pattern. "The Good Anna" and "The Gentle Lena" are similar life-histories, told undramatically, without rise or fall. Anna and Lena come from the same peasant stock as Félicité and lead equally dull lives of servitude. Anna was based on a real person named Lena Lebender who was Gertrude Stein's servant in Baltimore for five years, but she resembles Félicité as well. She has the same dour peasant mentality, the same thin, angular spinster's frame. Tireless and frugal, she sacrifices herself to indulge the soft, ample, helpless women she serves. Though not generous by nature, both Anna and Félicité perform works of mercy as a matter of course. Both are pious Catholics, but religion has nothing to do with their charity. Both are sentimental, Félicité about the son and daughter of the house and later about her parrot, Anna about her three dogs. Both endow their pets with human understanding and feeling. There are many other parallels, from the opening remark of each story to its close, but one in particular seems a clear act of homage to Flaubert: the good Anna is given a green parrot.

Flaubert is noted as an ironic observer of the manners, the provincial mentality, and the banal everyday speech of his native Normandy. Gertrude Stein is the Flaubert of Baltimore, without the irony. She is less clinical and documentary but equally patient in her observation of the poor of her own provincial metropolis. She penetrated to a Flaubertian degree the habits of mind and elemental feelings she recorded. She went beyond Flaubert to discover a new mode of expressing the inarticulate. Flaubert had discovered the subject in "*Un Coeur Simple*," but his literary discipline, the relentless quest for *le mot juste*, was directly at odds with such a subject. Gertrude Stein imitated the language of her inarticulate women and found an expression based not on precise words and syntax but on the cumulative effect of imprecise speech endlessly repeating itself. Above all she caught the rhythm of speech.

Gertrude Stein must have had an enormous capacity for listening to housekeepers. Her tales reproduce their endless droning monologues, full of banal moralizing, psychologizing, and philosophizing about empty lives.

> "Yes Mrs. Aldrich" said the good german woman to her mistress later, "Yes Mrs. Aldrich that's the way it is with them girls when they want so to get married. They don't know when they got it good Mrs. Aldrich. They never know what it is they're really wanting when they got it, Mrs. Aldrich. There's that poor Lena, she just been here crying and looking so careless so I scold her, but that was no good that marrying for that poor Lena, Mrs. Aldrich. She do look so pale and sad now Mrs. Aldrich, it just break my heart to see her. She was a good girl was Lena, Mrs. Aldrich, and I never had no trouble with her like I got with so many young girls nowadays, Mrs. Aldrich, and I never see any girl any better to work right than our Lena, and now . . ."

This is talk at its farthest remove from poetry, yet it has a certain rhythm and rhyme. Steady, regular, and monotonous, punctuated by the names repeated at more or less regular intervals, the monologue advances like a tide, very slowly, on the waves of rhythm, each wave adding ever so slightly to the forward movement. People, even articulate people, actually speak this way, as the transcripts of tape-recorded speech have demonstrated. Here is a passage from a poet's conversation:

> When I resumed writing in the fifties I resumed reading. I reread Apollinaire. I had never translated Apollinaire and I never translated any French poetry. It wasn't until I resumed writing in '53 with these poems that I resumed reading. It was then that I began to read Eluard. I never read too much of Eluard when I was in Paris. I began reading and translating him in 1953. I translated Villon and Eluard. I translated a lot of Eluard.

Gertrude Stein is sometimes acclaimed as the first to write down "the stream of consciousness." The expression was coined by her mentor at Harvard, William James, who may also have provided her with ideas on language and syntax. But while *Three Lives* records the subjective process, what she has caught is the rhythm of consciousness rather than consciousness itself, and what she reproduces is speech rather than the interior monologue. She does not get inside her characters in *Three Lives;* they do not even seem to have any interior awareness. Instead, like Félicité, they represent a certain mentality, a type not very definitely individualized. The explanation is that Gertrude Stein was trying to tell their stories in their own terms, in the light of their own very limited consciousness.

"Melanctha," the third of the *Three Lives* to be written, represents a further development in her method. Melanctha is a Negro girl with a totally different dialect and tempo; she is not only more intelligent and complex than the good Anna or the gentle Lena, her consciousness imposes itself more emphatically. In the two earlier stories the writing is fairly conventional, with some deliberate clumsiness of expression as it assumes a slightly German turn of thought and idiom. In "Melanctha," the prose is more highly cadenced and far more repetitious.

> "I certainly do think you would have told me. I certainly do think I could make you feel it right to tell me. I certainly do think all I did wrong was to let Jane Harden tell me. I certainly do know I never did wrong, to learn what she told me. I certainly know very well, Melanctha, if I had come here to you, you would have told it all to me, Melanctha."

This is Negro speech, but the same rhythm and repetition pervade Gertrude Stein's own writing, as though Melanctha herself were telling the story:

> Every day now, Jeff seemed to be coming nearer, to be really loving. Every day now, Melanctha poured it all out to him, with more freedom. Every day now, they seemed to be having more and more, both together, of this strong, right feeling. More and more every day now they seemed to know more really, what it was each other one was always feeling. More and more now every day Jeff found in himself, he felt more trusting. More and more every day now, he did not think anything in words about what he was always doing. Every day now more and more Melanctha would let out to Jeff her real, strong feeling.

In *The Autobiography of Alice B. Toklas* Gertrude Stein offers two different sources for her new style. One is her research in automatic writing at Harvard, which, she states, is "the method of writing to be afterwards developed in Three Lives and Making of Americans." The other is the rhythm of her long walks across Paris every afternoon to pose for her portrait. "During these long poses and these long walks Gertrude Stein meditated and made sentences. She was then in the middle of her Negro story Melanctha Herbert, . . . and the poignant incidents that she wove into the life of Melanctha were often these she noticed in walking down the hill from the rue

Ravignan." Further she adds, "She had come to like posing, the long still hours followed by a long dark walk intensified the concentration with which she was creating her sentences." Just as she had insisted on Cézanne's influence on *Three Lives*, so she now seems determined to associate "Melanctha" with Picasso's portrait, her art with his. "In the long struggle with the portrait of Gertrude Stein, Picasso passed from the Harlequin, the charming early italian period to the intensive struggle which was to end in cubism. Gertrude Stein had written the story of Melanctha the negress, . . . which was the first definite step away from the nineteenth century and into the twentieth century in literature."

It took more than three years to get the book in print because no publisher would accept it. Gertrude Stein finally decided to have it printed by a vanity press in New York. The publisher politely wrote that the typist had garbled her manuscript and one day sent "a very nice very american young man" to call about correcting her English. She tells this amusing story at her expense, adding that the publisher was later pleasantly surprised at the favorable notices the book received. His comment at the time he read proof had been, "I want to say frankly that I think you have written a very peculiar book and it will be a hard thing to make people take it seriously." The original printing of one thousand copies of *Three Lives*, published in 1909, lasted until 1920. Her next book, *The Making of Americans*, proved even more discouraging. Written in 1906–08 for the most part, it was not published until 1925. Not until the 1920s did Gertrude Stein gain any measure of recognition. Meanwhile she went on writing in isolation, as she put it, "for myself and strangers."

"One of the things that I have liked all these years," she wrote in *The Autobiography of Alice B. Toklas*, "is to be surrounded by people who know no english. It has left me more intensely alone with my eyes and my english. I do not know if it would have been possible to have english be so all in all to me otherwise. And they none of them could read a word I wrote, most of them did not even know that I did write. No, I like living with so very many people and being all alone with english and myself." This statement has several implications for her style. It was "my english" that she wanted to write, her own private language which she heard in her inner ear. When she visited England she was bothered by "the never ceasing sound of the human voice speaking in english." She preferred to listen to her memory of spoken English and to recreate the language in silence and solitude. She wrote in the lonely hours of the night, struggling with "those long sentences which were to change the literary ideas of a great many people." But since she had no immediate audience, she felt no immediate need to communicate, and her work was never subjected to criticism until long after it could be affected. As a result her style became progressively more ingrown and idiosyncratic.

The Making of Americans, almost one thousand pages long, can only be described as soporific. Here the insistent repetitions of *Three Lives* are carried to obsessive lengths. The rhythms of the sentences and paragraphs soon become incantatory and, even in the recording of Gertrude Stein's magnificent voice, hypnotic. In one of her lecture-readings, "The Gradual Making of The Making of Americans," she explains, "I began to get enormously interested in hearing how everybody said the same thing over and over again with infinite variations but over and over again until finally if you listened with great intensity you could hear it rise and fall and tell all that that there was inside them, not so much by the actual words they said or the thoughts they had but the movement of their thoughts and words endlessly the same and endlessly different." No reader shares her interest or her infinite patience. The book, which concerns the history of a German-Jewish family over three generations in America, deals with its subject so abstractly as to arouse no interest. Though based on the Steins, including Gertrude herself, the characters are impersonal and their experiences dim. Her history is without sequence of events, for she set out to destroy the past in order to create the continuous present.

This to her was the twentieth-century tense, as she explains in her lecture delivered at Oxford and Cambridge and published as *Composition as Explanation:* "In the first book there was a groping for a continuous present and for using everything by beginning again and again." In *The Making of Americans* she dwells in the continuous present by continuously using present participles and continuously repeating. Here is a fairly representative paragraph:

> This is then now to be a little description of the loving feeling for understanding of the completed history of each one that comes to one who listens always steadily to all repeating. This is the history then of the loving feeling in me of repeating, the loving feeling in me for completed understanding of the completed history of every one as it slowly comes out in every one as patiently and steadily I hear it and see it as repeating in them. This is now a little a description of this loving feeling. This is now a little a history of it from the beginning.

When Alice B. Toklas says of *The Making of Americans* that it is necessary to type or proofread Gertrude Stein's writing in order to appreciate it, the reader can only agree: the typist or proofreader has the advantage of being kept awake by his task. Even such a determined reader as Edmund Wilson admitted in *Axel's Castle,* "I confess that I have not read this book all through, and I do not know whether it is possible to do so."

In 1908 Gertrude Stein began writing "portraits." "Ada," her first, was a portrait of Alice Toklas, though no one would recognize the subject. She wrote a good many portraits in the next few years, mostly of the people who came to 27 rue de Fleurus; sometimes she gave their names as titles, but often the portraits were anonymous: "A man," "Two women," "Italians." The identity of the subjects did not matter so much as their type. Later she said that she supplied names for historical reasons, and as she went on writing portraits over the decades, enough to fill three or four volumes, they did indeed provide an interesting record of her acquaintance. Her portrait gallery includes the painters she collected and the friends she made through them—Apollinaire, Max Jacob, Vollard, Jean Cocteau, Erik Satie; *grandes dames*, climbing socially from Mabel Dodge to Edith Sitwell to the Duchesse de Clermont-Tonnerre; and, particularly in the twenties, American admirers and disciples—Carl Van Vechten, Jo Davidson, Sherwood Anderson, Hemingway, Harold Loeb, Virgil Thomson, Bravig Imbs.

The portraits vary widely in method and purpose. Originally they were meant to be psychological studies of "bottom natures." For that reason they were not supposed to reproduce a recognizable likeness but to get at the inner being. But gradually the scope was enlarged to include places and crowds, as in "Rue de Rennes" and "Flirting at the Bon Marché," and later rooms and food. Strictly speaking these were no longer portraits but scenes and still lifes. Later still, they became personal messages, such as "A Valentine to Sherwood Anderson," often containing private allusions, sometimes obscure even to the recipient. The portraits vary in style too. Many of them are written abstractly and participially to express continuous states of being; others are more concrete and declarative.

In "Portraits and Repetition," one of the lectures she gave when she toured America in 1934–35, Gertrude Stein has explained what she was trying to do. Just as every generation has a different way of seeing and composing, she says, so every generation must do portraits in a different way. Just as there is no plot in the three important novels written in her generation—"There is none in Proust in The Making of Americans or in Ulysses"—so her portraits are done without the traditional description of character. After making a distinction between portraits and description she goes on to distinguish between insistence and repetition, arguing that her writing is not based on repetition, but on constant variation, however slight. "A bird's singing is perhaps the nearest thing to repetition but if you listen they too vary their insistence." Through such minor variations Gertrude Stein is trying to record "the rhythm of anybody's personality" within the slow steady flow of consciousness, "what is moving inside them that makes them them." This is the fundamental essence of character. "We inside us do not change but our emphasis and the moment in which we live changes."

Further in "Portraits and Repetition" she offers another parallel to what she was doing in her portraits and in *The Making of Americans:*

> . . . I was doing what the cinema was doing. I was making a continuous succession of the statement of what that person was until I had not many things but one thing. . . . I of course did not think of it in terms of the cinema, in fact I doubt whether at that time I had ever seen a cinema but, and I cannot repeat this too often any one is of one's period and this our period was undoubtedly the period of the cinema and series production. And each of us in our own way are bound to express what the world in which we are living is doing.

At first the cinema seems to provide a valid parallel to her method, suggesting affinities with futurism; but in the long run her writing appears to be more like mass production of the same article over and over again. Her repetition seems static, since the printed page cannot present several variations to the eye at once, but only one at a time. She has produced something like a cinema film, but in arresting the eye at each frame she has presented a series of stills and destroyed the whole effect of *moving* pictures.

Writing, like music, is an art that exists in time, but she has suspended time and brought her writing as close as possible to the spatial art of painting. Here the analogy becomes more than a metaphor. Her portraits resemble nothing so much as those the cubist painters were producing during the same period. They abstract certain features from their subjects and project them in more or less nonrepresentational compositions. Her portraits, like theirs, can scarcely be recognized without titles, but when a title is supplied, features begin to emerge. In 1911 Picasso did a cubist portrait which was long mistaken for a landscape because he had put the name of the place where it was painted on the back. When he entitled it *The Accordionist*, the subject became recognizable, though only the painter or the sitter could say that the accordionist was Braque. In her portrait of Braque done in 1913, Gertrude Stein provides only one clue besides the title: "Brack, Brack is the one who put up the hooks and held the things up and ate his dinner." Braque, a tall man, helped hang the paintings at 27 rue de Fleurus.

From portraits Gertrude Stein went on to still lifes. She began looking at objects as the cubists did, analyzing and abstracting their properties, choosing ordinary household objects comparable to the bottles, pipes, and musical instruments that Picasso and Braque painted in their still lifes. In her next work, *Tender Buttons*, she came closest to what the painters were doing. The first of her objects most clearly suggests a cubist composition.

A CARAFE, THAT IS A BLIND GLASS

> A kind in glass and a cousin, a spectacle and nothing strange a single hurt color and an arrangement in a system to pointing. All this and not ordinary, not unordered in not resembling. The difference is spreading.

A carafe is just the kind of homely object that the cubist painters would choose, one that offers interesting possibilities of geometric analysis. Gertrude Stein is unable to diagram its planes and angles in writing, but she does something very similar by analyzing its nature, substance, color, and shape. It is "a blind glass" and "cousin" because it is akin to seeing glasses or spectacles. It is also punningly "*a* spectacle" and yet "nothing strange," an ordinary visual object. Presumably the carafe has no color of its own, but its angles diffract the colors of the spectrum, which merge into "a single hurt color" like that of a bruise. In rendering its shape as "an arrangement in a system to pointing," Gertrude Stein defines the very essence of cubism.

The rest of the composition is more abstract than descriptive, generalizing about the carafe as distinct from another "kind in glass." The second sentence may be interpreted as saying: and yet a carafe is extraordinary; it does not resemble glass in other forms, but it is organized ("not unordered") according to its own principles. The third sentence seems to follow from the second: a carafe differs from other glass objects in "spreading" to enclose a space.

To analyze Gertrude Stein's still lifes as riddles may be doing them an injustice. Perhaps she intended them merely as objects for contemplation. But the nature of writing is such that the reader always expects words to yield a meaning of some sort. Therefore *Tender Buttons* will be read, if at all, as a collection of imagistic riddles. As such they appeal to a particular taste of this century, which derives intellectual pleasure in unraveling the metaphysical conceits of John Donne, documenting the obscurities of T. S. Eliot, and decoding the polyglot puns of James Joyce. *Tender Buttons* can be approached in the same spirit. The titles provide the answers, but most of the puzzles require great ingenuity, and many appear to be indecipherable. Some are easy enough, whether visual:

> A PETTICOAT
>
> A light white, a disgrace, an ink spot, a rosy charm.

or conceptual:

> A TIME TO EAT
>
> A pleasant simple habitual and tyrannical and authorised and educated and resumed and articulate separation. This is not tardy.

or onomatopoeic:

A SOUND

> Elephant beaten with candy and little pops and chews all bolts and reckless reckless rats, this is this.

But others yield their secret less readily:

A METHOD OF A CLOAK

> A single climb to a line, a straight exchange to a cane, a desperate adventure and courage and a clock, all this which is a system, which has feeling, which has resignation and success, all makes an attractive black silver.

What is puzzling here is the shift from the visual to romantic associations to perhaps private references. The clock and the color may come from the author's personal acquaintance with cloaks, though one can readily imagine a clock in a desperate cloak-and-dagger rendezvous and the ideal cloak as being black, silver, or both. In any case the subject can readily be recognized, if not all the allusions. But a great many of the compositions in *Tender Buttons* seem to be based on private references that defy interpretation. A cutlet may be quite inscrutable, despite its brevity.

A CUTLET

> A blind agitation is manly and uttermost.

"Nothing changes from generation to generation except the thing seen and that makes a composition." This idea recurs throughout Gertrude Stein's critical writings from *Composition as Explanation* to *Picasso*. Every generation has a different way of seeing, a different way of composing, a different time-sense. She was acutely aware of generations and self-conscious about her role in her own generation. She prized originality above all as the sure mark of genius, and there is no denying her originality. Like Picasso she approached her work as research and went on ceaselessly experimenting, passing through styles and "periods." But perhaps what she produced was more important in theory than accomplishment, closer to science than art.

She was preoccupied with the two great concerns of twentieth-century literature, psychology and time. But for all her theorizing about "bottom natures," her work communicates very little of the subject she studied and claimed as her own in literature, the consciousness, the subjective process, the inner workings of the psyche. Again on the subject of time, her theory is more acceptable than her practice. "A composition of a prolonged present is a natural composition in the world as it has been these thirty years," she said in 1926, explaining her own works from "Melanctha" on. But when she tried to create the flux of time, what she produced was more like stasis. Her lectures and critical writings often have the air of rationalizations, explaining many years after the fact what she had originally tried to do. A wide disparity remains between theory and practice.

Her originality and her shortcomings both stem from the circumstances of her life in Paris: her association with painters and her isolation from an audience. Other writers have worked in isolation without becoming hermetic, but she was extremely independent and strong-minded to begin with, and readily became more eccentric. Her intelligence was always theoretical. Hence the abstract, conceptual nature of her work. Hence too her attempt to transfer the principles of one medium to another. She thought much in pictorial terms, writing portraits, still lifes, and landscapes. She was more successful in dealing with space and description than time and narration, which properly belonged to her medium. And she tried to do with words what the painters of the School of Paris had done with paint. The fauves and cubists had shattered the accepted canons of painting, radically altering perspective, representation, the very concept of reality. Gertrude Stein did something similar to literature, writing novels without narrative sequence, plays without character or conflict, and poetry without form. Her work resembles that of the cubists in certain particulars, but most of all in its fundamental iconoclasm.

If she was not published and not understood in her time, she felt sure that she would be accepted eventually. The fault lay with the public, which always lagged a generation behind the avant-garde. She could not serve "god and mammon," her artistic conscience and the demands of an audience. In the twenties the young came and sat at her feet, and the little magazines published her work, but it was her powerful personality that presided over that decade rather than her writings. Success finally came to her in the thirties when she compromised with her audience and produced her most accessible work, *The Autobiography of Alice B. Toklas*, *Lectures in America*, and *Picasso*. Now she became a celebrity. Her opera, with the benefit of Virgil Thomson's music, was a Broadway hit, and her lecture tour of the United States a triumphal progress.

Though she only visited her native land once in the forty-odd years she lived in Paris, Gertrude Stein remained entirely American. Her imagination always dwelt in her native land, peopled by such heroes as George Washington, Ulysses S. Grant, and Wilbur Wright. She was like Joyce, who always carried Dublin around in his head, but unlike Joyce she was at peace with her country and permanently in touch with its pulse—as if her American background was more real to her in France.

Much has been written about the Americanism of her writing, likening it to the wide empty spaces of an unshaped continent, the grid pattern of the American city, or skyscraper architecture. William Carlos Williams has made more sense of this interpretation than anyone else: "Stein's pages have become like the United States viewed from an airplane—the same senseless repetitions, the endless multiplications of toneless words, with these she had to work." Williams goes on to say that she could not escape her American past: "No use for Stein to fly to Paris and forget it." This remark is reminiscent of her own often repeated observation: "And so I am an American and I have lived half my life in Paris, not the half that made me but the half in which I made what I made."

3.

The Autobiography of Gertrude Stein and Alice B. Toklas

For all her individualism, Gertrude Stein longed for public recognition; her great ambition was to be published in the *Atlantic Monthly*. She finally achieved that ambition after she had been writing for thirty years, when in 1933 the *Atlantic* published excerpts from her forthcoming *Autobiography of Alice B. Toklas*. "*The* autobiography," as it was quite appropriately called in her circle, was her first public success. The reasons for its popularity are obvious enough. The book was readable and entertaining, full of gossip and memorable anecdote, written in the infectious primitive style that she now adopted. To this day it remains her most widely read and most successful book, if not her most important. It is even more beguiling now than it was thirty years ago when most of the writers and artists were less famous. With time it has acquired a legendary quality and has helped to make its author a legendary figure. The wag who called her "the Mother Goose of Montparnasse" captured in that phrase the whole essence of the book as a collection of fairy tales told by a fabulous narrator.

Many of the characters in the tales found themselves unable to appreciate what she had written about them. Leo Stein, as might be expected, was deeply wounded by her cavalier treatment. For a year he spluttered indignantly in letters to his friends about "that farrago of rather clever anecdote, stupid brag and general bosh," correcting her lies, her memory, her dates, and her facts. He saw the comedy all right but insisted on psychoanalyzing the comedian. "But God what a liar she is! If I were not something of a psychopathologist I should be very much mystified." In the humorless way of many Freudians he searched for buried motives when the explanation was all too apparent. "Practically everything that she says of our activities before 1911 is false both in fact and implication, but one of her radical complexes . . . made it necessary practically to eliminate me." One of his comments in particular reveals his limitations as a critic: "I simply cannot take Gertrude seriously as a literary phenomenon." A literary phenomenon she undeniably was, if nothing else.

The *Autobiography* offended others as well, and some of them replied in print. In February 1935, the little magazine *Transition* published a fifteen-page pamphlet entitled *Testimony against Gertrude Stein,* containing statements by Braque, Matisse, André Salmon, Tristan Tzara, Eugene and Maria Jolas, correcting some of her facts and refuting some of her claims. It is an interesting document, informative and expressive of the individual personalities, each approaching the truth in a different way. Matisse writes a point-by-point rebuttal that is as futile as it is meticulous, but valuable for its details about his early years. It is here that he credits Sarah Stein with being "the really intelligently sensitive member of the family." Maria Jolas is at pains to give a true account of the founding and editing of *Transition* and its relations with Gertrude Stein, whose falsifications she attributes to jealousy because *Transition* paid more attention to James Joyce. Tzara appears strangely out of character in accusing Gertrude Stein and Alice Toklas of fraud, megalomania, and publicity seeking—this from the promoter of dada! Salmon writes more in sorrow than in anger, corrects a number of mistakes, and recommends Fernande Olivier's book, *Picasso et Ses Amis,* for a more accurate account of the Rousseau banquet. Gertrude Stein had written that Salmon had an attack of delirium tremens during the banquet and had to be locked up in the cloakroom, where he had eaten Alice Toklas' hat in his frenzy; Fernande's version of the story is that Salmon had played a joke on the gullible Americans by eating soap and foaming at the mouth.

Braque's statement is the shortest and most dignified. It is also the most effective because of his authority. "Miss Stein understood nothing of what went on around her. I have no intention of entering into a discussion with her, since it is obvious that she never knew French really well and that was always a barrier. But she has entirely misunderstood cubism which she sees simply in terms of personalities." Here Braque has put his finger on Gertrude Stein's method. He goes on to explain that he and Picasso suppressed their individuality in their early research into cubism and did not care if others mistook their paintings. "Miss Stein," he continues, "obviously saw everything from the outside and never the real struggle we were engaged in. For one who poses as an authority on the epoch it is safe to say that she never went beyond the stage of the tourist."

The most devastating rejoinder came thirty years later from a writer who was more than a match for Gertrude Stein, who had studied her methods and now turned them against her. He was endowed with the same competitive psychology and had the further advantage of being a most accomplished writer of fiction. His book was also destined to become a permanent part of the legend. The ghost of Ernest Hemingway will continue to haunt the ghost of Gertrude Stein because she committed a crime against his reputation. Her real mistake was in underestimating this dangerous opponent and inciting him to revenge. The *Autobiography* includes a number of anecdotes at his expense, insidiously slighting him in ways that were most calculated to hurt, describing him as "yellow," "fragile," and "ninety percent Rotarian." Hemingway knew that he could only beat her by playing the same game, and he waited until his last years to even the score. His Paris reminiscences, *A Moveable Feast,* contain a full-length portrait of Gertrude Stein that shows how much he had learned from her. He employs her own tactics, praising her only to undermine her, snubbing "her companion" as a dim anonymous figure, attacking her where he thinks she is most vulnerable. The result is rather discreditable but undeniably artful. It is likely to be the last word.

Hemingway is one of the few who understood what Gertrude Stein was doing in the *Autobiography*. It was not surprising that readers who were deeply involved should regard the book as a parcel of lies. What is surprising is that other readers, including literary and art historians, have taken the book literally and cited its contents as fact. Hemingway understood this too when he wrote *A Moveable Feast* and knew it would be widely accepted as a historical document. Actually both books are ingeniously wrought fictions. The characters and events are all based on real people and their doings, but so are the characters and events of any fictional work. To a fiction writer his acquaintance and their experiences are merely raw material. His business is not to record them accurately but to improve them. Verisimilitude is his test, not veracity. And when he decides to write his memoirs, he is likely to fictionalize to some extent.

Usually the fictional autobiographer gives clues to his reader. That most notorious fictionalizer of his life, Ford Madox Ford, announces at the beginning of one book of memoirs, *It Was the Nightingale*, that he intends to write it as a novel. Hemingway suggests in his preface that *A Moveable Feast* may be read as fiction. Gertrude Stein gives no explicit warning, but the very title of her autobiography indicates a spoof, and the writing sounds tongue-in-cheek. Whereas Hemingway's book is entirely believable on the surface, hers seems meant to be taken with a grain of salt.

The *Autobiography* is highly inaccurate, with events revised to suit the author's convenience. Gertrude Stein treats facts with insouciance, ignoring those that do not interest her, modifying others, highlighting those she finds most dramatic or significant. In order to concentrate on a few main characters, she relegates the others to minor roles or suppresses them entirely; thus she alludes to "her brother" as though she had only one and attributes most of the achievements of the Stein family to herself. Her treatment of dates is particularly carefree. Picasso's age is still twenty-four in 1907 when Alice B. Toklas appears on the scene, because he was twenty-four when Gertrude first met him, and that seemed a fitting age for him to be. To bring Alice B. Toklas on at a climactic moment, the events of three or four years are concentrated into one. The early struggles of Matisse are telescoped so that Gertrude Stein can rescue him at a desperate moment by purchasing *La Femme au Chapeau.* She prefers the legend about Rousseau's days in Mexico to the fact that he had never been there and repeats the legend about the death of the wounded veteran Guillaume Apollinaire on Armistice Day while the crowd outside shouted "*à bas Guillaume.*" Gertrude Stein must have known that Apollinaire died two days before the armistice, but the legend was more poignant than the anticlimactic fact. Invariably she is more interested in telling a good story than telling the truth.

The best way to see what she has done and how well she has succeeded is to compare the *Autobiography* with Fernande Olivier's *Picasso et Ses Amis*. Fernande Bellevallée, as she was then, was Picasso's mistress during the decisive period from 1904 to 1912. She served as his model and shared his life through the five lean years he lived in Montmartre and then in Clichy through the exploratory years of cubism. In her book she set out to describe the artist's life as one who had lived at its very center. *Picasso et Ses Amis* is composed of brief disconnected sketches of the *bateau lavoir* group engaged in characteristic activities. It portrays, among others, the poets Max Jacob and Guillaume Apollinaire, the dealers Sagot and Vollard, the painters Marie Laurencin, van Dongen, Derain, Vlaminck, and Braque. Picasso is always the center of attention, and the others are seen in relation to him. The book is also a guide to Picasso's Paris, describing his disorderly studio and its contents, such favorite haunts as the Closerie des Lilas and the Lapin Agile, the Cirque Médrano and Saturday evenings at the Steins'.

All this is the stuff of legends, but Fernande is no maker of legends. Her book has great documentary value but less human interest than might be expected. She writes in fragmentary notes that do not always come to a point, and her overall purpose is not altogether clear, even to herself. Are these chapters in art history or chapters in the history of Bohemia? Her attitude is uncertain, as she cannot decide whether to sigh wistfully at those lost days of her youth, to reproach her old friends for having abandoned her, or to frankly admire Picasso's great talent. She does all three alternately.

Picasso et Ses Amis may very well have inspired *The Autobiography of Alice B. Toklas.* Some of Fernande's reminiscences first appeared in 1931, published by installments in *Le Mercure de France.* As an interested party Gertrude Stein would certainly have read the sketches when they appeared in the magazine. She must have seen the possibilities of the material and the opportunity to do far better herself. She could of course have done so without reading *Picasso et Ses Amis,* but the fact is that she did not write the *Autobiography* until the fall of 1932, and both books appeared the following year.

The difference between them was all the more striking. One became a best seller while the other went out of print and became a minor work of reference. No doubt some of the anecdotes originated with Fernande, but it was Gertrude Stein who made them famous. Her versions are better in every respect: more incisive, more characteristic, more vivid, more memorable. When there are discrepancies, the *Autobiography* is often more convincing.

When Fernande recounts the "duel" between Apollinaire and another writer, a duel which consisted of elaborate and prolonged negotiations between their seconds while the principals anxiously awaited the outcome, she provides a more factual account, complete with the itemized bill on which the story turns. Max Jacob, acting as Apollinaire's second, claimed expenses because he had to treat his antagonist's second to coffee, matches, a roll, a newspaper, an apéritif. Apollinaire was notoriously stingy, and the duel, once settled, turned to haggling. When Gertrude Stein tells the same story, she says she heard it from Fernande and Picasso at the time and did not have a very clear picture of the details, but her account is nonetheless more amusing and more pungent. The fact is that she is a practiced storyteller, while Fernande, despite her inside knowledge of Montmartre and ironic sense of humor, is an amateur.

The contrast is most apparent in their two versions of the banquet given in honor of Rousseau. Picasso had discovered a painting by Rousseau on sale at a junk dealer's for five francs. He displayed it prominently in his studio, decorated it with wreaths and flags, hung up a banner proclaiming "*Honneur à Rousseau,*" invited some thirty friends for dinner and anyone who wanted to come afterward. Among those at dinner were Gertrude and Leo Stein, Alice Toklas, and her friend Harriet Levy. Fernande of course was the hostess. Everything went wrong. The food that had been ordered from a caterer did not arrive. Some of the guests got drunk and disorderly. Several times the ceremony threatened to become a riot. Still, the evening proved a great success. Apollinaire read a poem he had written for the occasion, others sang and danced, Rousseau played his violin.

Fernande, who presents the banquet as a joke at Rousseau's expense, considers it ridiculous that he should be deeply moved by the honor. She depicts him as a naïve old clown, dozing off with candle wax dripping on his head. The *Autobiography* conveys the animated confusion of the party, reports Fernande's attempts to keep the peace, quotes her protests that this was a serious banquet, and describes it as the apotheosis of Rousseau—in short, reverses Fernande's interpretation and her own role. Over these and other versions of the event there will never be any agreement, but the *Autobiography* gives a most convincing account. It is not only livelier but much more circumstantial, and its details, true or false, have the ring of authenticity:

> Marie Laurencin sang in a thin voice some charming old norman songs. The wife of Agero sang some charming old limousin songs, Pichot danced a wonderful religious spanish dance ending in making of himself a crucified Christ upon the floor. Guillaume Apollinaire solemnly approached myself and my friend and asked us to sing some of the native songs of the red indians. We did not either of us feel up to that to the great regret of Guillaume and all the company. Rousseau blissful and gentle played the violin and told us about the plays he had written and his memories of Mexico.

One possible explanation of the discrepancy between the two accounts is that Gertrude Stein and Alice Toklas remained sober throughout the banquet. They had the advantage of being spectators, less involved in the agitation, better able to observe, and they outnumbered Fernande two to one. Between them they could remember more and compare notes, and in the years that followed they must have told the story over and over again. Gertrude Stein's anecdotes are like family jokes that improve with each telling and become transformed with age. She says she wrote the *Autobiography* in six weeks, but she and Alice Toklas had been rehearsing the materials for twenty-five years. In her circle these anecdotes are still being repeated, some of them sixty years old, as though they had never appeared in print.

Anecdote is the basis of her method. Gertrude Stein admits that she is a good gossip, fond of intrigue. The *Autobiography* is simply a succession of anecdotes and remarks, moving by free association the way gossip moves, from one person or episode to another. Although Gertrude Stein quotes her reprimand, "Hemingway, remarks are not literature," the *Autobi-*

ography proves otherwise. She cultivated a particular brand of bon mot and had an enormous repertory of little stories, usually told at someone's expense, often understated, leading to an anticlimax that concealed a sharp point. It was no easy matter to weave these scattered elements into a unified work. She managed to do so by using several devices. Chief of these was Alice B. Toklas.

If Alice B. Toklas had not existed, it would have been necessary to invent her. She makes an engaging character and an indispensable narrator. Fond of cooking, dusting, and needlepoint, she is the domestic member of the household, playing Martha opposite Gertrude Stein's Mary. She is the quiet member too, but all-observant and sly as a cat. Her innocent exterior belies her shrewd wit, for there is no doubt that she contributed her share to the store of anecdotes and epigrams in the *Autobiography*. Tactically, Alice B. Toklas is a most useful subterfuge, giving the narrative a point of view, a tone of voice, and a semblance of objectivity that permits Gertrude Stein to quote her own clever remarks and say flattering things about herself without seeming egotistical. Then there is always the presence of the real Alice Toklas outside the book, who is quoted as protesting against her autobiography as it is being written. These shifting planes of reality make the creation of Alice B. Toklas a humorous cubistic artifice.

Yet the book is quite seriously about Alice Toklas too. Its original title was to have been "My Twenty Five Years with Gertrude Stein," and its subject remains the story of their life together. Though for the most part self-effacing, Alice Toklas is always there. Gertrude Stein is doing the writing, but Alice Toklas is narrating; one even feels at times that she is dictating and that Gertrude Stein is her amanuensis. The book is not so much an autobiography as a portrait and self-portrait of each by the other.

Some measure of their close working relationship is indicated by Alice B. Toklas' statement that Gertrude Stein's handwriting "has always been illegible and I am very often able to read it when she is not." She was not only the expert on handwriting, she not only typed the manuscripts and read the proofs, she was Gertrude Stein's chief critic, publisher, adviser—and more. They lived their lives together in an intimacy that extended to all their activities and excluded all others. That is one reason why Leo, Michael, and Sarah Stein are never mentioned by name; neither is Harriet Levy, the companion who accompanied Alice Toklas to Paris and shared an apartment with her before she moved into the rue de Fleurus; even Etta Cone, her predecessor as Gertrude Stein's typist, is excluded by ridicule. The Steins were suppressed not only so that Gertrude could play the role of discoverer of modern art by herself, but because Alice Toklas had supplanted them and become Gertrude's family. So the *Autobiography* is hers too.

Thirty years later, when Alice Toklas published her memoirs in her own name, *What Is Remembered,* she disclosed what one had suspected all along, that she had contributed a good deal to the *Autobiography*. The style, the character, the point of view, the quiet delivery, the sly wit are all much the same. Many of the same anecdotes and epigrams are there, along with new ones in the same vein, and it becomes apparent that a good share of those in the *Autobiography* originated with Alice Toklas. (Only she could have quoted her father's remark when he was awakened with the news of the San Francisco earthquake and fire: "That, said he with his usual calm, will give us a black eye in the East.") *What Is Remembered* shows the same keen eye for the amusing and characteristic, the same childlike approach, often the same primer English, with abrupt, disconnected sentences creating incongruities and non sequiturs, as in the following complete paragraph:

> It was when I was seven or eight that my grandmother talked to me about music and took me to hear it. The first singer I remember was Judic, a gay though very old Parisian light opera singer. She wore an immense turquoise

> brooch surrounded by diamonds presented to her by the Emperor Louis Napoleon. That was my first introduction to the War of 1870.

Of her typing Alice Toklas says, "I got a Gertrude Stein technique, like playing Bach. My fingers were adapted only to Gertrude's work." Her style too is often like that of Gertrude Stein. She remembers a childhood experience as "frightening but romantic," speaks of Paris as "my home town," and writes of the first night she spent on French soil, "Under a hotel window French voices were singing French songs in the mild French air." She employs the same primitive sense of cause and effect: "From Córdova we went to Seville, where it was very hot and where I ate innumerable ices during the day, which disturbed Gertrude's stomach."

The similarity is most apparent in the handling of anecdotes. Here is one about the Matisse school:

> Olga Merson, a young and good-looking Russian, attached herself to one after the other of the young men. She was indifferent to their indifference to her charms. Eventually she took an especial interest in the *cher maître*. He was blondish and wore gold spectacles, making him look like a German professor. Was this in memory of her student days in Germany?

And another, with the same kind of understated conclusion:

> Crossing the Luxembourg one day I ran into Leslie Hunter, a San Francisco painter, a large burly Scotchman. He came to see me and took me on long, cold, winter walks and I took him to see the pictures at the rue de Fleurus, which shocked him profoundly. He wished he had never gone to see them. His painting was under the influence of Sir Thomas Lawrence.

Alice Toklas does not always write in this deadpan style. The most moving passage of *What Is Remembered,* the account of her first meeting with Gertrude Stein, rises to an eloquence that is beyond the reach of primer English:

> In the room were Mr. and Mrs. Stein and Gertrude Stein. It was Gertrude Stein who held my complete attention, as she did for all the many years I knew her until her death, and all these empty ones since then. She was a golden brown presence, burned by the Tuscan sun and with a golden glint in her warm brown hair. She was dressed in a warm brown corduroy suit. She wore a large round coral brooch and when she talked, very little, or laughed, a good deal, I thought her voice came from this brooch. It was unlike anyone else's voice—deep, full, velvety like a great contralto's, like two voices. She was large and heavy with delicate small hands and a beautifully modeled and unique head. It was often compared to a Roman emperor's, but later Donald Sutherland said that her eyes made her a primitive Greek.

Which came first, Alice Toklas or Alice B. Toklas? The author of *What Is Remembered* was surely influenced by the *Autobiography,* but there can be no doubt that she had influenced the *Autobiography* in the first place. Because she is self-effacing, Alice Toklas is easily overlooked and underestimated. She can be most clearly detected in her other book, *The Alice B. Toklas Cookbook,* where her elusive personality, like a subtle but indispensable spice, flavors the writing throughout.

What is most impressive about the cookbook is Alice Toklas' very considerable literary skill. A cookbook with a plot, it reminisces about the circumstances in which its recipes were gathered, from the time she began cooking for Gertrude Stein. The *Cookbook* can be read as a companion to the *Autobiography,* presenting a view from the kitchen on much of the same material. There are observations on Franco-American culinary relations; there are "Dishes for Artists," including "Bass for Picasso" and "Oeufs Francis Picabia"; there are Spanish recipes collected during their travels in Spain; there is a chapter about the restaurants they discovered in their first two cars, "Food to which Aunt Pauline and Lady Godiva led us," and another on "Food in the United States in 1934 and 1935," commemorating their one and only visit to their native land. There is also a good deal of out-of-the-way information usually omitted from cookbooks. One chapter tells about the cooks who worked for them, including the famous Hélène who proves to be much as she appears in the *Autobiography;* another tells about gardening at Bilignin, where they spent their summers, and another about foraging under the German occupation, with "Liberation Fruit Cake" as its happy ending. The *Cookbook* reveals a perceptive imagination at work. Alice Toklas is in every respect a worthy collaborator of Gertrude Stein.

In the *Autobiography* the character of Alice B. Toklas lends a tone of voice as well as a point of view. Her very name sets the tone, introducing Alice-in-Wonderland with a middle initial and a rather discordant surname. It was Gertrude Stein who insisted on that middle initial, overriding Alice Toklas' objections. An air of childlike naïveté clings to the character, who makes remarks with Wonderland logic, calling Gertrude Stein "a civil war general of either or both sides," or saying of her birthplace, "As I am an ardent Californian and she spent her youth there I have often begged her to be born in California but she has always remained firmly born in Allegheny, Pennsylvania." Like a child she often ignores time sequence. Thus she describes a friend of Raymond Duncan as "a very beautiful, very athletic English girl, a kind of sculptress, she later married and became the widow of the discoverer of the South Pole, Scott." Of Apollinaire's introduction to Marie Laurencin's mother, she reports, "Later just before the war the mother fell ill and died. Then the mother did see Guillaume Apollinaire and liked him." In the same vein but more knowing is Picasso's comment about Gertrude Stein's portrait, "Yes, he said, everybody says that she does not look like it but that does not make any difference, she will, he said."

The treatment of time in these instances is both primitive and sophisticated. Alice B. Toklas seems to have a very dim time sense; dates, seldom mentioned, are quite unreliable; the sequence of events is often confused, with stories told out of chronological order. Time is treated like perspective in modern painting, or for that matter, like character in the *Autobiography:* flattened and simplified to bring certain elements into the foreground and suppress others. Actually Gertrude Stein has perfectly good reasons for disrupting chronology. By this means she keeps the narrative returning to one pivotal point, the moment of Alice B. Toklas' arrival in Paris and the beginning of their twenty-five years together.

The second chapter, "My Arrival in Paris," presents the most determined manipulation of time. "This was the year 1907," the narrator announces, and she proceeds to list in the opening paragraph the accomplishments of that time, ranging from Picasso's portrait of Gertrude Stein (1906) to the publication of *Three Lives* (1909), from the beginnings of fauvism (actually 1905, though she cites Matisse's *Bonheur de Vivre,* which was painted in 1906) to "the heroic age of cubism," which only began three years later. She concludes this catalogue with an air of innocence: "I remember not long ago hearing Picasso and Gertrude Stein talking about various things that had happened at that time, one of them said but all that could not have happened in that one year, oh said the other, my dear you forget we were young then and we did a great deal in a year." Of course the memory compresses time, but in this case it is poetic justice that forces all these momentous events to take place simultaneously, bringing Alice B. Toklas on the scene at the most appropriate time.

The second chapter opens on a grand occasion, an evening at 27 rue de Fleurus, and proceeds through a series of dramatic moments. Actually Alice Toklas did arrive in Paris in September 1907, did meet Gertrude Stein on her first day there, did have dinner at 27 rue de Fleurus with Fernande and Picasso on her first Saturday night in Paris. This succession of experiences was breathtaking enough, and the account of her first Saturday evening is quite reasonably awestruck. It was indeed, as she says in the *Autobiography*, one of the most important evenings in her life. But fictional time sets in when she goes to the *vernissage des Indépendants* and sees paintings by Rousseau, Matisse, Braque, and Derain that can be identified from her descriptions. Actually she did go to the *vernissage* of the Autumn Salon (not the Indépendants, which was held in the spring) shortly after her arrival in Paris, but the *Autobiography* compresses the exhibitions of several years into one show in order to recapitulate art history from fauvism to the beginnings of cubism.

As Chapter II continues, Gertrude Stein takes Alice B. Toklas on a guided tour of Montmartre, crossing Paris by the more picturesque horse-drawn omnibus (rather than the motorbus which had started running from Saint-Germain-des-Prés to Montmartre the previous year), finding her way around the *bateau lavoir* (full of memories of events that had not yet taken place) to Picasso's studio. There in the intimacy of the artist's workshop they are able to witness the discovery of cubism, to see *Les Demoiselles d'Avignon* half finished, at a crucial moment just before the two archaic "Negro" figures were added. Alice B. Toklas feels "something painful and beautiful there and oppressive but imprisoned." Her description of the painting (not mentioned in *What Is Remembered*) appears to be entirely fictional, for she only sees the three "*demoiselles*," whereas Picasso's preliminary sketches all included other figures.

After the visit to Picasso's studio Alice B. Toklas proceeds to call on Fernande, temporarily estranged from Picasso. It is true that she took French lessons from Fernande to tide her over during a quarrel with Picasso, but the visit to Fernande serves a useful purpose in the *Autobiography*, permitting Gertrude Stein to introduce other wives and mistresses of artists and to work in a good many stories about the Bohemian life of Montmartre. While seeming to ramble casually, the account of Alice B. Toklas' introduction to Paris is carefully plotted and directed. The entire *Autobiography*, for all its ingenuous air, is controlled by a firm sense of purpose.

The legend of Gertrude Stein is always clearly before us. More than half the book deals with the prewar years in an attempt to place her in the creative history of that period. The first five chapters form a separate unit that might be entitled "Gertrude Stein and the New School of French Painting." In reporting the doings and sayings of Montmartre and Montparnasse they explain "how two americans happened to be in the heart of an art movement of which the outside world at that time knew nothing." And undeniably one great value of the *Autobiography* is that it captures the spirit of those early years before the painters became famous. Regardless of accuracy, it communicates more of the excitement of that time and transfixes its gestures more successfully than any history. A Saturday evening at the rue de Fleurus, the *vernissage* of one of the revolutionary exhibitions, the banquet for Rousseau, these dramatic moments group together the new painters of the day in the presence of their epoch-making works.

All things considered, *The Autobiography of Alice B. Toklas* is a masterful combination of reminiscence, art history, and fiction, weaving the lives of the painters and the history of modern art into the real and fancied reminiscences of the author and the narrator. Underlying all this artifice is the central thesis that Gertrude Stein and Pablo Picasso were the two great geniuses who discovered the twentieth century between them. That is the ultimate purpose that binds all these disparate elements together into one of the most ingenious autobiographies ever concocted.

THE GREAT WAR

CHRONOLOGY II

1914 Henry James, *The American Volunteer Motor-Ambulances in France*

1915 Mildred Aldrich gives bird's-eye view of the war in *A Hilltop on the Marne*
Edith Wharton directs refugee and hospital work, visits the front as V.I.P., reports fervidly in *Fighting France: From Dunkerque to Belfort*

1916 Ellen La Motte, *The Backwash of War: The Human Wreckage of the Battlefield as Witnessed by an American Hospital Nurse*
Poems of Alan Seeger, killed in action July 4 while serving with French Foreign Legion. "I have a rendez-vous with Death"
Barbusse, *Le Feu*

1917 Woodrow Wilson declares war to make the world safe for democracy
Cummings, Slater Brown, and Dos Passos go to France with Norton-Harjes Ambulance Corps
Eight Harvard Poets

1918 Hemingway joins Red Cross, wounded on the Italian front
Apollinaire, *Calligrammes*

1919 Versailles Peace Conference

1920 Dos Passos, *One Man's Initiation—1917*
Pound, *Hugh Selwyn Mauberley:*

> There died a myriad,
> And of the best, among them,
> For an old bitch gone in the teeth,
> For a botched civilization.

Prohibition

1921 Dos Passos, *Three Soldiers*

1922 Cummings, *The Enormous Room*
Eliot, *The Waste Land*

1923 Cummings, *Tulips and Chimneys*

1924 Ford, *Some Do Not*, first volume of *Parade's End*

1925 Hemingway, *In Our Time*

1929 Remarque, *All Quiet on the Western Front*
Hemingway, *A Farewell to Arms*

1932 Dos Passos, *1919*
Céline, *Journey to the End of Night*

4.

The View from the Windows of Nowhere

"World War One," E. E. Cummings once said, "was the experience of my generation," but it could hardly be said that his own experience was typical. Although among the first to go overseas after the United States entered the war, he saw more of Paris than he saw of the front, and more of a French prison than of either. Cummings appears to have had no illusions about the war and certainly no desire to be drafted. He volunteered for the ambulance service, partly to avoid the army, partly "to do something useful and to see France at the same time." As he explains in his autobiographical *i: Six Nonlectures*, "Being neither warrior nor conscientiousobjector, saint nor hero, I embarked for France as an ambulance-driver." He sailed on the *Touraine* on April 28, 1917; on board he met William Slater Brown, with whom he soon became the closest of friends.

Cummings and Brown were both New Englanders of the nonconformist variety. Cummings, born and raised in Cambridge, the son of a Unitarian minister who had once taught at Harvard, had inherited all the individualism of the New England tradition but none of its stuffiness. Irreverent toward all institutions, fundamentally satiric, anarchic, and bawdy, he was a true Yankee nonetheless. Slater Brown was if anything more dissident. To this day Brown takes an ironic view of his origins, describing Webster, Massachusetts, where he grew up, as an ugly mill town and putting the blame on his great-great-grandfather who had built the mills and introduced child labor into America. Brown hated Massachusetts and took the earliest opportunity to escape by enrolling at Columbia College. When the United States was about to declare war, he went to Washington with an antiwar delegation in an effort to prevent Congress from voting in favor of the declaration. When this effort failed, he and a friend decided, ". . . if we couldn't stop the war we could hurry over there and see what it was all about." Finding that the quickest way of getting over to France was to join the Norton-Harjes Ambulance Corps, they signed up within a week and were among the earliest Americans to land in France.

Brown and Cummings took the train from Bordeaux to Paris with a group of Norton-Harjes volunteers. When the train reached the outskirts of Paris the other members of the group were herded off at the wrong station; Brown and Cummings stayed on till the train had reached the Gare d'Orléans, which was their proper destination, and reported to Norton-Harjes headquarters, which sent them to a hotel. They were thus separated from their group, which was billeted elsewhere, and their records got lost in the files somehow, so that they managed to have a month's leave in Paris before they saw any service. They thoroughly enjoyed that month, discovering the attractions of Paris in the spring, walking about its streets ten or twenty miles a day, buying books and reproductions of Cézanne and Matisse, going to the Ballet Russe every night they could. They saw Stravinsky's *Petrouchka* many times and attended the premiere of *Parade* with Satie's mechanical music and Picasso's cubist décor. When the audience booed *Parade*, Cummings was outraged and threatened to fight; Brown remembers "Cummings yelling all sorts of dirty words in French." They also gravitated to a side of Paris that never ceased to fascinate Cummings in later years, the Paris of the Commune, the world of popular uprisings and demonstrations. "Monsieur

Brown . . . & I," he wrote home, "have already participated in all the grèves of Paris (She is practically, or has been, in a state of revolution)." And of course they were beguiled by the feminine side of Paris, "the finest girls God ever allowed to pasture in the air of this fresh earth."

The effect of that first month in Paris was profound and lasting, an essential part of Cummings' education. "After Harvard," he says in "i & selfdiscovery," one of his "nonlectures," "I thank (for selfdiscovery) a phenomenon and a miracle." The phenomenon was New York City, where he had spent the months before going to war; the miracle was Paris. Although he later chose to live in Greenwich Village, Paris was his second home, to which he returned again and again for prolonged stays—about a dozen times altogether. He loved the Village, but a miracle compared favorably with a phenomenon: "Whereas —by the very act of becoming its improbably gigantic self— New York had reduced mankind to a tribe of pygmies, Paris (in each shape and gesture and avenue and cranny of her being) was continuously expressing the humanness of humanity."

In Paris he found a world such as he had never known in New England or New York. When he speaks of the freedom of Paris, he means not so much an escape from Anglo-Saxon prohibitions as the frank acceptance of the whole man which was so vital a part of his outlook. His discovery of this new world precipitates a string of joyous paradoxes.

> Now, I participated in an actual marriage of material with immaterial things; I celebrated an immediate reconciling of spirit and flesh, forever and now, heaven and earth. Paris was for me precisely and complexly this homogeneous duality: this accepting transcendence; this living and dying more than death or life. . . . Everywhere I sensed a miraculous presence, not of mere children and women and men, but of living human beings; and the fact that I could scarcely understand their language seemed irrelevant, since

> the truth of our momentarily mutual aliveness created an imperishable communion. . . . Now, finally and first, I was myself: a temporal citizen of eternity; one with all human beings born and unborn.

After a month the ambulance service caught up with its two stray volunteers and assigned them to a unit near the front. Cummings' comment upon arrival was hardly enthusiastic. "The entrance of the camp here was much unprepossessing," he wrote in a letter home, "as ever just the people we left America to avoid are found here." The same letter contains two further comments which might have caused a military censor to frown: "As you doubtless know, the famous cathedral not far away, still in the possession of the Allemands, has kept the French fire from the town of which it is the crown. The refusal of the French to knock up their old glories angers the English considerably. I think it's the first passably pleasant thing about the war." And the letter closes melodramatically, "I shall write later when I, too, have nearly gone insane under fire, like the poor poilus who are all praying for a wound to take them out of the trenches."

Cummings and Brown drove an ambulance together for three months, without seeing much action. In his letters Cummings referred to "the front" in quotation marks and reported chiefly boredom, resentment of routine and odious superiors. His only friend was Brown, and they fraternized as much as possible with the French. "Nous sommes, Brun et moi, toujours camarades avec les français qui nous appellent Edouard V et Guillaume II." Cummings was soon at home in French and wrote his letters in that language with rapidly increasing fluency. He and Brown ended up living with the French soldiers assigned to their unit.

Slater Brown remembers that he and Cummings were the only Americans in their unit who were fond of the French and wanted to master their language. They used to go to the French soldiers' café, where they talked with troops *en repos* from the front and learned a great many French songs. Brown recalls one occasion when the French soldiers insisted that they sing "Tipperary." "So Cummings and I got on the table and all we knew was the chorus, but Cummings thought we ought to be able to do more than sing the chorus. So he began. He made up all the words leading up to the chorus—impromptu and all in rhyme too. I remember that the last two lines that he sang were 'And to her maidenhead I softly, softly send.' And I joined in the chorus, 'It's a long way to Tipperary. It's a long way to go.' I'm sorry that I can't remember the other passages because it was all as neat as that. And quite, you know, ad-lib. Cummings could always do things like that."

Ironically, their fondness for the French got them into trouble. As Brown explains, their chief took an immediate dislike to him and Cummings "because we consorted with the French and he couldn't understand how any true-blooded American could prefer the French soldiers to their own countrymen." He also suspected them because they kept to themselves and, Brown thinks, because they used to take long walks in the evening. (Once when they were out walking they kept hearing a strange sound overhead, until finally some Frenchmen warned them they were walking straight toward no man's land; the whining sound they heard was that of machine-gun bullets.) Brown says their superior did everything he could to get them into trouble because he wanted to get rid of them. And the charges he finally brought against them were serious, for he declared them undesirable in the military zone and too dangerous to be sent home. He condemned Brown as the real "Germanophile" of the two but also charged that Cummings "expressed pro-German feelings and endeavored to come into contact with French soldiers with suspicious intentions." They were turned over to a French tribunal because their unit was attached to the French army and subject to military law.

The charges seem preposterous now, and Brown's letters, which were supposed to serve as evidence, could hardly be construed as pro-German. Brown thinks that the charges were taken seriously because he wrote about the mutinies that had demoralized the French army during the spring of 1917 and threatened to bring the war to an end. Very few Americans ever heard about these mutinies; fewer still heard about them from French soldiers. To a French military court Brown's sympathies may have seemed dangerous. And Cummings, who could easily have been cleared, condemned himself when he remained loyal to his friend. Thus they ended up in a French prison camp at La Ferté Macé, Cummings detained temporarily, Brown sentenced to a concentration camp for the duration of the war.

Actually Cummings was held for three months, despite all the efforts of American authorities to obtain his release, and Brown, who had visions of being locked up for a Thirty Years War or a Hundred Years War, was finally released after five months. Both were promptly sent home, and both were drafted into the American army the following summer; but Brown, who had lost too many teeth from scurvy, was soon discharged, and Cummings spent an anticlimactic six months waiting out the war. When drafted he gave his occupation as artist ("Specialist in Cubism") and offered himself as an interpreter, but his talents were never required, and he soon learned to hate the military life.

After the war Cummings' father continued to be indignant about the treatment his son had received at the hands of the French. Dr. Cummings had used all kinds of influence to obtain his son's release from prison, even addressing a letter to Woodrow Wilson, and two years later he was still determined to sue the French government for a million dollars. Brown, who stayed at the Cummings' summer home in 1920, can remember that Dr. Cummings used to argue endlessly with his son, urging him to write an account of his imprisonment to be used in the lawsuit. E. E. Cummings had much more common sense than his father, Brown says, and finally agreed to write the story on condition that it would not be used in a lawsuit. Thus it happened that Cummings wrote *The Enormous Room* and turned the manuscript over to his father, who had it published. But several of Cummings' letters show that he had already been working on his "French notes" for a year and a half before this, slowly writing "the Story Of The Great War Seen From The Windows Of Nowhere," painstakingly weaving a fabric, "so that every inch of it seems good to me."

Brown stayed with Cummings while he wrote the book, helping him remember their adventures together. But Cummings relied mainly on the notebooks he had kept in prison, sketching his fellow inmates, recording conversations, endlessly taking notes on whatever went on around him. His portraits, so fresh and vivid, seem to come directly from the notebooks, and Brown says that the people at La Ferté Macé are all accurately described. But *The Enormous Room* is more than straight documentary; the experience is brought to life by Cummings' highly original style and by his ability to capture the essence of character in action. "He was a wonderful mimic," Brown recalls. "In prison he was always mimicking. He used to mimic some of the *plantons* and he particularly liked to give a performance imitating the *Surveillant*. All the prisoners would gather around to hear these and roar with laughter at his imitation of the *Surveillant* giving a lecture on being clean and washing one's face and shaving every morning."

In *The Enormous Room* Cummings' scorn for all representatives of authority is matched by his pity for those unfortunates whose crime was "thinking during warlike moments recently passed." Ultimately he questions some of the ideals for which "The Great War for Humanity, etc." was supposed to be fought, since the war deprived him of his rights, exposed him to the strange ways of justice, and locked him up for an indefinite period on unspecified charges. The resulting narrative is not "one of the very best of the war-books," as T. E. Lawrence and Robert Graves regarded it, but one of the best prison books. Like most writing about prison experiences, it regards the establishment with a jaundiced view. Despite its lighthearted tone, a fierce irony prevails; in this acid Cummings etched his portraits, black or white. His fellow prisoners are for the most part saintly, his custodians usually villainous.

The narrative begins at the ambulance service camp with Cummings and Brown cleaning their chief's vehicle, a form of penance to which they were well accustomed. They prided themselves on being the dirtiest men in their unit, appropriately named *Section Sanitaire 21* and surrounded by what the French called "*La Boue Héroïque*," the heroic mud. During their three months' service they had made no effort to endear themselves to "the Norton Harjes fraternity," least of all to their chief, who now denied them leave because, as it turns out, he had other plans for them. To Cummings' great delight, they were whisked away by the French military police, treated as suspicious characters, and interrogated separately. Cummings was given a chance to repudiate his friend but chose to share his fate; when asked if he hated the Boches, he perversely replied, "*Non. J'aime beaucoup les français.*"

The story is told as an allegory, with parallels to John Bunyan's *Pilgrim's Progress.* It opens in the Slough of Despond, which is not the heroic mud but *Section Sanitaire 21.* After being tried and found wanting, the pilgrim makes the long journey by train with two gendarmes to the internment center at La Ferté Mecé. There he spends three months in Limbo awaiting the Last Judgment, though, as he explains, time does not exist in prison. As he enters the world of timelessness, the allegory shifts from pilgrimage to microcosm. The Enormous Room which he shares with some sixty others suggests a church in its architecture; its occupants resemble nothing so much as gargoyles. Cummings sees them with a painter's naked eye, grotesque creatures from an overpopulated canvas by Hieronymus Bosch. Some are repulsive, but many he loves, for all their deformity; the saintliest he calls, after John Bunyan, the Delectable Mountains. Cummings' allegory is of course political rather than religious, though in the broadest sense it is both. His concern is moral, man's inhumanity to man in the form of the system against the individual. But what is most touching about the book is Cummings' own tenderness toward his fellow man.

In camp he had ingratiated himself with the French soldiers by being "in contrast to *les américains*, not bent upon making France discover America but rather upon discovering France and *les français*." In the Enormous Room he broadened his acquaintance to include all the Allies and quite a few neutral nations besides. (La Ferté Macé was a screening depot for aliens who had served time in French prisons and were awaiting deportation or assignment to a concentration camp.) As far as Cummings could tell, none of his fellow prisoners were guilty of treason, and most of them were hapless innocents. At every opportunity he protested that he had come to France because he loved the country and its people. Even though he learned to hate "the great and good French government," his book bears witness to his affection for the ordinary Frenchman, the more ordinary the better.

The Enormous Room is Cummings' first piece of sustained writing; as such it presents an interesting record of his stylistic evolution. He already possessed a unique speaking style, which Dos Passos describes as "comical ironical learned brilliantly-colored intricatelycadenced damnably poetic and sometimes just naughty." He discovered his literary style in the process of writing the book, progressing from facile parody to a voice that is distinctively his own. He began in a mock-heroic vein, with archaic or pompous cadences degenerating occasionally into slang. The pomposity of official rhetoric was entirely appropriate to his subject; the archaism suggests that he had been reading too much eighteenth-century satiric prose in preparing to write his own.

His writing is saturated with French. The book was finished three years after his sojourn at La Ferté Macé, but with his notebooks to prompt him, Cummings naturally lapsed into his former idiom. Much of the dialogue is in French, and the narrative is full of French expressions. Cummings writes in a kind of pidgin, bastardizing both languages in the manner of American soldiers who have picked up some French and are amused by the mixture: "My *affaires* were mostly in the vicinity of the cuisine, where lodged the *cuisinier*, *mécanicien*, *menuisier*, etc." From the French he borrows many army and prison expressions which are either untranslatable or would lose some of their effect in translation. He uses English cognates like "regard," "mount," "descend," and "inquietude" in their French sense, and coins such French-sounding phrases as "refind *la liberté*," and "this sort of blaguing." He scrambles the vocabulary and renders the turn of phrase of one language in the other: "M'sieu' Jean . . . they have no hearts, *la commission;* they are not simply unjust, they are cruel, *savez-vous?* Men are not like these; they are not men, they are Name of God I don't know what, they are worse than the animals." Not only *The Enormous Room* but all Cummings' later writing is sprinkled with French, and his mastery of a second language undoubtedly gave him greater flexibility in his experiments with idiom and syntax.

His first book clearly shows the elements that went into his style, the play on language and grammar, the use of typography for maximum effect. Cummings is irresistibly drawn to banality and cliché, which he teases into freshness by coining unexpected variations: "spic not to say span," "ready without being rough," "about sixteen feet short and four feet narrow." He produces similar surprises by inverting negatives, whether in simple phrases ("full of unfear"), or in more complicated constructions that have to be worked out: ". . . weather conditions on Sunday were invariably more indescribable than usual." His grammar is sometimes deliberately and comically pedantic, sometimes highly inventive: "three very formerly and even once bonnets," "the black, evil, dull, certainly not coffee," "I will get upon the soonness of the train and ride into the now of Paris." Cummings may seem to toss off such lines without taking thought, but they are as meticulously worked out as algebra. So is the typography which makes its appearance in

The Enormous Room, the use of capitals to indicate emphasis, volume, or inflection. One prisoner sings

> mEET me to-nIght in DREamland,
> UNder the SIL-v'ry mOOn.

Another has

VIVE LA LIBERTE

tattooed on his chest, a motto which under the circumstances deserves to be printed as a headline. Spacing and punctuation are also used expressively. When Cummings is marched off by gendarmes, they want him to "HurryHurryHurryHurryHurry-Hurry." A childish song the prisoners sing in chorus is carefully rendered, with its accelerated refrain ("Quackquackquack") and its measured close:

Quack.
    Quack.
        Quack.
            Qua-
                ck.

Cummings writes as a poet, his language richer than ordinary prose. He depicts his gendarmes as pigs "chomping cheek-murdering chunks" and observes of one that "a mist overspread the sensual meadows of his coarse face." He is also a painter with an original way of looking, forever visualizing people as animals or disembodied objects. Here is how he sees the three men who interrogate him:

> I looked into six eyes which sat at a desk.
>
> Two belonged to a lawyerish person in civilian clothes, with a bored expression plus a moustache of dreamy proportions with which the owner constantly imitated a gentleman ringing for a drink. Two appertained to a splendid old dotard (a face all ski-jumps and toboggan-slides), on

> whose protruding chest the rosette of the Legion pompously squatted. Numbers five and six had reference to Monsieur, who had seated himself before I had time to focus my slightly bewildered eyes.

Often his observations are in notebook form. Cummings quotes one specimen of the "telegraphic technique" he used in taking notes, and a number of other passages are written in the same cryptic shorthand. His account of Sunday Mass, for instance, seems to have been copied directly from his notebooks, along with the memories of another Sunday when he and Brown were free.

> *Dimanche:* green murmurs in coldness. Surplice fiercely fearful, praying on his bony both knees, crossing himself . . . The Fake French Soldier, alias Garibaldi, beside him, a little face filled with terror . . . the Bell cranks the sharp-nosed *curé* on his knees . . . titter from bench of whores—and that reminds me of a Sunday afternoon on our backs spent with the wholeness of a hill in Chevancourt, discovering a great apple pie, B. and Jean Stahl and Maurice *le Menuisier* and myself; and the sun falling roundly before us.

Increasingly toward the end of the book he writes in this telegraphic manner, which merges into his own style, that of his poetry which he was in the process of discovering. The thirteenth and final chapter is the most interesting stylistically. As Cummings is released from prison, the staccato phrasing reflects his disoriented state. But grammar helps him to find his way out of this bad dream.

> 'I? Am? Going? To? Paris?' somebody who certainly wasn't myself remarked in a kind of whisper.
>
> '*Parfaitement.*'—Pettish. Apollyon. But how changed. Who the devil is myself? Where in Hell am I? What is Paris

> –a place, a somewhere, a city, life, to live: infinitive. Present first singular I live. Thou livest. The *Directeur.* The *Surveillant.* La Ferté Macé, Orne, France. 'Edward E. Cummings will report immediately.' Edward E. Cummings. The *Surveillant.* A piece of yellow paper. The *Directeur.* A necktie. Paris. Life. *Liberté. La liberté. 'La Liberté'*–I almost shouted in agony.

Here and elsewhere Cummings uses punctuation to maximum effect, as he was later to do in his poetry. In *The Enormous Room* he also resorts to the paradoxes and parentheses that give unexpected twists to his meaning. Here is a typical specimen of early Cummings:

> The Great American Public has a handicap which my friends at La Ferté did not as a rule have–education. Let no one sound his indignant yawp at this. I refer to the fact that, for an educated gent or lady, to create is first of all to destroy–that there is and can be no such thing as authentic art until the *bons trucs* (whereby we are taught to see and imitate on canvas and in stone and by words this so-called world) are entirely and thoroughly and perfectly annihilated by that vast and painful process of Unthinking which may result in a minute bit of purely personal Feeling. Which minute bit is Art.

Finally in *The Enormous Room* Cummings displays the elusive element of timing. Some years later, when asked to explain his technique, Cummings wrote in the foreword to a volume of poetry, "Like the burlesk comedian, I am abnormally fond of that precision which creates movement." In conveying the agitation of a train arrival in Paris ("Bump, slowing down. BUMP-BUMP.") he rings the changes with precision and timing.

> Some *permissionnaires* cried 'Paris.' The woman across from me said 'Paris, Paris.' A great shout came up from

every insane drowsy brain that had travelled with us—a fierce and beautiful cry, which went the length of the train. . . . Paris where one forgets, Paris which is Pleasure, Paris in whom our souls live, Paris the beautiful, Paris *enfin.*

The Englishman woke up and said heavily to me: 'I say, where are we?'

'Paris,' I answered, walking carefully on his feet as I made my baggage-laden way out of the compartment. It was Paris.

5.

The Education of John Dos Passos

On December 16, 1917, three days before Cummings' release from La Ferté Macé, John Dos Passos wrote to Mrs. Cummings asking for news of her son. "I sympathized with him so thoroughly, and my letters being anything but prudent," wrote Dos Passos, "that I expected I'd be in the same boat; but the censor evidently didn't notice me—so I am still 'at large,' as the blood & thunder militarists would say of us." Cummings came home in time to answer the letter himself. On January 22, 1918, he wrote to Dos Passos recounting his adventures during the previous four months. By then he had been back long enough so that life in Cambridge had begun to pall, and homesickness for Paris had set in. His letter, written in idiomatic French, concludes, "Ah mon Dos, que je me gène, que je m'ennuie pour la Ville Immense, la Ville Réale, la Femme Superbe et Subtile qui s'appelle—tu le sais—Paris."

Dos Passos and Cummings had much in common besides a love for Paris. At Harvard they had been friends, fellow contributors to the *Harvard Monthly*, and members of the Harvard Poetry Society; their work first reached the outside world in a collection called *Eight Harvard Poets*. In 1917 Dos Passos joined the Norton-Harjes Ambulance Corps and went to France two months after Cummings. There he reacted similarly to the war, the French soldier, brass hats, regimentation, and militarism in general. Although he had tried the year before to join the ambulance service and the Commission for Relief in Belgium, Dos Passos had no more illusions about the war than Cummings and much the same motives in volunteering. He wanted to be of use, and the idea of serving with the French army appealed to him. He had childhood memories of Paris, spoke French with complete fluency, and admired the French. By nature less intransigent than Brown and Cummings, he was never imprisoned, but he too proved to be insufficiently warlike, spoke his mind too frankly, and wrote letters that revealed less than total acceptance of official propaganda at a time when dissent was considered tantamount to treason. No charges were ever brought against him, but wherever he went he was pursued by suspicions that could never be cleared. He saw much more of the war than Cummings and was as profoundly affected.

Eight Harvard Poets is the work of sensitive, cultivated young men who have led a sheltered existence. They may have been attracted, as Cummings certainly was, to the lower-class life of bars and brothels and burlesque shows. There has been a long tradition at Harvard of visiting the Old Howard and the dives of Scollay Square, but Harvard men have gone there as tourists from more privileged circumstances. In the first decades of this century they may have been cultivating a taste for low life that belonged to another tradition, that of the nineteenth-century aesthetes and decadents of Oxford and Paris. The Harvard poets read Oscar Wilde and Huysmans; they affected the attitudes of the mauve decade; their verse was imported *fin de siècle*, modeled after the contents of *The Yellow Book*, smooth, competent, and derivative. Their subsidized volume bespoke leisure spent in harmless frivolity, shallow paradox, secondhand emotions, attenuated Romanticism—in a word, inexperience.

Twenty years later, in the introduction to a portfolio of George Grosz's drawings, Dos Passos reviewed his aesthetic education. "My generation in college was full of callow snob-admiration for the nineties. I can still remember the fashionable mood of gentle and European snobmelancholy the Whistler pastels produced, so like that of Debussy piano pieces, little scraps of red and yellow and green coming out of the dove-colored smudge. At that I think the titles affected me more than the pictures. Still I must have been visually stirred because I soon got hold of a box of pastels and began to make dovecolored smudges of my own." Dos Passos persisted as a painter, eventually progressing beyond "pastel blurs" to the brilliant colors which illustrated his *Orient Express;* he had two one-man shows in New York and did considerable stage designing, including the curtain for Les Ballets Nègres, which first presented Josephine Baker in Paris. But his first approach to painting was literary and ninetyish. He had started looking at paintings after reading Whistler's *Gentle Art of Making Enemies* and had read about the French impressionists in George Moore's *Confessions of a Young Man,* a book which gave him the impression that the painters were "literary figments like the Goncourts." Even contemporary art was confused with literature in his mind and left only a dim memory. "The Armory Show was a real jolt, though I can't remember any picture I saw there, and it is mostly associated in my mind with a torn yellowbacked volume of Van Gogh's letters a friend lent me along with a terribly bad French translation of *Crime and Punishment.* In spite of all the kidding about the 'Nude Descending Stairs,' I didn't recognize it when I saw it again at the Museum of Modern Art in New York. The most I got from cubism at the time was the tingling feeling that a lot of odd things I didn't know about were happening in the world."

Like other Harvard aesthetes, Dos Passos was suddenly overtaken by history. He has since described himself as "a bookish young man of twenty-two who had emerged half-baked from Harvard College and was continuing his education driving an ambulance behind the front in France." His experience transformed him from a dilettante into a deeply engaged political writer, from a minor poet into a leading chronicler of his time. His first two books were war novels, and much of his writing since has dwelt on Verdun and Versailles. What a whaling ship did for Melville, the Great War did for Dos Passos: "It was my university, World War I."

As Dos Passos has frequently explained, the war came first as a shock to members of his generation who had grown up "during the quiet afterglow of the nineteenth century," comfortably assured of progress, civilization, freedom, and peace. "To us, the European war of 1914–1918 seemed a horrible monstrosity, something outside of the normal order of things like an epidemic of yellow fever in some place where yellow fever had never been heard of before." Next came the feeling of disillusion. Dos Passos believed that Woodrow Wilson acted contrary to American traditions when he entered the war, but he felt the betrayal of the New England tradition even more keenly.

> I was studying at Harvard up to the spring of 1916 and followed with growing astonishment the process by which the professors, most of them rational New Englanders brought up in the broadminded pragmatism of William James or in the lyric idealism of Ralph Waldo Emerson, allowed their mental processes to be so transformed by their conviction of the rightness of the Allied cause and the wickedness of the German enemy, that many of them remained narrow bigots for the rest of their lives. . . . I can still remember the sense of relief I felt in taking refuge from the obsessions of the propagandists of hate in the realities of war as it really was. The feeling was almost universal among the men of my generation who saw service in the field.

Dos Passos also experienced the excitement of the war, the sense that it was something to see, an experience not to be missed: "Most of us just out of college were crazy to see what war was like."

Like Cummings he wanted to see the war but not in the army at first. Eventually he served in the army, more willingly than Cummings. Dos Passos who "disapproved of war as a human activity," who was disqualified by his myopia, and who was persona non grata with the military in Europe, nevertheless went to great lengths to enlist in 1918 after the ambulance service was disbanded. Only by returning to the United States and exerting influence did he finally succeed in becoming a buck private in the medical corps toward the end of the war. "I've always been glad that I did," he says. "It was the most valuable part of my education during these years." The army put him in the position of the underdog, much as Cummings' internment had done. Like many sons of the professional class who served as enlisted men, he was thrown in with the working class for the first time in his life. At Harvard the common man had been an abstraction in political economy; now he knew him personally.

More than his experiences at the front it was the army that set Dos Passos at odds with the established order. "We experienced to the full the intoxication of the great conflagration, though those of us who served as enlisted men could hardly be expected to take kindly to soldiering, to the caste system which made officers a superior breed or to the stagnation and opportunism of military bureaucracy. Waste of time, waste of money, waste of lives, waste of youth. We came home with the horrors. We had to blame somebody."

His first book, *One Man's Initiation—1917*, conveys many of his attitudes toward the war. It is not a very good novel but an interesting document, a firsthand account of the war by a man who managed to see much and hear more, an intelligent piece of reporting that explains the disillusionment of his generation. The book sketches another pilgrim's progress from the embarkation of his troopship to its arrival in Bordeaux, then by train to Paris and on to the front, where he learns what war really means: rain, mud, bombardments, gas attacks, horrible deaths. All this is told with the rawness of direct sensation, still fresh as the moment it happened. The book is based on a journal Dos Passos kept during July and August 1917, recording the nauseous smells and unrelenting noise, the terror and boredom, and the lessons of war. A series of impressionistic fragments, it has no plot, but a very clear message, brought out through ironic situations and contrasts.

Martin Howe, the protagonist, is an immature idealist who has much to learn. His education begins on shipboard as he overhears rumors about German atrocities and the immoralities of Paris. He talks with an American girl full of patriotic zeal who would like to exterminate all the Huns. At a café in Paris he finds himself looking into the eyes of a youth whose face has been shot off. In a village near Verdun he watches French soldiers riding by in camions, being driven unwillingly to their deaths. He discovers that there is no hatred between French and German soldiers. Each chapter makes a bitter comment on the meaningless slaughter and its inhuman consequences. On leave in Paris Howe hears of an authentic atrocity from an Englishman who has witnessed the cold-blooded murder of a wounded German prisoner. When Howe himself meets a German prisoner at the front, he feels only compassion; when the German is wounded and dies in his arms, he achieves a sense of atonement.

The book reaches a climax of sorts in what is transparently a political debate, as Martin Howe talks with four French soldiers about their hopes for the postwar world. They conclude that a socialist revolution is needed to guarantee humanity a world free of wars and slavery. The book is dedicated "to those with whom I saw rockets in the sky a certain evening at sunset on the road from Erize-la-Petite to Erize-la-Grande," and Dos Passos seems to be commemorating a political discussion like that of the French soldiers in his book. In any event Martin Howe's education is completed that evening. The final irony arrives a few pages later as he learns that all his French friends have been killed in action.

One Man's Initiation has much in common with another book about the war and its effect on those who lived through it, Ernest Hemingway's *In Our Time*. Both report the sights and sounds of war in a series of disconnected fragments. Both record dialogue objectively and try to report without comment, relying instead on the irony of circumstances to move the reader. The irony is often heavy, particularly in the Dos Passos book, which was intended more as protest than as art. Dos Passos wrote the first draft of *One Man's Initiation* on the ship as he returned from France. "To get my feelings off my chest, to tell my side of the story," he explains in his memoirs, he put Martin Howe "through everything I had seen and heard that summer on the Voie Sacrée."

Dos Passos' second novel, *Three Soldiers,* describes the lot of the common soldier. Based only in a general sense on his army experience, it is not autobiographical like his novel about the ambulance service. *Three Soldiers* is a more conventional piece of fiction, both in its smooth-flowing narrative and in its fictitious characters and events. Yet Dos Passos tends to regard the book as history: "I always felt that this might not be any good as a novel but that it would at least be useful to add to the record."

Dos Passos now calls such historical fictions "contemporary chronicles." Character and event may be entirely fictitious, but they are representative of their time. His three soldiers, a store clerk from San Francisco, an Indiana farm boy, and a student from the East Coast, together with others who appear briefly, represent different parts of the country and different walks of life. Their army experiences are meant to be typical. The opportunist Fuselli begins with hopes of promotion and manages to evade combat duty but contracts venereal disease and ends up on permanent K.P. in Paris. Chrisfield conceives a passionate hatred for a sergeant and has his revenge on the battlefield when he finds him wounded and kills him. After the armistice, when another sergeant suspects his crime, Chrisfield becomes a deserter hiding out in Paris. John Andrews, the third soldier, is the real protagonist, the main figure during most of the book. He is a man very much like the author, whose misfortunes express Dos Passos' protest against the humiliation and injustice of army life. Andrews, who could easily obtain a discharge six months after the armistice, chooses to desert instead and, when discovered by the military police, faces a long prison term.

The novel concludes pessimistically, with all three soldiers defeated. Its underlying attitudes, which are the same as those of *One Man's Initiation,* reappear in most serious American novels of both wars. In his protest and anarchism Dos Passos anticipates Cummings; in his disenchantment, Hemingway. Toward the end of *Three Soldiers,* John Andrews, in revolt against the system, makes a statement that sums up Cummings' view of society in *The Enormous Room:* "organizations growing and stifling individuals, and individuals revolting hopelessly against them, and at last forming new societies to crush the old societies and becoming slaves again in their turn." In the same speech Andrews also repudiates military language, "those pompous, efficient words: detachment, battalion, commanding officer," much as Hemingway in *A Farewell to Arms* was later to condemn such obsolete obscenities as "sacred, glorious and sacrifice and the expression in vain." John Andrews goes A.W.O.L. by jumping into the Seine, just as Hemingway's Lieutenant Henry was to make his separate peace by diving into another river. Hemingway and Cummings did not necessarily imitate Dos Passos; all three simply reacted in the same way to military servitude and the war's monstrous delusions.

The writer who first gave an influential voice to the war's disillusionments was the French novelist Henri Barbusse. *Le Feu,* which won the Prix Goncourt in 1916, was one of the most widely read novels of the Great War. Translated the following year as *Under Fire: The Story of a Squad,* it undoubtedly had more influence on American writing than is recognized. Nowadays it makes less compelling reading than the best war novels but still tells more about life and death in the front-line trenches. As a *poilu* Barbusse experienced war at its worst; his book makes it possible to understand the way it was, reporting in detail the gruesome deaths, the ubiquitous rotting corpses, the unbearable noise, fatigue, cold, and wet that numbed the senses and made one almost forget the ever present likelihood of haphazard death. The book is dedicated to the memory of comrades who fell at his side at Crouÿ and on Hill 119; Barbusse makes a point of writing in the language used by soldiers and concludes with a soldiers' debate about war.

Obviously *One Man's Initiation* was inspired by Barbusse. Dos Passos read *Le Feu* several months before he joined the ambulance service and was deeply affected by the book, not only then but later in France when he collaborated with Robert Hillyer on a novel that was never finished, a novel about one Martin Howe. Consciously or not, Cummings and Hemingway were affected also, not to mention others. Certain particulars in *Le Feu* reappear in *The Enormous Room*, others in Hemingway's war fiction; in *A Farewell to Arms* Lieutenant Henry reads the book while convalescing in Milan; and in his anthology of war writing, *Men at War*, Hemingway comments, "The only good war book to come out during the last war was 'Under Fire' by Henri Barbusse." Whether or not they borrowed from Barbusse, all agreed with him in their reaction to the war, Dos Passos and Cummings most explicitly. Both were no doubt natural born anarchists, but without the war they might never have articulated their feelings. Both talked with a good many French anarchists during 1917, the year of mutinies in the French army. Their subsequent experience of regimentation confirmed them in opposition to the system, whatever it happened to be.

After the armistice, when the army allowed some soldiers to attend European universities on detached service, Dos Passos continued his education in Paris, listening to lectures at the Sorbonne but learning more in the streets and cafés and theaters. He spent four impressionable months there between February and June of 1919, enjoying the life of the city. At the same time he was working furiously on his second novel and throwing off an occasional poem. Later collected in *A Pushcart at the Curb*, his imagistic poems about Paris in the spring are grouped under the title "Quai de la Tournelle," to commemorate the place where he often did his writing, in the apartment of the playwright John Howard Lawson, a friend he had met in the ambulance service.

Much of *Three Soldiers* takes place in Paris during the same period, as John Andrews is assigned to the Sorbonne Detachment. After months of desperate ennui and slavery, Paris gives him freedom, beauty, love, and music. Andrews, a composer, is now able to work on "the Queen of Sheba music" inspired by Flaubert's *Tentation de Saint Antoine* and the music of Debussy. "There is nowhere except Paris where one can find out things about music," he says during an intermission of *Pelléas et Mélisande,* anticipating a generation of American composers. "I think I have been happier this month in Paris than ever before in my life." During that month he has had a love affair with a pretty socialist, and now he is talking to a beautiful bluestocking who seems like a creature out of Debussy's imagination. He has also found pleasure in the aged beauty of Paris, which he compares favorably to the vigorous ugliness of America. The book is full of lyrical descriptions of Paris, but later it also presents the ugly side of the city when Andrews is attached to a labor battalion, and later still he hides out in a lower class bar where he meets other deserters hoping for a revolution on May Day. Dos Passos was not discharged from the army until July 1919; when the Sorbonne Detachment was disbanded, he found himself back at an army depot doing meaningless labor, until one day he went A.W.O.L., traveled to headquarters, and obtained his discharge; he returned to Paris in time to celebrate Bastille Day.

That first peacetime spring was a memorable season in Dos Passos' life, one that kept reappearing in his writing. "The horsechestnuts were in bloom," he reminisced in the mid-thirties. "We knew that the world was a lousy pesthouse of idiocy and corruption, but it was spring. We knew that in all the ornate buildings under the crystal chandeliers, under the brocaded hangings the politicians and diplomats were brewing poison, huddled old men festering like tentcaterpillars in a tangle of red tape and gold braid. But we had hope. What they were doing was too obvious and too clear. It was spring. The first of

May was coming. We'd burn out the tentcaterpillars. . . . Loafing around in little old bars full of the teasing fragrances of history, dodging into alleys to keep out of sight of the M.P.s, seeing the dawn from Montmartre, talking bad French with taxidrivers, riverbank loafers, workmen, petites femmes, keepers of bistros, poilus on leave, we young hopefuls eagerly collected intimations of the urge towards the common good."

"Paris really was the capital of the world that spring of the Peace Conference," he has written most recently in his memoirs, *The Best Times*. But he always remembers those days with a mixture of exhilaration and doubt. "It looked as if every man or woman in the United States who could read and write had wangled an overseas job. Relief was the great racket. Those who couldn't disguise themselves as relievers came as journalists or got attached to government commissions." Among the most incongruous he met was Dean Briggs from Harvard, an old-fashioned New England schoolmaster who symbolized values that were entirely out of place amid "the sham and fustian of the Peace Conference." The enounter suggests how much Dos Passos had learned since Harvard. The Peace Conference marked a most important stage in his political education.

Paris also educated him in the arts. During the war he had spent his leaves in picture galleries; in the spring of 1919 he had plenty of opportunity to become acquainted with what was going on in painting and music; and during the postwar years he often visited Paris, appreciating the artistic ferment that attracted his generation there: "The war had taught us Paris. We were hardly out of uniform before we were hearing the music of Stravinsky, looking at the paintings of Picasso and Juan Gris, standing in line for opening nights of Diaghilev's Ballet Russe. 'Ulysses' had just been printed by Shakespeare and Company. Performances like 'Noces' and 'Sacre du Printemps' or Cocteau's 'Mariés de la Tour Eiffel' were giving us a fresh notion of what might go on on the stage." At the time Dos Passos was still undecided between painting, writing, and theater; in Paris he admired the latest in all the arts.

A chapter in his memoirs entitled "*La Vie Littéraire*" is devoted largely to Paris in the early twenties. He returned to Paris with Cummings in 1921 and visited there repeatedly during the next three years. Dos Passos was a traveler, forever journeying back and forth, with an occasional stopover in Paris between trains. He never stayed long, but he managed to meet a number of artists and take part in some of their activities. He met Joyce and Picasso, strolled along the quais with Léger, helped Larionov and Goncharova paint sets for the Ballet Russe, marched in a dada manifestation led by Tristan Tzara. And of course he knew the resident Americans. He came to despise "the huddle of literary expatriates round Montparnasse," disliking literary people in general and Bohemians in particular, but he was acquainted with the principal characters of that village. He went the rounds with Donald Ogden Stewart, lost money at the horse races by betting on Harold Stearns's tips, endured Scott Fitzgerald's drunken scenes. In Paris he made lasting friendships with two Americans he respected, Ernest Hemingway and Gerald Murphy. He went to Pamplona one year with Hemingway and visited the Murphys on the Riviera a number of times. In its unpretentious, matter-of-fact way, "*La Vie Littéraire*" epitomizes the American Paris of the twenties. It reads like an abstract of the two major expatriate novels, *The Sun Also Rises* and *Tender Is the Night.*

Much of what Dos Passos learned in Paris found its way into his own writing, particularly his great trilogy *U.S.A.* The middle volume, *1919*, describes the Paris he had known during the war and the Peace Conference, but quite apart from subject matter, the whole trilogy seems to have been inspired by the modernism of postwar Paris. In the mid-twenties Dos Passos adopted a number of experimental techniques that he was to perfect in *U.S.A.*, many of them borrowed from the visual arts and music rather than literature. His use of typography and montage, his shifts in tempo and texture, all suggest the experimental spirit of Paris. The techniques did not necessarily originate there, but they were most widely practiced in that international center of the arts, and it was there that Dos Passos was most likely to become acquainted with them. "After all," he remarks in *Orient Express*, "Paris, whether we like it or not, has been so far a center of unrest, of the building up and tearing down of this century. From Paris has spread in every direction a certain esperanto of the arts that has 'modern' for its trademark."

U.S.A. is both the most ambitious and the most successful of Dos Passos' works. In retracing three decades of American experience, this "contemporary chronicle" brings together fiction with history, biography, and autobiography. Originally Dos Passos did not conceive of it as a novel at all but as "a series of reportages similar to those the French were publishing at that time." He set out to capture contemporary life in all its multitudinous phenomena, momentous or trivial; he sought to project a composite view of his times by focusing from different angles. Here was historical fiction to match the complexity of the twentieth century. An undertaking of such scope and multiplicity called for new techniques to supplement the basic fictional element, and Dos Passos devised three: the Newsreel, the Camera Eye, and the capsule Biography. These are scattered throughout the novel, which is itself divided into a number of plots, following the rise and fall of a dozen major characters, whose interweaving lives cumulatively provide the representative experience of a generation.

The whole is a montage, and the overall method of cutting and piecing is that of the cinema, although the individual elements are taken from other media. The Newsreel and the Camera Eye are somewhat misleadingly named, for one is composed mostly of newspaper headlines, never of images, while the other, unlike the camera, is almost totally subjective. They usually follow one another, often with interesting results, as they alternately register the most public and private view of contemporary events, sometimes in total disagreement. Similarly the biographies of the men who shape history contrast with the fictional lives shaped by history.

Each of the four strands has its own basic style. The prose

of the fictional portions varies with the character, more or less adopting his idiom. The Newsreels are written in a pop style drawn from the mass media, full of cliché, sentimentality, and oversimplification. The impression is that conveyed by a cursory glance at the front page of the daily newspaper while a radio supplies snatches of song and slogan in the background.

How are you goin' to keep 'em down on the farm
After they've seen Paree

If Wall street needed the treaty, which means if the business interests of the country properly desired to know to what extent we are being committed in affairs which do not concern us, why should it take the trouble to corrupt the tagrag and bobtail which forms Mr. Wilson's following in Paris?

ALLIES URGE MAGYAR PEOPLE TO UPSET
BELA KUN REGIME

11 WOMEN MISSING IN BLUEBIRD MYSTERY

Enfin La France Achète les stocks Américains

How are you goin' to keep 'em away from Broadway
Jazzin' around
Paintin' the town

Typographically the most arresting, the Newsreel is also the most nervous in tempo, as the mechanical rhythm of the press alternates with popular songs, the bland voice of advertising with headlines shrieking violence and profits indiscriminately. The Camera Eye has a smoother, flowing style, unpunctuated and uncapitalized, as befits the stream of consciousness which it registers in a series of impressionistic images somewhat reminiscent of the poems Dos Passos wrote in Paris after the war.

there were always two cats the color of hot milk with a little coffee in it with aquamarine eyes and sootblack faces in the window of the laundry opposite the little creamery

> where we ate breakfast on the Montagne St. Geneviève huddled between the old squeezedup slategrey houses of the Latin Quarter leaning over steep small streets cosy under the fog minute streets lit with differentcolored chalks cluttered with infinitesimal bars restaurants paintshops and old prints beds bidets faded perfumery microscopic sizzle of frying butter

The Biographies vary considerably, but their basic style is a driving rhetorical free verse. Like entries in a rather dramatic, frequently ironic *Who's Who*, they communicate facts with telegraphic terseness.

> By 1917 the Allies had borrowed one billion, nine hundred million dollars through the House of Morgan: we went overseas for democracy and the flag;
>
> and by the end of the Peace Conference the phrase *J. P. Morgan suggests* had compulsion over a power of seventy-four billion dollars.
>
> J. P. Morgan is a silent man, not given to public utterances, but during the great steel strike, he wrote Gary: *Heartfelt congratulations on your stand for the open shop, with which I am, as you know, absolutely in accord. I believe American principles of liberty are deeply involved, and must win if we stand firm.*
>
> (Wars and panics on the stock exchange,
> machinegunfire and arson,
> bankruptcies, warloans,
> starvation, lice, cholera and typhus:
> good growing weather for the House of Morgan.)

The poet in Dos Passos is most evident in the Biographies and in the lyrical passages of the Camera Eye.

A French critic notes that the experimental techniques of *U.S.A.* were all anticipated in France. Dos Passos' remark that they were in the air is a better explanation than a catalogue of sources. The French novelist most frequently cited as a forerunner is Jules Romains, with his theory of "unanimism," which calls for equal representation of all elements of society in a collective novel. Yet Dos Passos did not read Romains before writing *U.S.A.* and later, when he did read Romains, found him rather boring.

In Paris Dos Passos could absorb theories like simultanism or futurism, ideas about typographic or cinematic effects, and the ideal of total art. Without necessarily tracing techniques back to their origins he could have derived from Apollinaire the visual possibilities of printing, from Stravinsky the compulsive rhythms of the twentieth century, from the surrealists the random selection and juxtaposition of materials with startling results, and most of all from the cubists the whole analytic approach to his medium. *U.S.A.* is in a sense a cubist novel, with its elements dismantled, fragmented, and redistributed. Cubistic too is its use of collage, the scraps of newspaper clippings and songs introducing an element of authentic reality into the composition. The manuscripts of the Newsreels are literally collages, pasted up from the newspapers Dos Passos used as source material.

In his use of shifting styles and techniques, he owes most to the example of that Irish Parisian, James Joyce. But the writer he most resembles is Blaise Cendrars, a kindred spirit and world traveler like himself. Dos Passos first read Cendrars in Paris during the war. *La Prose du Transsibérien* was a title to catch his eye, evoking his earliest memory: as a four-year-old Dos Passos was taken aboard the Trans-Siberian Express at the Paris Exposition of 1900. The form of this long poem must have captivated him as much as its memories of a railroad trip across Siberia during the Russo-Japanese War. Here in irregular free verse Cendrars caught the rhythms of the railroad, which were to haunt Dos Passos through the twenties when he made similar journeys. In 1926 he wrote a tribute to Cendrars, "Homer of the Transsiberian," in which he translated passages from his poetry. In the winter of 1929–30 he toured the cafés of Paris with

Cendrars, spent a gastronomic week as his guest in Périgord, and was taken on some hair-raising one-armed drives over mountain roads. (Cendrars had lost his right arm in the war.) On the homeward voyage he translated another long poem by Cendrars, *Panama.* Under this title he collected his several translations of Cendrars, including "Prosody of the Transsiberian," selections from *Kodak Documentaire*, and another sequence of travel poems. This book was published in 1931, between the first and second volumes of *U.S.A.*

To a writer like Dos Passos the appeal of Cendrars was irresistible. In addition to his love of travel and adventure, Cendrars had a remarkable eye for the contemporary scene and directed an open mind toward unlikely sources of poetry in the mass media. He tried his hand at journalism and movie-making. Before the war he invented his own poetry of the modern city, celebrating the noisy confusion of streets, subways, cars, and factories, the busy world of machinery motivated by money and revolving around the central symbol of the Eiffel Tower. He fashioned a "telegram poem" out of a news story that appeared in *Paris-Midi* about four escaped convicts in Oklahoma. In the middle of *Panama* he inserted a prospectus from the Denver Chamber of Commerce. Along with Apollinaire, he liberated poetry of punctuation, thereby creating the fluid unstopped line that runs through so much modern verse. He developed a flexible prose poetry, written in shifting meters and forms, organized casually, almost haphazardly. Dos Passos assimilated Cendrars so completely that he did not need to imitate. In spirit, form, and style Cendrars's poetry became the very fiber of *U.S.A.*

The best volume of the Dos Passos trilogy, *1919*, is also the one that tells most about the education of its author. If the trilogy itself was motivated by the Sacco-Vanzetti case, its central volume grew out of the war and its aftermath. Dos Passos was writing about something that was very immediate to him, that aroused his deepest convictions, yet already belonged to his youth and evoked nostalgia. Through the songs and headlines of wartime and through his own private impressions he was able to recapture the emotions of that period. The objective Newsreel and the subjective Camera Eye, though often at odds, complement each other more closely than at any other point in the trilogy; the very disagreement between documentary and commentary intensifies the novel's sardonic view of the Great War.

The fictional element of *1919* is once again drawn from the author's observation of the war and the discreditable peace that followed. Its principal characters are Joe Williams, a merchant seaman who is torpedoed three times, only to have his skull bashed in during a barroom brawl on Armistice Day; Richard Ellsworth Savage, a Harvard man who serves with the Norton-Harjes Group in France, with the Red Cross in Italy, and later in the army as a captain; Eveline Hutchins, who spends two years in Paris with the Red Cross; and Anne Elizabeth Trent, who is seduced by Captain Savage and dies in a plane crash while stunt-flying with a French war ace over Paris. Dick Savage is not only the central character whose life crosses all the others, but the representative figure of his generation—beginning as an idealist in 1917 but selling out to join the power establishment in 1919.

His wartime adventures are very much the author's own, even down to minor incidents. He sails to France on the same ship, travels with similar companions to the same places, where he has the same experiences—as poet, ambulance driver, and "grenadine guard." In a few pages Dos Passos quickly recapitulates the five months of *One Man's Initiation—1917*. Then Dick Savage drives an ambulance across France to Italy, where his pacifist sentiments make him suspect, returns to Paris in an attempt to clear his reputation, and failing, sails home. At this point his career deviates from the author's. He abandons his principles, accepts a commission, returns to France, and only too willingly becomes one of the bright young men on the fringes of the Peace Conference.

The Camera Eye parallels the Dick Savage plot, with impressions of swimming in the Marne, the garden at Récicourt,

Dick Norton's farewell to his "gentlemen volunteers" under shellfire–impressions that reappear in *The Best Times*–and evocations of French landscape, history, wines, gastronomy. (Camera Eye 33 reflects a deep appreciation of French culture and an easy familiarity with its literature; elsewhere Dos Passos' writing shows that he was well read in the French novelists; Anatole France is the patron saint of *1919*.) Then as the author's life diverges from the Dick Savage plot, the Camera Eye dwells on shipboard K.P. amid rumors of the armistice (Dos Passos sailed back to France on Armistice Day), clerical work in the medical corps, fatigue duty piling scrap iron while waiting for a discharge, and the relief of becoming a civilian again. The Camera Eye views Paris during the Peace Conference but with a totally different perspective from that provided by Dick Savage and his sort.

Through the composite view provided by the Camera Eye, the Newsreels, and the several fictional characters, Dos Passos projects a montage of Paris as it appeared to Americans during 1917–19. The book is full of the sights of Paris in wartime, the zeppelin raids on moonlit nights, the bombardments of Big Bertha, the evacuation of the wounded directly from the front into the city, Armistice Day, the May Day demonstrations, and the buzzing corridors of the Crillon Hotel during the Peace Conference. Most vivid is the Camera Eye (39) which sums up Paris as Dos Passos returned to it after military service.

> Paris of 1919
> paris-mutuel
> roulettewheel that spins round the Tour Eiffel red square white square a million dollars a billion marks a trillion roubles baisse du franc or a mandate for Montmartre
> Cirque Médrano the steeplechase gravity of cellos tuning up on the stage at the Salle Gaveau oboes and a triangle   la musique s'en fout de moi says the old marchioness jingling with diamonds as she walks out

on Stravinski but the red colt took the jumps backwards and we lost all our money

la peinture opposite the Madeleine Cezanne Picasso Modigliani

Nouvelle Athènes

la poesie of manifestos always freshtinted on the kiosks and slogans scrawled in chalk on the urinals L'UNION DES TRAVAILLEURS FERA LA PAIX DU MONDE

revolution round the spinning Eiffel Tower

that burns up our last year's diagrams the dates fly off the calendar we'll make everything new today is the Year I Today is the sunny morning of the first day of spring We gulp our coffee splash water on us jump into our clothes run downstairs step out wideawake into the first morning of the first day of the first year

Here Dos Passos conveys his own enthusiastic response to Paris immediately after the war. But he also reports faithfully on the activities of other Americans on hand. Paris is the center of events in *1919*, headquarters and crossroads of the A.E.F., scene of the peace treaty, capital of the world, the place where all paths cross and where characters keep returning. Indeed for many Americans the Battle of Paree remained the chief memory of the war.

6.

Typographic Verse

E. E. Cummings was a typical twentieth-century French poet, his French translator concluded, after noting how much Cummings had in common with a dozen of his contemporaries in France. As a painter Cummings could best be described as belonging to the School of Paris, whose leading practitioners he always admired. In the twenties Cummings thought of himself primarily as a painter, though finally with the success of his poetry he was willing to concede that he was an "author of pictures, a draughtsman of words." Paris helped make him the kind of artist he was, both in words and pictures.

Cummings lived in Paris for two and a half years in the early twenties and was there off and on through the twenties and thirties. In March 1921 he sailed for Europe with Dos Passos on a Portuguese freighter. Cummings was "pining for Paris," Dos Passos recalls in *The Best Times,* and "didn't feel himself again until we climbed off the train at the Gare d'Orléans in La Ville Lumière." There he settled down in the heart of the old Latin Quarter. When his father urged him to return to New York to read proof on *The Enormous Room,* Cummings wrote back that "it would be extremely foolish to leave just then, for the pays des libres et le chez-eux des braves." A subsequent letter explains why he thought it foolish to leave: "May in Paris is the most of all mosts everanywhere." He stayed in Paris through three successive springtimes, returned for another stay in 1924–25, and again in 1926 and 1928.

"Every time Cummings got any money he'd go back to Paris," Marion Morehouse Cummings recalls. She first went with him in 1933, and she remembers six or seven subsequent visits. His letters from the thirties show that his love of Paris remained undimmed. In 1931, when he went to Russia to write *Eimi,* he stopped off four times as long in Paris to study Russian with an émigrée. On that visit he witnessed Joffre's funeral and rediscovered France, "which certainly has more in it than the rest of creation multiplied by itself." Despite the constant winter rains and the undesirables of Montparnasse, he was not disappointed when that eternal Parisian springtime came around. "Paris, nowanights, reeks with Etrangers," he wrote in April, "ah, but the trees are budding, & we've seen certain hours-without-rain!" Again on a visit in 1937 he wrote: "Paris is Paris, needless to add. The banks of the Seine are filled with fishermen so busy passing through a number of financial political economic and other crises that they scarcely find time to scratch each other. Le Quatorze Juillet was plus gai than I've ever danced it: despite a somewhat incendiary predominance of busloadsupon-busloads of gardes mobiles with tinderbies and rifles, aussi tanks and zouaves, merely a few 'reds' turned out and nearly nobody (apparently) paid any attention to them."

This letter is reminiscent of Cummings' poem about an earlier demonstration in which the police outnumbered the communists fifty to one.

16 heures
l'Etoile

the communists have fine Eyes

some are young some old none
look alike the flics rush
batter the crowd sprawls collapses. . . .

In Paris the communists had inherited the historic tradition of the communards, and though Cummings' visit to Russia had given him the horrors, his sympathies remained with the common people. The Paris he preferred was the plebeian world of bars and cabarets and other entertainments. This predilection is shown in his letters expressing continued fondness for demonstrations and dancing in the streets. The simple pleasures he found in Paris are most clearly evoked in an article he wrote for *Vanity Fair*, contrasting the tourist's "Gay Paree" with the native's "*Paname*."

> Always, the *Jardin du Luxembourg* has its wooden horses to ride and its tiny ships to sail; and in the Elysian Fields *guignols* twinkle like fireflies. Barges and *bateaux mouches* glide (and will forever glide) through the exquisite river; from which old gentlemen, armed with prodigious poles and preternatural patience, will forever extract microscopic fish. Beneath "Paree," beneath the glittering victory of "civilization," a careful eye perceives the deep, extraordinary, luminous triumph of Life Itself and of a city founded upon Life—a city called "Paname," a heart which throbs always, a spirit always which cannot die. The winged monsters of the garden of Cluny do not appear to have heard of "progress." The cathedral of Notre Dame does not budge an inch for all the idiocies of this world.
>
> Meanwhile, spring and summer everywhere openingly arrive.
>
> Lovers capture the *Bois*.
>
> In crooked streets young voices cry flowers.

In the early twenties Paris was also a gregarious American society. Old friends from Harvard or the ambulance service kept turning up, bringing new friends with them: Scofield Thayer, Stewart Mitchell, Slater Brown, John Howard Lawson, Gilbert Seldes, Lewis Galantière. Most of them had gone on from undergraduate publications like the *Harvard Monthly* to work on *The Dial*, *Broom*, and other literary magazines in which Cummings' poems began to appear. Cummings also met the resident poets. He had tea at Ezra Pound's studio and spent an evening with Archibald MacLeish at his house in suburban Saint-Cloud. Not all his evenings were staid. In a letter to Slater Brown, Cummings reports:

> ⓐ that Dos, Seldes & self had a party
> ⓑ " E. E. Cummings was lugged to the rue des Grands Augustins police station for having pissed opposite the Calvados Joint of rue Gît le Coeur (time 3 A M)
> ⓒ that Dos accompanied me; & even entered the station—only to be thrown out protesting
> ⓓ that Seldes, despite great tipsiness, followed Dos. . . .

Cummings was finally saved by diplomatic intervention when Seldes appealed to Paul Morand, a contributor to *The Dial* who happened to be an undersecretary at the Quai d'Orsay. In the same letter to Brown, Cummings mentions another celebration with Dos Passos, this one at Malcolm Cowley's place at Giverny; the letter gives no details but suggests the spirit of the occasion as Cummings expresses relief that his host was not injured.

Cummings' life in Paris was not confined to the American literary colony. He became acquainted with the French poet Louis Aragon (whom he later translated into what looks at times like original Cummings), with Michel Larionov of the Ballet Russe (whose portrait he sketched), and he met Picasso (to whom he paid tribute in a poem). He admired Cocteau's ballet *Les Mariés de la Tour Eiffel* much as he had appreciated *Petrouchka* in 1917, and he wrote an enthusiastic article about Cocteau's drawings when they were published. Cummings had been an early observer of the artistic ferment in Paris. In his commencement talk at Harvard, "The New Art," he had shown an awareness most unusual in a college student of 1915, citing Matisse, Brancusi, Satie, Stravinsky, and Gertrude Stein as he surveyed the latest experiments in all the arts. Even considering that the Armory Show had come to Boston in 1913 and *Tender Buttons* had been published in New York in 1914, Cummings was better informed than most professional critics about what was happening in the arts in Paris—this before he was twenty-one and before he had been abroad.

During his first postwar sojourn in Paris, Cummings probably produced more paintings than poems. In December 1922 he shipped fifty-nine water colors to Slater Brown in New York. Cummings' painting often reflects the influence of Paris, with individual works showing an affinity for Derain, Vlaminck, Léger, Matisse, and, most of all, Cézanne. In one of his letters he identified his palette as Cézanne's; his composition is frequently reminiscent of Cézanne's, and his New Hampshire mountain scenes distinctly recall the French master's many paintings of Mont Sainte-Victoire. *CIOPW*, a volume of reproductions published in 1931, includes many Parisian scenes done in the style of Paris: impressionistic views of the Seine, drawings entitled *gonzesse* and *l'amour*, portraits and caricatures identified as *bois de Boulogne*, *boulevard Montmartre*, and *porte Saint-Denis*.

Inevitably the city also appears in his poetry.

> Paris; this April sunset completely utters
> utters serenely silently a cathedral
> before whose upward lean magnificent face
> the streets turn young with rain. . . .

Some poems refer to specific Parisian settings, such as the Hotel Meurice, "Dragon st," and "Fields Elysian." More often Paris provides a backdrop, a cathedral, café, quai, or boulevard merely suggesting the scene. Paris is the setting for a good many of his love poems, and French is the language of love. Dialogue and scraps of French appear frequently in his early poetry, often unexpectedly. "Pay" can readily be recognized as a bilingual pun in a satirical poem about "Peacepeacepeace" and the unknown soldier, but "Mairsee" appears without warning in a phonetic exercise that begins "oil tel duh woil doi sez" and continues in the same vernacular throughout. Cummings sometimes writes French with an exaggerated American accent that makes it hard to translate, particularly when the context is misleading. The Hotel des Artistes appears unexpectedly as "the hoe tell days are/teased" when there is no reason to expect a hotel, much less one with a French name. The ending of another poem, "and the duckbilled platitude lays & lays/and Lays aytash unee," requires a considerable adjustment before it makes sense as a satiric comment on the United States. But language and setting are superficial details when compared to the pervasive influence of the modern style.

Cummings found his voice as a poet during the years he was most exposed to Parisian influences. His first volume of poetry, *Tulips and Chimneys,* appeared in 1923, after he had been living in Paris for two and a half years. In 1925 he published two more volumes and won the Dial Award for that year. In announcing the award the editors of *The Dial* observed: "The two books of verse published this year are not as some think, made up of poems written more recently than those of his first volume. With the exception of a few poems written in 1915 and earlier, the whole lot is the result of six years of acute activity, 1917–1923, during which, to use his own expression, he wrote 'literally millions of poems.'" *The Dial* goes on to summarize Cummings' biography, mentioning his wartime experience and concluding, "Since then he has lived, for reasons of economy, mainly in France." The announcement appeared in January 1926; in June of that year Cummings published still another volume of poetry, the last that was to appear for five years. Taken together, the four volumes represent the entire period in which Cummings emerged as a modern poet, a period he spent mostly in Paris.

At Harvard Cummings had written fluent verse that might have been collected into an anthology illustrating the history of English poetry from the Elizabethans through the late Romantics. He continued to imitate his elders for some time after leaving Harvard, even persisting in the archaic poetic diction of the "thee-thou" school. His first three volumes still contain lines and even whole poems that might have been lifted from a dozen different poets. Neither the models nor the results were bad for apprentice exercises, but they were scarcely the work of a twentieth-century poet. The first poem in *Tulips and Chimneys* sounds like Keats out of Milton, going on for stanza after stanza with more rhetoric than meaning:

> Chryselephantine Zeus Olympian
> sceptred colossus of the Pheidian soul. . . .

And his third volume, *XLI Poems,* contains a sequence of sonnets that seems deliberately to trace his evolution from the old masters to his own distinctive style, from such stately Shakespearean lines as

> i do excuse me, love, to Death and Time

to his own proper colloquial voice

> by god i want above fourteenth.

Although derivative work continued to appear in the poems written between 1917 and 1923, Cummings' originality asserted itself more and more, quite unmistakably in the new poems that followed. His work became progressively freer in form, more unconventional, more "modern." In this he was following the trend that had started with Eliot and Pound, with its origins in French symbolism. At Harvard he had received what might be called the classic education in modern verse. He may not have known Eliot, who had just returned from Paris as a graduate student, but he knew Foster Damon who was then reading Laforgue and Verlaine and who enthusiastically shared such discoveries as *Tender Buttons* and *Des Imagistes.* And he met Amy Lowell, whose formidable presence in Boston made his generation fully aware of imagism. In 1916 she spoke to the Harvard Poetry Society on the subject of *vers libre* and disagreed curtly with Cummings on the subject of Gertrude Stein.

Cummings' modernism is most apparent in his tendency to experiment with form, typography, and syntax. At first he seems to be mainly striving for effect, breaking up the poem's form arbitrarily and eliminating punctuation and capital letters without any compelling reason. Gradually his usage becomes more meaningful as he devises new rules for punctuation, capitalizing, and grammar—a kind of algebra with its own internal logic. At first glance his most experimental poems look like the work of a drunken typesetter, with capitals and punctuation scrambled, lines, words, and syllables fractured, the whole structure staggering down the page. Ultimately his dislocations lead to a new mode of expression and a new significance in the pattern on the printed page, whether in such relatively simple exercises in onomatopeia as

```
                              pho
      nographisrunn
      ingd  o  w,  n  phonograph
                      stopS.
```

or in far more complicated pieces of notation, like the following, which treats both the subject and the medium "analytically," in the cubist sense of the word:

```
inthe,exquisite;

morning    sure      lyHer eye s exactly sit,ata little roundtable
among otherlittle roundtables Her,eyes    count    slow(ly

obstre poroustimidi ties surElyfl)oat iNg,the

ofpieces ofof sunligh tof fa l l in gof throughof treesOf.

(Fields Elysian

the like,a)slEEping neck a breathing a  ,lies
(slo wlythe wom an pa)ris her
flesh:wakes
         in little streets. . . .
```

Like the cubists dismantling objects and reassembling them as new forms, Cummings takes the elements of language and printing apart to give them a new meaning. If ever a literary composition could be called cubist, this poem deserves the name far more than anything Gertrude Stein wrote.

Cummings imitated *Tender Buttons* once in a poem that begins

any man is wonderful
and a formula
a bit of tobacco and gladness
plus little derricks of gesture. . . .

But otherwise he did not adopt Gertrude Stein's method, and though he respected her early experiments, he was not subject to her influence. Joyce was a much more likely influence during the years when Cummings was developing most, for installments of *Ulysses* began to appear in *The Little Review* in 1918, and the book was published in Paris in 1922. But the writer Cummings most strikingly resembles is the experimental French poet Guillaume Apollinaire.

Before the war Apollinaire made a name for himself not only as a poet but as the great apologist for the cubist painters. In 1913 he published two important books, gathering his poems in a volume called *Alcools* and his art criticism in *Méditations Esthétiques: Les Peintres Cubistes.* Because of his close association with Picasso and his friends, Apollinaire has often been called a cubist poet, and indeed in the last few poems he wrote while assembling *Alcools,* he attempted to carry out the principles of simultanist painting borrowed from his friend Robert Delaunay. In this and other respects *Alcools* represents a new departure in French verse, but the boldest change of all came with Apollinaire's last-minute decision to eliminate all punctuation. Since then many other poets have found punctuation unnecessary—in English as well as French.

Later in the same year Apollinaire wrote an iconoclastic manifesto for a futurist exhibition, *L'Antitradition Futuriste,* calling for the suppression of punctuation, syntax, prosody, and typographic symmetry, along with other grammatical and literary conventions. The manifesto was no doubt meant as a joke, but Apollinaire carried out much of this program in his subsequent work. In 1914 he began to produce the typographic compositions he called "*calligrammes,*" in which he patterned letters and words to form the outline of a house, a watch, a fountain, falling rain, constellations, the Eiffel Tower.

S
A
LUT
M
O N
D E
DONT
JE SUIS
LA LAN
GUE É
LOQUEN
TE QUESA
BOUCHE
O PARIS
TIRE ET TIRERA
TOU JOURS
AUX A L
LEM ANDS

This kind of topiary verse was nothing new, although it had not been used for ages. What seemed strange was that an accomplished lyricist should adopt a form which appealed to the eye rather than the ear. The words had to be puzzled out, and the music was lost in the process. The result was a picture rather than a poem. But it was the very quaintness of this device that appealed to Apollinaire's sophisticated humor.

"*Calligrammes,*" his final book of verse, appeared in 1918, the year of his death. Composed mostly of occasional poems written in 1913–16, this collection tells the story of his experience as a soldier at the front. It includes, along with some perfectly regular poems, two kinds of calligrams: picture-poems, properly speaking, and other typographical forms. These may be designed in a variety of ways to achieve certain effects, like the sound of a bombardment:

Du coton dans les oreilles

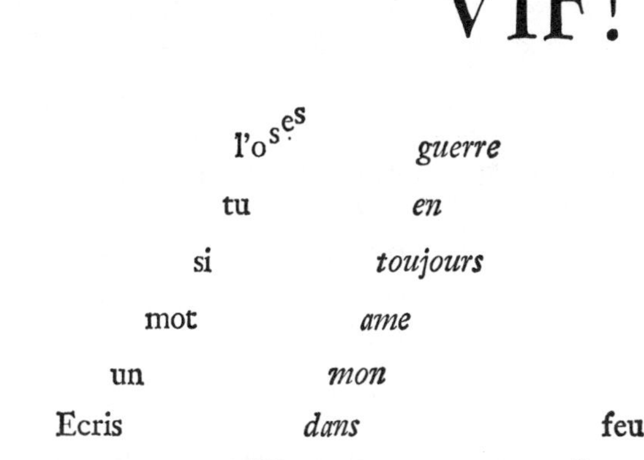

d'impacts le

points crache

? *Les* féroce

troupeau

Ton

OMÉGAPHONE

Or the layout and the varying typefaces may be designed like posters and billboards to arrest the attention. Like his friend Cendrars, Apollinaire believed in borrowing from the mass media for the proper stuff and techniques of modern poetry.

What he was trying to do is explained in his final critical pronouncement, *L'Esprit Nouveau et les Poètes:* "Typographical devices, employed with great daring, have given rise to a visual lyricism almost unknown before our time. These devices are capable of being carried much further, to the point of bringing about the synthesis of the arts–music, painting, and literature." Further in the same statement he singles out th element of surprise as one of the mainsprings of modern poetry.

Cummings was not one to theorize much about poetry and art. But in his practice he began where Apollinaire left off. The similarity between the two is so remarkable that it leads one to speculate about coincidences. Apollinaire seems to have lost his singular talent in 1916 when he was wounded in the head and trepanned; Cummings began to write experimental verse in the Apollinairean manner in 1917. That was the year of his first arrival in Paris and of *Eight Harvard Poets,* which announced his transition from juvenilia to something like his mature manner. Four of Cummings' eight contributions to that volume are regular sonnets; the other four are written in free verse, unpunctuated, with lines broken up and scattered down the page. In printing his poems thus Cummings went far beyond the gradual loosening of form that characterized free verse in English.

Cummings had probably come across Apollinaire during the previous year. He could have heard Amy Lowell lecture on "The New Manner in Modern Poetry" in 1915, but more probably he heard about that lecture from someone like Foster Damon and read her article on the same subject published in the *New Republic* a week after her appearance before the Harvard Poetry Society in 1916. In her lecture and in the article she began by deploring current fads, singling out "Guillaume Apollinaire as chief priest, who wrote 'ideographic poetry,' or poems printed so as to represent a picture of a railroad train with puffing smoke, or some other thing of the sort." No wonder she later disapproved of Cummings' aberrations. In retrospect one of his calligrams seems an acknowledgment to Apollinaire and a mischievous salute to Miss Lowell, as it depicts

```
                a lo
               co
               mo
                  tive    s pout
                                ing
                                  vi
                                  o
                                  lets
```

Cummings produced few picture-poems of this sort. If he took Apollinaire's methods as a point of departure, he pursued them much further and came closer to realizing Apollinaire's aims in "visual lyricism." Many of Apollinaire's *calligrammes* were greetings to friends, dashed off in a hurry. Cummings was a subtler, more painstaking calligrapher. Most of his calligrams are not strictly pictorial, but they are graphic for all that. They are usually dynamic representations of seas breaking, birds flying, bells ringing, snow falling. Cummings has a power beyond mere description to convey being and motion so that they can be heard, seen, and felt. His grasshopper is a good example.

```
                              r-p-o-p-h-e-s-s-a-g-r
                        who
     a)s w(e loo)k
     upnowgath
                     PPEGORHRASS
                                              eringint(o-
     aThe):l
             eA
               !p:
S                                                       a
                            (r
     rIvInG                           .gRrEaPsPhOs)
                                                   to
     rea(be)rran(com)gi(e)ngly
     ,grasshopper;
```

This poem is not a picture of a grasshopper but an abstraction of the grasshopper's quintessence, which is action. The grasshopper composed in the last line is totally uninteresting after the wild disintegrating leap that catches the eye and tenses the muscles. While it lasts, the poem comes closer than any picture to being a grasshopper. The punctuation, the letters, and the typography all work together in a kinesthetic experience of grasshopperness. Here is "that precision which creates movement" of which Cummings confessed to be abnormally fond.

The grasshopper appeared in a volume entitled *No Thanks* and dedicated to the fourteen publishers who had refused it. They were probably put off by the scurrilous contents rather than Cummings' experiments, but this volume does contain the most extreme examples of his typographical technique. Several of these besides the grasshopper represent being in motion. Not the most agitated, but perhaps the most complex, is the following:

ondumonde"

(first than caref
ully;pois
edN-o wt he
n
,whysprig
sli

nkil
-Y-
strol(pre)ling(cise)dy(ly)na(
mite)

:yearnswoons;

&Isdensekil-
ling-whipAlert-floatScor
ruptingly)

ça-y-est
droppe5
qu'est-ce que tu veux
Dwrith
il est trop fort le nègre
esn7othingish8s
c'est fini
pRaW,IT;O:
allons
9
&
.

(musically-who?

pivoting)
SmileS

"ahlbrhoon

The subject of this poem is a Negro boxer named Panama Al Brown who was a familiar figure in the Paris ring between 1926 and 1938. The poem suggests that Cummings saw him fight in 1928, when he became, as the referee announces, "ahlbhroon [bantamweight champi]ondumonde." Like a number of Cummings' poems this one ends with a return to its beginning. Inside the parentheses the poem recreates first the boxer's murderous tactics, then the comments of the spectators as his opponent falls, "writhes nothingish," and is counted out. The most astonishing part of Al Brown's career came years later when he lost his title, and Cocteau—of all people—managed his comeback campaign. "Al Brown was a poem in black ink," wrote Cocteau, unwittingly describing the poem Cummings had written. The composition not only outlines the boxer in action but reports the whole scene through scraps of conversation and incidental details. Cummings here combines the calligraphic method with the simultanism that Apollinaire had also introduced into poetry.

Cummings would have been an original poet if Apollinaire had never existed. But the similarities between them are inescapable and extend far beyond technique. Apollinaire was just the sort of man to appeal to Cummings, a great talker like himself, a frequenter of disreputable bars, a curious observer of the modern metropolis with an eye for its vulgar charms. Both were anarchic individualists, irreverent, bawdy, and humorous; both were satiric yet sentimental; both had a weakness for the naïve and the clever. Apollinaire was a professional pornographer for a time, Cummings the most candidly and joyously erotic of American poets. Both made poetry of the city's ugliness, appreciating its sordid neighborhoods and dubious characters. Both wrote about the war, Apollinaire being one of the few French poets to do so. *Calligrammes* reads like a journal of his war experiences, sketched and jotted down at the time, like the notebooks Cummings kept during the war. Its subject matter was likely to appeal to Cummings in 1918, its form and spirit to stay with him long after the war was over. His poetry seems a continuation of Apollinaire's, though none the less original for all that. He does not give the impression of having been suddenly influenced and converted, as Eliot was by Laforgue. Rather he seems to have become more definitely himself, to have discovered his true self through Apollinaire. As a result the resemblance is more thoroughgoing than that which exists between Eliot and Laforgue or any other modern American and French poet. The similarity between them is so remarkable as to suggest nothing less than a transmigration of souls.

DADA AND SURREALISM

CHRONOLOGY III

1913 Armory Show. School of Paris educates New York, Chicago, even Boston. Public scandalized at *Nude Descending a Staircase*

1915 Picabia and Duchamp arrive in New York, form anti-art triumvirate with Man Ray

1916 Man Ray's first dadaistic exhibit. "Take a useful object and make it into something useless"

1917 R. Mutt's ready-made immortal, not immoral

1918 Duchamp's last word on painting: "*Tu m'*"

1920 Duchamp and Man Ray help Katherine Dreier found her museum of modern art, Société Anonyme

1921 First and last issue of *New York Dada*
Man Ray joins Paris dada, takes up photography for a living, discovers Montparnasse, Kiki, and rayographs

1923 Man Ray's first movie a riot

1924 Pope Breton's first surrealist manifesto

1925 Man Ray exhibits with surrealists

1928 Surrealists celebrate fiftieth anniversary of hysteria

7.

Paris Comes to New York

To a young man in New York before the war Paris seemed the capital of the world. "During the day at my desk, overlooking the river," he remembered in his autobiography half a century later, "I watched the liners leaving their docks en route to France and wondered if I could ever get to Paris, that Mecca of art." Born in Philadelphia and raised in Brooklyn, Man Ray grew up with the dream of Paris that haunted all Americans who wanted to be artists. While working in an office he was doing his best to learn about art by painting and going to museums in his spare time. He preferred the impressionists to any older school, and he was ready for more recent art. This he found at the gallery of Alfred Stieglitz at 291 Fifth Avenue, at that time the best place in America to learn about contemporary art. There he saw Cézanne water colors, Brancusi bronzes, Picasso collages, and the work of American painters who had just returned from Paris—John Marin, Marsden Hartley, and Arthur Dove. Always a craftsman, he supported himself by doing lettering, layouts, and drafting in advertising and engineering offices, but a job was only a living, and he never allowed that to distract him from his purpose.

Like any artist Man Ray learned through his eyes, but he also learned from the company he kept. At the Ferrer School, where he painted in the evenings, he became acquainted with

Samuel Halpert, who had studied with Matisse, and met the Frenchwoman who became his mistress, later his wife. He did sketches of her "in pure French tradition," after Degas and Toulouse-Lautrec. She introduced him to the works of the writers most closely allied with modern art from cubism to surrealism: Rimbaud, Lautréamont, Mallarmé, and Apollinaire. When Halpert and others came to call, with wine and French conversation, he imagined himself "transported to Paris."

On February 17, 1913—the most important date in the history of American art—the Armory Show opened in New York. Man Ray was twenty-three that year and like all artists who attended the show was profoundly impressed. Organized by a group of New York artists with the purpose of introducing the American public to new developments in art, the Armory Show created a sensation both in the good and bad sense, arousing the basic philistinism but also the curiosity of the press and public. Although it included twice as much American art, the European works aroused far more interest, ridicule, and hostility, for they opened up a startling new world. The Americans seemed tame by comparison to the fauves, and the cubists stole the show. After Matisse the artists who attracted the greatest attention were the three Duchamp-Villon brothers, Jacques Villon, Raymond Duchamp-Villon, and Marcel Duchamp, whose *Nude Descending a Staircase* achieved a notoriety that has lasted to this day and became synonymous with all that was outrageous in modern art. Picabia, the only foreign artist on hand for the opening, was also widely publicized, while Picasso was not shown to best advantage, with the result that the public had a somewhat lopsided view of cubism.

The School of Paris was remarkably well represented, thanks to the efforts of such American artists in Paris as Jo Davidson, Alfred Maurer, and Walter Pach, who found many works for the exhibition. Paris was represented not only by a multitude of French painters going back to Ingres and Delacroix but by many foreign artists who had gravitated there, from Archipenko to Zak. And the show demonstrated the continuing influence of

Paris on American art. Mary Cassatt was exhibited among the French impressionists, as was only proper, and among the Americans in the next room were other native impressionists who had been trained in Paris, as well as Whistler, who had been there before them. Among the younger Americans were several who showed the latest French tendencies, notably Patrick Henry Bruce, a former pupil of Matisse, and Morgan Russell, who with Macdonald-Wright was starting an offshoot of cubism called synchronism.

Whether or not it succeeded in educating the public taste, the Armory Show had a decisive effect on American art. For although at least half the American artists in the show had worked in Paris, many were out of touch or out of sympathy with recent developments. Les Anciens de l'Académie Julian, for instance, too old-fashioned to appreciate contemporary movements, devoted their annual reunion to a burlesque of the new "fads." Yet despite such opposition, half a dozen New York galleries were exhibiting modern art a year after the show, including the last-minute work of the synchronists, Russell and Macdonald-Wright. Painters like Weber and Maurer, who had been fiercely criticized a few years before, were now understood, and the old postimpressionist Prendergast was finally appreciated. Younger artists like Demuth and Sheeler, to mention but two, were encouraged to continue in the direction they had taken in Paris. Cézanne emerged as the dominant influence and cubism as a major trend in American art.

Like most painters of the younger generation, Man Ray took up cubism, but only for a brief period. During 1913–14 he did a series of cubist canvases culminating in his monumental comment on the outbreak of the war, *A.D. MCMXIV*. He continued to work in flat cubistic forms for another year or so, but moved steadily away from his original models to his own personal interpretation. In 1914 he had a canvas in the synchronists' exhibition, and in 1915 his first one-man show was sponsored by one of the new galleries that had opened in the wake of the Armory Show. By then, however, he was no longer interested in the work he had been doing, and although he caught the fancy of a big collector who bought a number of paintings, nothing could induce him to return to a style he had abandoned. All his life Man Ray was to move on to new styles, new techniques, new media, with no concern for the market.

By 1915 he had come upon a movement that appealed to him far more than cubism. As everyone knows, dada was founded in 1916 at the Cabaret Voltaire in Zurich by two Rumanians, two Germans, and an Alsatian, who were all refugees from a war they could not believe in. But the dada spirit already existed in New York in a circle of refugees from Paris which centered around Picabia and Duchamp. The invidious question of priority is not worth arguing. The truth is that dadaism existed before the movement promoted by the shrill voice of Tristan Tzara. Apollinaire, a close friend of Duchamp and Picabia, anticipated dada theory and practice. Picasso in his collages and constructions invented the favorite dada forms, often with dada humor. *Alice in Wonderland* is a better piece of dada than anything written in the twentieth century; writers like Gertrude Stein and E. E. Cummings were dadaists, even though they had nothing to do with the movement. "Who made Dada?" Man Ray asked many years after the movement was dead. "Nobody and everybody. I made Dada when I was a baby and I was roundly spanked by my mother. Now everyone claims to be the author of Dada." He placed himself in the history of dada in this statement, written for the catalogue of a retrospective exhibition: "I might claim to be the author of Dada in New York. In 1912 before Dada. In 1919, with the permission and with the approval of other Dadaists I legalized Dada in New York. Just once. That was enough. The times did not deserve more. That was a Dadadate."

In France the battle between the artist and the bourgeois had been going on since Flaubert, and the urge to scandalize the philistines was perennial. The international movement that invented the name "dada" used mischief for the same purpose, but with the motive compounded to intolerable proportions. Dada was an attempt to provoke a bourgeoisie so stupid that it could tolerate a world war. Underlying dada's gaiety and nonsense was a profound despair; hence the spirit of negation and nihilism. Dada was against, since there was nothing to be for: against politics, religion, art, against all systems that made up society, against reason which only served as a disguise for madness. Under such bloody circumstances the only reasonable response was illogic, the only decent comment blasphemy and obscenity.

New York was far from the war in 1915, but dada found its truest expression in art there. Duchamp and Picabia were both by nature endowed with that mixture of absurd humor and skepticism that characterized dada, and the war deepened their sense of irony. Picabia, after service as a general's chauffeur for a time, managed to get himself sent on a mission to Cuba, his father's homeland, to buy molasses for the army; he never got to Cuba because he stopped off in New York and found life to his liking there. Duchamp, rejected for miliatry service and finding wartime Paris intolerable for a civilian, went to New York, where he joined a circle that included his old friend Picabia, the cubist Gleizes, the composer Varèse, Man Ray and other American artists, and their hospitable Maecenas, Walter Arensberg. Although they formed what might be called a salon and published an occasional issue of a little magazine, these friends did not constitute a movement like the Zurich dadaists. They had no program, they did not issue manifestoes, they staged no demonstrations, they merely produced dada art.

While the Zurich dadaists were noisily formulating principles and taking positions, Duchamp and Picabia quietly went about their business of subverting art. They had long since settled such questions as realism versus abstraction and were now confronting nothing less than suicide. As anti-artists they went to the limits that dada demanded. Their philosophical nihilism found its best expression when both stopped painting and used their talents in the destruction of aesthetic canons. They not only annihilated their own art, they blasphemed against all that was sacred, Duchamp drawing a mustache on the *Mona Lisa,* Picabia labeling a toy monkey *Portrait de Cézanne,* both with derisive punning captions. They abandoned humanism in favor of the mechanical world that was destroying mankind, Duchamp exercising the ingenuity of a Leonardo to design machinery with no function, Picabia in his mechanical drawings inventing machines with human characteristics, then reversing the process in portraits depicting men as machines (Stieglitz a camera, Picabia himself an auto horn).

Duchamp carried his anti-art logic to its ultimate conclusion with his "ready-mades," taking an ordinary mass-produced object like a corkscrew or a snow shovel, adding a title, and displaying it as art. His most successful ready-made was a porcelain urinal entitled *Fountain* and signed "R. Mutt 1917." When this masterpiece was submitted to the Society of Independent Artists, newly founded by analogy to the Salon des Indépendants (which in 1912 had objected to Duchamp's *Nude Descending a Staircase*), the organizing committee would not exhibit the offending object. Since the Society was founded on the principle that there would be no jury to judge or reject, Duchamp had succeeded brilliantly in testing its principles, challenging his fellow artists, and exposing the committee of which he was himself a member. Scandalizing the bourgeois was nothing by comparison to this supreme dada gesture.

His defense was another bit of dada, as *The Blind Man,* a little magazine published by Arensberg and Henri-Pierre Roché in honor of the exhibition, reproduced the rejected art work in a photograph by Stieglitz and protested that Mr. Mutt's fountain was not immoral, "no more than a bath tub is immoral. It is a fixture that you see every day in a plumber's show window." As for the objection to plumbing, that was totally unfounded. "The only works of art America has given are her plumbing and her bridges." Nor did it matter that Mr. Mutt did not make it. "He CHOSE it. He took an ordinary article of life, placed it so that its useful significance disappeared under the new title and point of view—created a new thought for that object." Duchamp and Man Ray are sometimes identified as the editors of *The Blind Man*, and the article is even attributed to Duchamp, although it is signed by Louise Norton, who was a real person. The authorship is not important, since the statement doubtless originated with Duchamp, along with the theory that was later to develop into the pop art movement of the 1960s.

Man Ray became the third member of the New York anti-art group, exhibiting his first dada paintings and objects in 1916. Hans Richter in writing the history of dada assigned a role to each member of the triumvirate, classifying Picabia "as the passionate *destroyer*, Duchamp as the detached *anti-creator*, and Man Ray as the tireless, pessimistic *inventor*." From the start Man Ray was distinguished for his fertile imagination, skill in execution, and variety of techniques. He was particularly good at mechanical contraptions like his 1916 *Self Portrait*, with his hand print in the middle of the "face," two electric bells for eyes, and instead of a mouth a push button that did not work. He also showed his particular brand of humor in hanging a work at an angle so that anyone looking at it would try to set it straight, only to have it swing back at an angle again. One of his first dada works was entitled *Découpage* because pieces of the painting were cut away so that the background served as part of the composition. A collage was labeled *Décollage* when he used no glue. Like other dadaists, he was fond of fanciful titles, sometimes incorporated into the composition, where they served as comments or added irrelevance to the mystification.

True to the anti-art spirit Man Ray soon abandoned traditional techniques and materials in favor of the most commonplace. He was probably the first to paint with spray gun and stencil, a technique considered sacrilegious at the time. If he painted in oil he took pains to make it look like something else. He had no use for marble or bronze or for sculpture in any traditional sense, but was fascinated by everyday materials and their possibilities. He liked to transform pieces of junk into a fantastic or ironic ensemble with a provocative title. His objects were never ready-mades (although composed of equally banal elements), but combinations of existing materials that showed wit and ingenuity. Instead of "ready-made" he used the term "by itself," indicating that the object existed without that pretentious creature the artist. His whole orientation was against the veneration of art as something sacred and unique. Far from valuing his creations, he did not care if they were lost or destroyed; it was the *idea* that mattered, for he could always reconstruct the works themselves. In his later years he has often reproduced his early objects, and he has no objection when they are copied or even mass-produced by others.

New York dada soon dwindled to two artists. Picabia left for Barcelona in the summer of 1916, returned for a time in 1917, then left for Switzerland, where he entered into contact with Tzara's group. Duchamp remained in New York working on his major creation, *The Bride Stripped Bare by Her Bachelors, Even*, an elaborate piece of engineering in glass which occupied him from 1915 to 1923. Several of Man Ray's works done between 1916 and 1919 show a certain affinity to Duchamp's ballet of geometric forms, notably *The Rope Dancer Accompanies Herself with Her Shadows*, *Admiration of the Orchestrelle for the Cinematograph*, and *Seguidilla*. On the other hand, Duchamp's last painting, *Tu m'* (1918), resembles Man Ray's aerographs of the same period. There is a kindred element of hoax in all these works, a parody of art and technology in the painstaking use of inappropriate techniques.

The two men became close friends and collaborated on a number of projects, such as their research into optical illusions and three-dimensional films. Both were intrigued by such effects (anticipating op art) but had to suspend their investigations when Duchamp's motor-driven *Appareil Rotatif, Optique de Précision* disintegrated, sending panes of glass flying in all directions and almost decapitating Man Ray. Both were also interested in photography; Duchamp thought it might supplant art, and Man Ray saw the possibility of getting away from painting and its whole aesthetic. The first tangible product of their collaboration was a photograph with the punning title *Elevage de Poussière* (Raising Dust), showing the dust formations that settled on the glass *Bride* over a year and a half. The dust had the great dada merit of being gratuitous, a random work of art.

Paradox and contradiction, those dada attitudes, have always played a part in their work, so it seemed quite natural that Duchamp should become a New Yorker while Man Ray ended up living in Paris. But, although they have much in common, they differ radically as artists. Duchamp, essentially cerebral and nihilistic, is possessed of a remorseless intelligence, pursuing his destructive logic to the point of futility. A hero to contemporary artists, who are catching up with his theories forty or fifty years later, he is really an anti-hero, for he stopped creating art in 1923 and thereafter used all his art in chess, just as earlier he had approached art as a game requiring the same concentration and abstraction as chess. Man Ray is also a chess player with a wry, skeptical sense of humor, but he has always been primarily a maker. His eyes are turned outward to the visible world, and his intelligence, as a French critic has said, is in his hands. Although his approach to art is often theoretical, he has made it his motto that there are no problems, only solutions. He does not like to be considered an experimenter, feeling that he has anticipated his results. Nevertheless he has investigated a greater variety of techniques and media than almost any other artist of his time.

In 1920, under the guidance of Duchamp, the art collector Katherine Dreier started a museum of modern art, the first in America, devoted to the cause of "Art, not personalities." Man Ray, who was also in this venture, suggested the name Société Anonyme, an expression he interpreted literally. Duchamp laughed and explained that this was a legal term for an incorporated company, Miss Dreier was also amused, and the Enterprise became Société Anonyme, Inc. To its first exhibition Man Ray contributed a work consisting of an unfurled lampshade hanging in a spiral from the skeleton of a dressmaker's dummy. The night before the opening the janitor mistook the lampshade for rubbish and threw it out, whereupon Man Ray promptly made a more durable replica out of metal painted to look like the original paper. Neither looked like a lampshade; hence the title, *Lampshade.* Both fulfilled his dada principle of taking a useful object and making it into something useless.

New York Dada was the final expression of a movement that had never declared itself one, a single issue of a four-page magazine published by Duchamp and Man Ray in April 1921. Picabia had been their publishing colleague, contributing to Stieglitz's monthly *291*, then founding his own *391* after he left New York. The Zurich dadaists were great propagandists, Tzara particularly, forever publishing broadsides and magazines to publicize themselves with photographs, personal jokes, insults, and gossip. *New York Dada* was quiet by comparison, with more anonymous nonsense than polemics. As usual with dada magazines, the text was printed in every direction, but with none of the agitated typography borrowed from Apollinaire and the futurists. The contents included the inevitable dada puns, the inevitable declaration by Tzara, a cartoon by Rube Goldberg, a photograph by Stieglitz, allusions to Marsden Hartley and Joseph Stella (who belonged to the Arensberg circle and the Société Anonyme), but no evidence of the editors. "How unusual for Dada," Man Ray later remarked, but the New York dadaists were always more subtle than the others, more inclined to disguise than to glorify themselves, more oblique in their humor. They are represented on the cover of *New York Dada* in Man Ray's anonymous photograph of a perfume bottle with a punning French label and the anagram of the pseudonym Duchamp had recently adopted, Rrose Sélavy. The lady with the beautiful breath whose photograph appears on the label, proves on close and informed inspection to be Rrose himself.

8.

The Mechanical Eye

The only date mentioned in Man Ray's *Self Portrait* is July 14, 1921, the day of his arrival in Paris. Immediately upon arrival he found himself in the midst of the dada movement, as Duchamp introduced him to Louis Aragon, André Breton, Paul Eluard, Théodore Fraenkel, Jacques Rigaut, and Philippe Soupault. Tzara was away for the summer, so Duchamp put him up in Tzara's room. Man Ray not only celebrated Bastille Day in Montmartre with the dadaists, he was taken up as a regular member of their group, frequented their café, and joined in their activities. Dada was primarily a literary movement in Paris, so the poets welcomed an artist, particularly one who already had an international reputation among dadaists. Dada magazines had been advertising his name and work.

Since the arrival of Tristan Tzara in 1919, Paris had become the capital of dada, with all kinds of demonstrations, festivals, expositions, and riots, not to mention innumerable publications. By the time Man Ray arrived on the scene, dada was in its declining stages, the period of feuds. Picabia had formally resigned from the movement, though he continued to publish his dada magazine under various names and remained a dadaist all his life. Breton, who had never been a dadaist at heart, professed loyalty and orthodoxy while attempting to overthrow Tzara and subvert the movement. The intrigues and power struggles of dada at this stage seemed a parody of all politics. Man Ray was not interested in politics and as a foreigner had little trouble remaining neutral through the wars of dada and surrealism, on good terms with all factions. He was banished temporarily by Breton once, but that happened to almost every surrealist sooner or later.

Man Ray had his first one-man show in Paris in December 1921, a modest retrospective of thirty-five works, most of them recent but some going back to 1914. He had brought with him a heavy trunk full of airbrush paintings and objects like his *Export Commodity*, an olive jar filled with ball bearings in oil, and *Inquiétude*, the works of an alarm clock in a glass case filled with tobacco smoke. Shortly after his arrival, when Soupault decided to open a gallery, Man Ray was the first to be invited to exhibit. The catalogue welcomed him with dadaistic greetings from the artists Hans Arp and Max Ernst as well as the Paris poets. Man Ray, who felt he was never understood in New York, had arrived in Paris. Henceforth his work was to appear regularly in all dada and surrealist exhibitions, beginning with the international Salon Dada the following June.

His one-man show attracted many visitors but no sales, so he decided to take up photography for his livelihood. Stieglitz had originally introduced him to the camera, and he had experimented with photography about the same time he developed his aerograph technique, which was not photography at all but an attempt to produce photographic effects with paint. His attitude toward photography has always been somewhat ambivalent; his autobiography is full of contradictory statements on the subject, sometimes regarding photography as an art, sometimes as a technical skill, sometimes as a mass medium. He seems to protest too much when he claims to be totally uninterested in the question whether photography can be an art. On the one hand he maintains that it never interfered or competed with his painting and that the two are not to be compared; on the other he frequently compares them by citing instances when

Leo, Gertrude, and Michael Stein, probably 1907. (The Cone Collection formed by
'r. Claribel Cone and Miss Etta Cone of Baltimore, Maryland)

2. Picasso, *Portrait of Leo Stein*, 1906. (The Cone Collection formed by Dr. Claribel Cone and Miss Etta Cone of Baltimore, Maryland)

FOUR PORTRAITS

4. Picasso, 1906. (The Metropolitan Museum of Art, Bequest of Gertrude Stein, 1946)

5. Vallotton, 1907. (The Cone Collection formed by Dr. Claribel Cone and Miss Etta Cone of Baltimore, Maryland)

3. Matisse painting Michael Stein's portrait. (San Francisco Museum of Modern Art, Gift of Nathan Cummings)

OF GERTRUDE STEIN

6. Lipschitz, 1921. (The Cone Collection formed by Dr. Claribel Cone and Miss Etta Cone of Baltimore, Maryland)

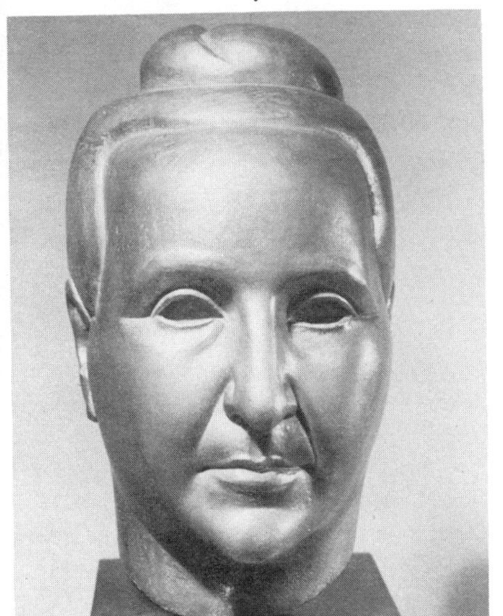

7. Picabia, 1928. (Gertrude Stein Collection, Yale University Library)

8. Alice Toklas and Gertrude Stein, 1922. Above Gertrude Stein's head the portrait of Madame Cézanne that inspired *Three Lives*. (Man Ray photograph, Courtesy of Juliet Man Ray)

9. E. E. Cummings. (Courtesy of Harcourt Brace Jovanovich)

10. John Dos Passos in Ambulance Corps uniform. (Courtesy of Lois Sprigg Hazell)

11. Man Ray, *Self-Portrait*, 1916. (Courtesy of Juliet Man Ray)

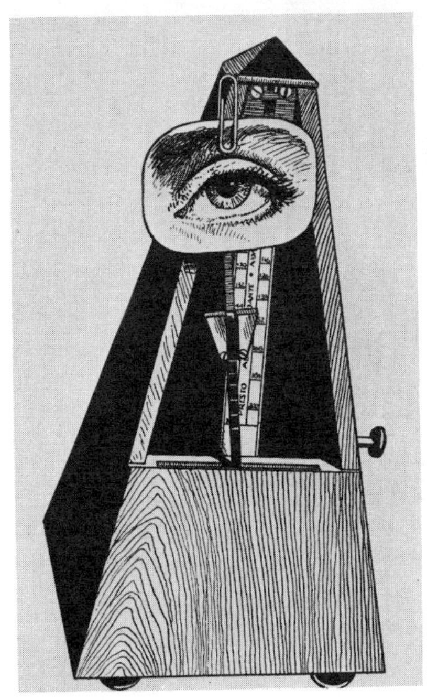

12. *Object of Destruction*, a drawing by Man Ray that appeared in the surrealist number of *This Quarter* (September 1932). This work was also called *Object to Be Destroyed* (1923) and renamed *Indestructible Object* (1957). (Courtesy of Juliet Man Ray)

13. Man Ray with one of his chess sets and *Observatory Time—The Lovers.* (Courtesy Juliet Man Ray)

14. *Clock Wheels,* 1925 Rayograph. (Courtesy of Juliet Man Ray and Yale University Art Gallery, Collection Société Anonyme)

he photographed as he painted or introduced photographic effects into his art. The fact is that Man Ray is best known as a photographer, and he resents that fact, not wishing to be typed or limited to one medium.

During the period he spent in Paris between the wars he acquired a reputation for his highly original photographic art. As a photographer he also became the "official recorder of events and personalities," as he says, likening himself to a notary public, "who sits there recording all the comings and goings of people, when they get married, when they get divorced, when they have children, or change their mistresses." Picabia started him on his career by asking him to photograph some paintings. Man Ray had first taken up photography when he needed reproductions of his own work and had subsequently done photography for Duchamp and for the Société Anonyme, on the sound principle that an artist was best qualified to photograph art works. Picabia recommended him to other painters and to art dealers, bringing him more business and at the same time introducing him to the artists of Paris. Thus began his friendship with Picasso, Braque, and Brancusi, among others, and his archives documenting modern art with the camera, much as Vasari had recorded the lives of Renaissance painters through personal anecdotes. Man Ray never limited himself to his "hack-work," as he calls it, but always made a point of photographing the artist in his atelier.

His portraits soon became fashionable. Picabia introduced him to Cocteau, who was pleased with his work and sent his friends to be photographed. Cocteau knew everyone in Paris, both in the arts and in the aristocratic society that patronized the arts. Thanks to him Man Ray added portraits of the young French composers to his collection and photographed Proust on his deathbed. He was taken up by the aristocracy and did their portraits, photographed their houses, attended their revels, and once directed them as performers in a film. Such wealthy noblemen as the Comte de Beaumont and the Vicomte de Noailles were great patrons of the avant-garde.

Some months after his arrival in Paris Man Ray discovered the Bohemian world of Montparnasse. Montmartre, which had been the artists' favorite quarter before the war, was now taken over by night clubs, and the artists had moved across the city to Montparnasse. The dadaists did not go there as a rule, for the idea of an artists' colony was against their principles, but Man Ray liked the atmosphere and took a room in the Hôtel des Ecoles in the heart of the quarter. To him Montparnasse seemed like a small town populated almost entirely by artists and writers. He liked the life of cafés and studios and settled down with a mistress—a model and cabaret singer who was locally famous as Kiki de Montparnasse. Without abandoning his French friends, he acquired a more cosmopolitan acquaintance and became the official photographer of the Americans of Montparnasse.

Not satisfied with portraits and documentary photographs, he went on to more experimental work. One night when working in his darkroom he hit upon his "Rayograph" process of making photographs without a camera by placing objects directly on photographic paper, then exposing it to light. The paper registered silhouettes in compositions that looked like abstract paintings. Fascinated by this method, he explored the possibilities further, producing shadows, shades, and textures, thus creating an effect like collage. The rayographs had an enormous success. Tzara, who had come to live in the same hotel as Man Ray, was the first to hear of the discovery, considered it a perfect dada art form, and even helped make some rayographs. He wrote the introduction for an album of rayographs published in 1922 under the title *Les Champs Délicieux* and took the occasion to launch into an attack on painting.

In his autobiography Man Ray records the explanation he gave at the time he produced his first rayographs: "I was trying to do with photography what painters were doing, but with light and chemicals, instead of pigment, and without the optical help of the camera." He sought similar effects with other developing techniques. When he printed some nude photographs, he made them look like drawings by eliminating depth and photographic detail. In developing portraits he sometimes used a process called "solarization," overexposing the negative until it bleached into a positive with sharply etched outlines. His album, *Photographs, 1920–1934, Paris,* shows an impressive range of techniques, matching the painter's art in variety and effect. At the same time his painting was influenced by his photography. In 1923 he painted a portrait of Duchamp, *Rrose Sélavy,* which simulated photography but which, he says, was "neither a painting nor a photograph."

Paris was the scene of much experimentation in the cinema during the twenties, so it was inevitable that Man Ray should proceed from still photography to moving pictures. He had already collaborated with Duchamp in this medium both in New York and Paris and had designated himself "*Directeur de Mauvais Movies*" when he signed Picabia's autograph collage, *The Cacodylatic Eye.* In 1923 he acquired a camera and began filming at random, mostly moving objects in his studio, such as revolving spirals and the light patterns on a buxom nude torso (presumably Kiki's). His first film, a three-minute affair, was made for a dada manifestation called *Le Coeur à Barbe* (The Bearded Heart), which included music, poetry readings, a play by Tzara, and films by Hans Richter and Charles Sheeler. Tzara, who had announced that Man Ray would be on the program, urged him to finish his film with some moving rayographs. This he did, sprinkling salt and pepper, pins and thumbtacks, on the film, then assembling the rayograph sequences with those he had filmed before. *Le Retour à la Raison* can only be regarded as an experiment, though it produced some interesting effects, the most successful being the dance of the pins and tacks on the film.

Man Ray entitled his film *The Return to Reason,* knowing that it was scheduled to appear at the end of the program and that the dada antics were bound to be mad. In his autobiography he says the film provoked a riot, also a predictable part of any dada performance, but the riot was serious in this case, caused by the bitter rivalry between Breton and Tzara. *Le Coeur à Barbe*, staged in July 1923, was the last dada manifestation. The following year Breton published his first surrealist manifesto, which marked the beginning of a new movement. Too solemn for dada's humor, too systematic and authoritarian for dada's anarchy, he codified its random impulses and added the whole apparatus of Freudian psychology. Under dada everyone had been a president; among the surrealists only Breton was the pope, and he excommunicated readily. Surrealism was more specifically preoccupied with irrational psychology, its art tending toward the hallucinatory, the visionary, and the dreamlike, but basically the movement was a direct outgrowth of dada, incorporating the same ideas.

By 1924 dada had run its course as a movement, but the dada spirit was eternal. That was the year that Picabia collaborated with a dadaist of almost sixty summers, the composer Erik Satie, on a ballet called *Relâche* (the word used on theater posters to announce that the theater was closed), in which Duchamp appeared briefly in a nude tableau of Cranach's *Adam and Eve*, and Man Ray made a more modest appearance (fully clothed), sitting in a chair onstage and occasionally walking back and forth. Both appeared again in a film shown during the intermission, playing chess on the roof of the theater. *Entr'acte*, filmed by René Clair but conceived and directed by Picabia, was the masterpiece of dada cinema.

Like his friends, Man Ray remained a dadaist at heart, although identified with the surrealists hereafter. Like most dadaists he attended Breton's meetings and exhibited his works at the first surrealist exhibition in 1925. But, as he points out, these were the same works that had appeared in his dada show four years before. One of them, *The Enigma of Isidore Ducasse*, was prominently reproduced in the surrealists' magazine *La Révolution Surréaliste*. The work in question, a sewing machine wrapped in burlap, could be interpreted as a symbol of the artist's subconscious mechanism, and Isidore Ducasse, venerated as a precursor of surrealism, had provided one of the surrealists' favorite texts: "Beautiful like the fortuitous meeting, on a dissection table, of a sewing machine and an umbrella." The only trouble with this interpretation is that the object was made in 1920, before the surrealist movement existed, and the title, which did not appear in the magazine, may have been added later. Still, Man Ray was quite willing to join the surrealists, and they took him up as the dadaists had done before. They liked his mysterious rayograms, his aerographs and objects, and reproduced his work in *La Révolution Surréaliste* more frequently than that of any other artist. When the Galerie Surréaliste opened in 1926, his works were the first to be shown, along with some primitive art from Oceania.

Naturally his work did not change overnight when surrealism was founded, and it is not surprising that his surrealist friends were critical of his second film, *Emak Bakia* (1926), though Man Ray himself thought they should appreciate its surrealistic qualities: "irrationality, automatism, psychological and dream-like sequences without apparent logic, and complete disregard of conventional storytelling." The film was probably influenced not by the surrealists but by Duchamp, with whom Man Ray collaborated about this time on a seven-minute production called *Anemic Cinema.* Duchamp, forever experimenting, was still trying to achieve the illusion of depth and had constructed another machine for the purpose, rotating disks in spiral patterns to create a three-dimensional effect. For variety he alternated the designs with inscriptions full of alliterative anagrams and puns. Though an interesting experiment, the film is appropriately named.

Emak Bakia achieved a similar rotating monotony whenever Man Ray used a turntable—revolving always at the same speed—to produce abstract designs. These he combined, as in his first film, with naturalistic sequences filmed at the villa on the Basque coast that gave the film its name. The scenes succeed each other in a disconnected series: shots taken from a car traveling at high speed, legs endlessly stepping down from the running board, a pair of legs doing the Charleston, fish amid waves and seaweed. The film shows that he was still too fascinated with the novelty of moving pictures, experimenting with such tricks as slowing the motion, reversing the action, superimposing one image on another, and turning images upside down. Back in Paris he introduced a more coherent sequence when he filmed the brisk arrival of Jacques Rigaut in a taxi carrying a briefcase, but gave it a dada twist as the briefcase contained only shirt collars, which Rigaut proceeded to tear up, one after another. Kiki provided a surrealistic touch at the end, appearing in a close-up with eyes heavily painted on her eyelids, which opened, revealing her eyes.

Man Ray called *Emak Bakia* a "*cinépoème*," but that description fits his next film, *L'Etoile de Mer* (1928), much better. The title was taken from a poem by Robert Desnos, a surrealist who was noted for his automatic writing while in a state of trance. The lines of the poem were rather disconnected, but Man Ray wove them into a pattern of images to create a poetic scenario centering around two feminine symbols of beauty, Kiki and the starfish (*l'étoile de mer*). The film has a dim sort of love story, with several encounters between a man and a woman and at the end a rival who takes her away, but the story only serves as an excuse to show Kiki undressing and to introduce Desnos fleetingly as the man who finally captures beauty. Otherwise the film is a lyrical meditation, its scenes linked by the free association of the camera eye: newspapers blowing over the ground pursued by a man's feet, a train running through abstract light patterns, suburban houses passing row on row, a harbor, La Santé prison, a starry sky, and recurrently, the woman and the starfish. Though disconnected, the scenes are vivid and haunting, the visual symbols fully realized, and all parts work together in an effective piece of surrealism.

L'Etoile de Mer is no longer the work of an amateur but one of the most accomplished short films of its time. Man Ray achieved some remarkable visual effects when he coated his lens with gelatin so that the disrobing scene would pass the censors. The blurred focus created an effect like painting, with a cubistic breakup of outline in some of the close-ups and impressionistic brushwork in landscapes and figures. The technique proved so effective that he used it through most of the film, with only an occasional clear shot to remind the eye of normal vision or to bring an object into clear focus. He made maximum use of the camera's resources in dramatizing the contrast between the fixed symbolic form of the mounted starfish and the biological reality in a close-up of its innumerable wriggling tentacles.

His last film, *Les Mystères du Château du Dé* (1929), was commissioned by the Vicomte de Noailles, who wanted a documentary of his newly completed modernistic villa on the Mediterranean. The title suggests the amusing scenario Man Ray invented in carrying out his assignment, rendering a tour of the establishment as a mystery story and taking his visual motif from the cubic forms of "the Château of the Dice." The dice naturally suggested a literary theme, Mallarmé's poem *Un Coup de Dés,* which was a favorite text of the surrealists because it dealt with the subject of chance. One critic sees the film as entirely surrealistic, haunted like the empty spaces of de Chirico's paintings. This interpretation is possible, for Man Ray liked a mystery, but the spookiness is hard to take seriously; it seems more likely that he meant it to be a parody of scary movies.

Les Mystères du Château du Dé begins with a trip from wintry Paris to the south of France, passing through scenes that illustrate the cubic motif even before the arrival at the "château." The camera then makes its tour of the empty rooms, while melodramatic subtitles create an air of suspense, and finally brings the place to life in filming the guests at their sports. Considering the nature of the assignment, the film accomplishes its purpose cleverly. The noble patron was so pleased that he offered to back a full-length film, but Man Ray had already made up his mind to abandon a medium which with the advent of sound was becoming too complicated for one man to handle by himself. He was willing to collaborate with one or two friends, as he did in the thirties, once with the poet Jacques Prévert, another time with Breton and Eluard, but in neither case did they complete more than a few scenes.

During the twenties and thirties Man Ray continued to work in a variety of media besides film. He made two of his most provocative objects shortly after his arrival in Paris: *Cadeau* (Gift), a flatiron with a row of tacks down the middle, and *Object to Be Destroyed*, a metronome with an eye attached to the moving arm. Both met a suitable fate. *Cadeau*, intended as a gift for Philippe Soupault, was stolen from his gallery, or according to another version of the story, was offered as a prize but stolen *by* Soupault. *Object to Be Destroyed*, so called because Man Ray had intended to destroy it publicly, was in fact destroyed many years after it was made, when a band of students from the Beaux-Arts demonstrated against dada and surrealism. The work was promptly reproduced with a new title, *Indestructible Object*, and has since been mass-produced.

Man Ray's aerographs, drawings, objects, chess sets, and rayographs appeared regularly in all the surrealist exhibitions and in the successive surrealist magazines. Exhibitions usually singled him out as one of the leading exponents of surrealism. In 1934 he finished his most dramatic surrealistic painting, *Observatory Time—The Lovers*, a pair of enormous lips floating against a twilight sky with the Paris Observatory on the horizon. In 1937 he published a book of drawings, *Les Mains Libres*, with poems written by Eluard as illustrations; among the drawings was a convincing imaginary portrait of the Marquis de Sade, of whom, strangely enough, no genuine portrait exists.

Surrealism reached its climax in Paris with the International Surrealistic Exhibition of 1938, in which all the surrealists tried to outdo each other. The first sight to greet the public was Dali's *Rainy Taxi* in the lobby, with water falling in torrents on the occupants. The next was *Surrealist Street*, a corridor filled with mannequins fantastically decorated by the artists, Man Ray's with large tears rolling down her cheeks and soap bubbles issuing from clay pipes in her hair. The entire extravaganza had been staged by Duchamp, who hung hundreds of coal sacks from the ceiling, covered the floor with dead leaves, and installed a mossy pool with ferns on its banks. Man Ray, who was in charge of lighting, left the gallery in the dark for the opening night and handed out flashlights.

Man Ray would never have left Paris if the Germans had not come. Although he occasionally visited New York on business, he had never a thought of staying there, thoroughly content, he says, with "the easy, leisurely life of Paris, where one could accomplish just as much and of a more satisfying nature." Paris appreciated his individualism and gave him a prestige he never enjoyed in New York. Paris shared his values and his guiding principles in work and play: "the pursuit of freedom and the pleasure it produces." His ambitions were limited, as was his view of the human race, distinguished, at its best, by the creation of "gratuitous emblems." He did not insist on being taken seriously; he thought of art as a harmless pursuit, unlike most human activities, and asked only for freedom to enjoy this pleasure.

When the Second World War started, life continued as usual in Paris, so he stayed on. When the Germans invaded France, he joined the exodus, but returned to Paris when Pétain capitulated. His autobiography gives an excellent account of how it felt to be in Paris before and after the occupation. The Germans told him he could stay and work for them, but he could not stand the sight of those gray-green uniforms. In the summer of 1940 he made his way to Lisbon and took a boat to New York. Dali and René Clair sailed with him, and other European artists were on their way to America, where the surrealist movement took a new lease on life. "New York was always twenty years behind Paris in its appreciation of contemporary art," Man Ray remarks in his autobiography. As if to confirm this statement, Breton landed in New York on July 14, 1941, twenty years to the day after Man Ray's arrival in Paris.

IN MONTPARNASSE

CHRONOLOGY IV

1918 Hemingway stops off in Paris en route to Italy, immediately goes to watch Big Bertha shells landing

1920 Pound's first Paris letter for *The Dial.* Pound settles in studio at 70 bis rue Notre-Dame-des-Champs

1921 Hemingway goes to Paris as roving correspondent

1922 Shakespeare and Company publishes *Ulysses* on Joyce's birthday, February 2

Hemingway, "A Canadian With One Thousand a Year Can Live Very Comfortably in Paris," *Toronto Star Weekly* (February 4)

1923 Hemingway contributes six "chapters" of *in our time* to the Exiles' Number of *The Little Review,* edited by Margaret Anderson, Jane Heap, and Ezra Pound

Three Stories & Ten Poems published by Contact Publishing Company

1924 *in our time,* dedicated "to robert mcalmon and william bird, publishers of the city of paris"

Hemingway becomes assistant editor and contributes three stories to Ford's *Transatlantic Review*

Fitzgerald finishes *The Great Gatsby* on the Riviera, begins *Tender Is the Night*

1925 Ernest Walsh launches *This Quarter* with "Homage to Ezra" and "Big Two-Hearted River"

1926 *The Sun Also Rises*

1927 *Men Without Women*

1929 *Transition*'s "Revolution of the Word"

Harry Crosby commits suicide

A Farewell to Arms

9.

On the Seacoast of Bohemia

> "You're an expatriate. You've lost touch with the soil. You get precious. Fake European standards have ruined you. You drink yourself to death. You become obsessed by sex. You spend all your time talking, not working. You are an expatriate, see? You hang around cafés."

Thus in *The Sun Also Rises* Hemingway sums up the clichés of the twenties about expatriation. Since then the very word "expatriate" has become a kind of cliché, more or less synonymous with "the lost generation" and equally unsatisfactory. To a disapproving America the word then connoted escapism, irresponsibility, and debauchery. To literary historians now it suggests a young American writer of the twenties deracinated by the war and alienated from his native land by "puritanism"—another cliché. The expatriate thus becomes a caricature of Harold Stearns on the one hand or Ernest Hemingway on the other. The chief objection to such oversimplifications is that they disregard the positive side of the phenomenon, namely the attractions of living abroad that had drawn Americans ever since the early days of the republic. No one has ever called Benjamin Franklin an expatriate, though he was more at home in Paris and stayed longer than the vast majority of Americans who went there in the 1920s.

To clear the air it is best to sort out the different types of Americans abroad, and to consider their motives for staying. Before the war relatively few Americans could afford to live abroad, but in the prosperous twenties their numbers increased. In 1927 the American Chamber of Commerce estimated that there were fifteen thousand Americans resident in Paris; the police reckoned thirty-five thousand. The discrepancy may reflect two different clienteles. Obviously not all the Americans in Paris were doing business. A great many of them were really tourists who stayed on, young people who had not yet settled down in life and who were sustained by checks from home. They were not in any sense exiles, for they mixed almost exclusively with their compatriots and always had the intention of returning home at some future date. Their contacts with the French were restricted mainly to waiters and shopkeepers. Since European life was not easy to penetrate, they generally stayed on the surface. Montparnasse, where the greatest number of them congregated, became an American village.

Paris attracted more Americans in the twenties than at any time before or since. The war was partly responsible, as the American Legion demonstrated by choosing Paris as the place to celebrate the tenth anniversary of American intervention. Prohibition also had its influence, for the younger generation wanted to get away from the whole repressive temper of American mores. But it was not so much the fleshpots as the freedom of Paris that attracted the young, not Babylon but Bohemia. To the middle-aged summer tourist out on a spree Paris may have had the aura of a glorified Folies Bergère; to his son or daughter it suggested the romantic life depicted in George Moore's *Confessions of a Young Man*, Du Maurier's *Trilby*, or Murger's *Scènes de la Vie de Bohème*. Murger's Bohemia, despite its factual origins, was no more real than Puccini's, a sentimental state of mind that romanticized the misery of poverty-stricken artists. The Bohemia discovered by the Americans of the twenties was even more unreal, a Land of Cockaigne in which one could play at starving in a garret for art's sake without being either poor or creative. Paris was a place that evoked all the sentimentality of the nineteenth-century Bohemia, that permitted the young to lead the artist's life with none of its disadvantages, that tolerated or ignored Americans and allowed them to be as carefree and unconventional as they wished without the disapproval of society.

For these Americans Paris consisted mainly of a cluster of sidewalk cafés along the Boulevard du Montparnasse. This was a relatively new neighborhood out beyond the Latin Quarter that became the headquarters for artists and writers in the twenties. Here at the Café du Dôme, La Rotonde, or Le Select, Americans gathered to spend their days. They took readily to the café, an institution in a country where men do not usually invite friends home. Living in hotel rooms, the Americans also found it convenient to conduct their social lives in public. The cafés of Montparnasse were their clubs, where they read their American newspapers, received letters from home, and met other Americans who like themselves had little to occupy them besides an occasional trip to the Morgan Bank or American Express to cash a check. It was a pleasant way to pass one's days, and time lost its American urgency at the slow tempo of the café *terrasse*.

The man who more than any other created the image of the expatriate was Harold Stearns. In his case the word fits, for Stearns made an issue—almost a career—of expatriation. He first made a name for himself as a critic of the American way of life when he edited a symposium on the subject, *Civilization in the United States*, and dramatized his attitude by sailing for Europe on the day he completed the book, July 4, 1921. Not only the date but the year was well chosen, for the postwar exodus got properly under way in 1921. Thereafter for twelve years Stearns was a familiar figure around Montparnasse, where he was regarded by some as a prominent citizen, by others as one of the village characters. He was in fact both, an intellectual who was considered the chief spokesman of the exiles and by his own admission one of the oldest clients at the Select. In *Exile's Return* Malcolm Cowley records one opinion of Stearns: "People used to look down at him sleeping on a café terrace and say, 'There lies civilization in the United States.'" Samuel Putman presents a more sympathetic view in *Paris Was Our Mistress.* Stearns long contemplated a book on Rabelais, an author as difficult as Joyce in medieval French; Putnam, the great modern translator of Rabelais, was impressed by Stearns's learning and brilliance on the subject.

Sinclair Lewis singled out Stearns as his chief target when he criticized the preciosities of Montparnasse in an article published in the *American Mercury* in October 1925.

> Nowhere in America itself is this duty-ridden earnestness of the artist and his disciples so well shown as at that Brevoort and cathedral of American sophistication, the Café Dôme in Paris.
>
> Among the other advantages of the Dôme, it is on a corner charmingly resembling Sixth avenue at Eighth street, and all the waiters understand Americanese, so that it is possible for the patrons to be highly expatriate without benefit of Berlitz. It is, in fact, the perfectly standardized place to which standardized rebels flee from the crushing standardization of America.
>
> On view at the Dôme is the great though surprisingly young author, who by his description of vomiting and the progress of cancer, in a volume of sixty-seven pages issued in a limited edition of three hundred copies, has entirely transformed American fiction. There is the lady who has demolished Thomas Hardy, Arnold Bennett, and Goethe. And king of kings, Osimandias of Osimandiases, supremest of Yankee critics, *ex cathedra* authority on literature, painting, music, economics, and living without laboring, very father and seer of the Dôme, is that Young Intellectual who, if he ever finishes the assassinatory book of which we have heard these last three years, will tear the world up by the

> roots. He is going to deliver unto scorn all the false idols of the intelligentsia, particularly such false idols as have become tired of lending him—as the phrase is—money.

In attacking the Left Bank highbrows Lewis was taking vengeance on those writers who had rudely rejected him from their fraternity, regarding him with contempt as a commercial success. Still, he nursed a wistful desire to be accepted by Montparnasse while writing best sellers. In his Nobel Prize address in 1930 he was generous in his praise of other American writers, particularly the young, "most of them living now in Paris, most of them a little insane in the tradition of James Joyce, who, however insane they may be, have refused to be genteel and traditional and dull."

Harold Stearns was neither as megalomaniacal as Lewis depicted him nor as idle. He was a relatively harmless, rather pathetic castaway who supported himself meagerly as a newspaperman. His autobiography, *A Street I Know*, reveals a lonely man who tried to drown his sorrows. Somewhat given to self-pity, he characterized himself as "just an uprooted, aimless wanderer on the face of the earth," but it is true that he was cast adrift by the death of his wife and took comfort in the saying that in Paris life passes like a dream. On the one occasion when he visited the United States he discovered that he was homesick for Paris and returned with relief. He described the Café Select as "a seething madhouse of drunks, semi-drunks, quarter-drunks, and sober maniacs," yet he sat there night after night, often until dawn, drinking champagne and enjoying the company. "It was a useless, silly life," he wrote in retrospect, "and I have missed it every day since."

In Paris he discovered a talent and acquired a reputation for handicapping the races. As "Peter Pickem" he became a legendary character, an oracle with an uncanny knack for picking long shots. In 1923 he went to the races for the first time and picked the winner of the Grand Prix de Paris, an outsider that looked like the horse in Hemingway's story published that same year, "My Old Man." Stearns had found the great passion of his life. The happiest pages in his autobiography are those which capture the color and excitement of the racetracks around Paris. After three years as an amateur handicapper he became the racetrack reporter for the Paris edition of the *Chicago Tribune*. The job paid little besides living expenses, but to Stearns it meant the ideal combination of work and pleasure. Seven afternoons a week he went to one of the seven racetracks around Paris; by early evening he had written his column and was free to relax at the Select as late as he wished.

He explained why he was content with such a life in his "Apologia of an Expatriate," written as a letter to Scott Fitzgerald and published in *Scribner's Magazine*. Fitzgerald in a characteristic act of kindness had offered to get the letter published and suggested as a topic "Why I Go On Being Poor in Paris." In giving his reasons Stearns confessed that he knew all "the bitterness of being an expatriate," living as he did in humiliating circumstances on the edge of poverty; he admitted that America was full of vitality, while Europe was old and disillusioned; yet he had many reasons for staying. He had been driven out of America by the postwar trend toward standardization, philistinism, and intolerance, "the emergence of articulate mediocrity, armed with self-assurance, a full stomach, and a tenacious determination to destroy anything better than itself." He questioned whether Fitzgerald was writing as well as he could in a society where all values were cheapened. In Paris Stearns had found the values of an established civilization, not the least of which was tolerance. Here he was left alone to live as he pleased, free to work or to make a fool of himself, at ease with himself and society. At the time he thought he would end his days in Paris, and he would have stayed on longer than he did if he had not gone temporarily blind and lost his job.

The world of Harold Stearns has been preserved in the memoirs of Jimmie the Barman, *This Must Be the Place*. A former prizefighter from Liverpool, Jimmie had a loyal following among the serious drinkers of Montparnasse as he worked in one bar after another. He was best known as the barman of the Dingo during the mid-twenties, and already in 1934, his book struck the elegiac note so familiar to memories of Paris, harking back to those vintage years when francs were plentiful and friends carefree. His reminiscences were taken down by a stenographer, edited by one of his drinking friends, the American newspaperman Morrill Cody, and provided with an introduction by another, Ernest Hemingway. Jimmie's talk was no doubt more entertaining in its proper setting; when translated to the printed page it goes flat, but the book documents a side of Montparnasse history that would otherwise have been lost. It serves as a social register of the Anglo-American bars, a record of an unusual assortment of people.

Jimmie divides his clientele into four categories: artists, writers, and newspapermen (40 percent), tourists (25 percent), students (10 percent), and the remaining 25 percent composed of "the regulars, the hangers-on, the disillusioned (mainly as a result of love complications) and the habitual drunks." The tourists and students were considered outsiders; the writers, the newspapermen, and the disillusioned got along fine, and Jimmie remembers them fondly. Most of his favorite customers appear extravagant, charming, and irresponsible; many of them seem to have had unhappy lives and come to the bar for conviviality. Among the noteworthy are "the first American to come to Montparnasse, forty years ago," "the most Montparnassian American in the world, for he was born in the building over the Dôme when that institution was still a little *bistro*," and an improbable character named Sam Weller who set up a business in Paris called the Necessary Luxuries Company. Jimmie has a weakness for such characters, which is understandable, since they were such an important part of his business. He mentions hundreds of them, bizarre, romantic, possibly rich or noble, although some of the Balkan titles would be hard to verify.

Usually he tells anecdotes about them; sometimes he merely catalogues their names and exploits:

> . . . Peter Powel, the photographer, who lost his American citizenship during the war because he fought in the French army, but later regained it; Captain Smith, who went from London to Italy in a canoe; the woman who was ashamed because she had a decided moustache on her lip, though when she had it removed she became a beauty; Bud Fisher, the creator of Mutt and Jeff; Sam Dashiel, an American journalist, and Hilda, his very English, ex-Tiller-girl wife; Captain Bunny Christiansen, who, though his legs were paralysed, was a great success with the ladies; Bea Mathieu, who represents the fashion column of *The New Yorker* in Paris; Rea Brown and Flo McCardle, friends of Bea's, and also in the fashion game; Countess de Vitali, a great friend of Pat and Duff; Stephanus Eloff, the grandson of General Kruger, of Boer War fame; the American Indian who entertained the Dingo by dancing on nails and swallowing fire or sticking pins into his skin; Jack Dempsey, who visited us once but said nothing; May Manning, the English model; Edward Titus, the husband of Helena Rubinstein, who published *This Quarter;* Lena Hutchins, with her strange Swiss accent and a grey streak in her hair; Victor Pattou, "the Greek God," famous for his looks and magnetic powers; George Gibbs, who was the spitting image of Douglas Fairbanks and liked to be taken for him; John Paul Jones, who died of tuberculosis contracted during the war; Bubbles Williams, whose international romances once occupied considerable space in the American newspapers; Mrs. Van Ness and her daughter, Betty, who was brought up in the Dingo; Louise Coons, a writer from Kentucky; Mary Seigert, known as Mary Queen of Scots, and very much liked; and Morton Hoyt; and Martin Somers; and Marjorie; and Hildegarde Martin; and Miss Marney; and Charles Grey; and Glen Goetz; and so many, many more.

The Dingo bar provided the characters for *The Sun Also Rises.* Two of them are mentioned here, Pat Guthrie and Duff Twysden, to whom Jimmie later devotes a chapter entitled "Brett and Mike," providing the sad sequel to the novel, a story of true love that ends in suicide. Other customers recruited for the novel appear in characteristic anecdotes: Harold Stearns the butt of a joke about a horse that wanted a drink, Ford Madox Ford fond of giving parties at a *bal musette* near the Place de la Contrescarpe, Harold Loeb proud of his bridge and boxing, and the "best-known person in Montparnasse in those days . . . Mitzy—officially the Duke of Mitzicus of Greece—who acted as guide and interpreter for all newly arrived English and Americans." Hemingway himself figures in the annals of the Dingo, as Jimmie remembers long conversations about boxing and bullfighting, and an anecdote worthy of *The Sun Also Rises* that was told by a friend of Hemingway's, Mike Ward. "'I got in a terrible fight about you yesterday,' Mike said. 'I was in the H— bar and I heard two men talking about you. I couldn't hear what they were saying, but I kept hearing the name Ernest Hemingway. So I went over to them and I said, "Are you friends of Ernest Hemingway?" And they said, 'No.' So I socked them both!'"

According to Jimmie, *The Sun Also Rises* gives an excellent picture of Montparnasse in the twenties; but at the time quite a few people thought otherwise, and not merely those who appeared in the book. Robert McAlmon, who frequented the Dingo, knew everyone in Montparnasse, and accompanied Hemingway to Pamplona twice, thought he had romanticized too much in the novel. McAlmon gives anything but a romantic view of the original circumstances in his memoirs, *Being Geniuses Together.* He also records the novel's reception in 1926, when people complained that Hemingway had ignored the productive residents of Montparnasse, creating the impression that the place was populated by disillusioned drunks. The novel is evidence enough that its author stayed away from bars during working hours, but the impression remains. Hemingway himself remarked in his introduction to Jimmie's memoirs, "Like everyone else in Montparnasse, the most interesting part of his life was before he crossed to the left bank of the Seine, but like almost everyone else there, he did not realize it." Hemingway remembered it as "a dismal place," and while he may have been thinking only of its bars and derelicts, that is the Montparnasse he immortalized.

He never had much good to say about Montparnasse. In an article written for the *Toronto Star Weekly* in 1922, "American Bohemians in Paris a Weird Lot," he may have considered it his task to cater to the prejudices of a stuffy Canadian reading public, but then again he may have been expressing his own opinions. His disgust sounds genuine enough: "A first look into the smoky, high-ceilinged, table-crammed interior of the Rotonde gives the same feeling that hits you as you step into the bird house at the zoo." And he tends to editorialize in distinguishing between serious artists and those who pose as artists but spend their days in talk. Again in 1929, in his introduction to *Kiki's Memoirs*, he makes the same distinction between "workers" and "bums." Speaking of the era of Montparnasse, which was overrated to begin with and which had just ended, he comments: "Montparnasse for this purpose means the cafés and the restaurants where people are seen in public. It does not mean the apartments, studios and hotel rooms where they work in private." And in "The Snows of Kilimanjaro," he remembers coming back to Paris after witnessing the horrors of the Greco-Turkish War, which affected him so profoundly that he could not bear to discuss it. "And there in the café as he passed was that American poet with a pile of saucers in front of him and a stupid look on his potato face talking about the Dada movement with a Roumanian who said his name was Tristan Tzara, who always wore a monocle and had a headache."

The serious writers and artists who went to Paris could not afford to spend all their time in bars or cafés and were inclined to resent the idlers who gave them a bad name. Dos Passos expressed a common complaint in his remark about "the huddle

Ezra Pound, John Quinn, Ford Madox Ford, and James Joyce at Pound's Paris studio, 3. Ford and Joyce sitting on Pound's homemade chairs. (Reproduced with the permission The Poetry/Rare Books Collection of The University Libraries, SUNY at Buffalo)

16. Ernest Hemingway at Shakespeare and Company, probably photographed by Sylvia Beach in 1922. (Princeton University Library, Sylvia Beach Collection)

17. Hemingway standing with Sylvia Beach in front of Shakespeare and Company. (Princeton University Library, Sylvia Beach Collection)

18. George Antheil. (Photograph by Man Ray, Courtesy of Juliet Man Ray)

19. George Antheil climbing up to his apartment above Shakespeare and Company. (Princeton University Library, Sylvia Beach Collection)

20. Virgil Thomson, Herbert Elwell, Walter Piston, and Aaron Copland chez Nadia Boulanger just before the all-American concert, May 5, 1926. (Photograph by Thérèse Bonney)

21. Gertrude Stein and Virgil Thomson, 1927. (Photograph by Thérèse Bonney)

22. Scene from *Four Saints in Three Acts*, "Saint Teresa half in and half out of d
(Photograph courtesy of Virgil Thomson)

23. Henry Miller, 1932. (Brassaï photograph)

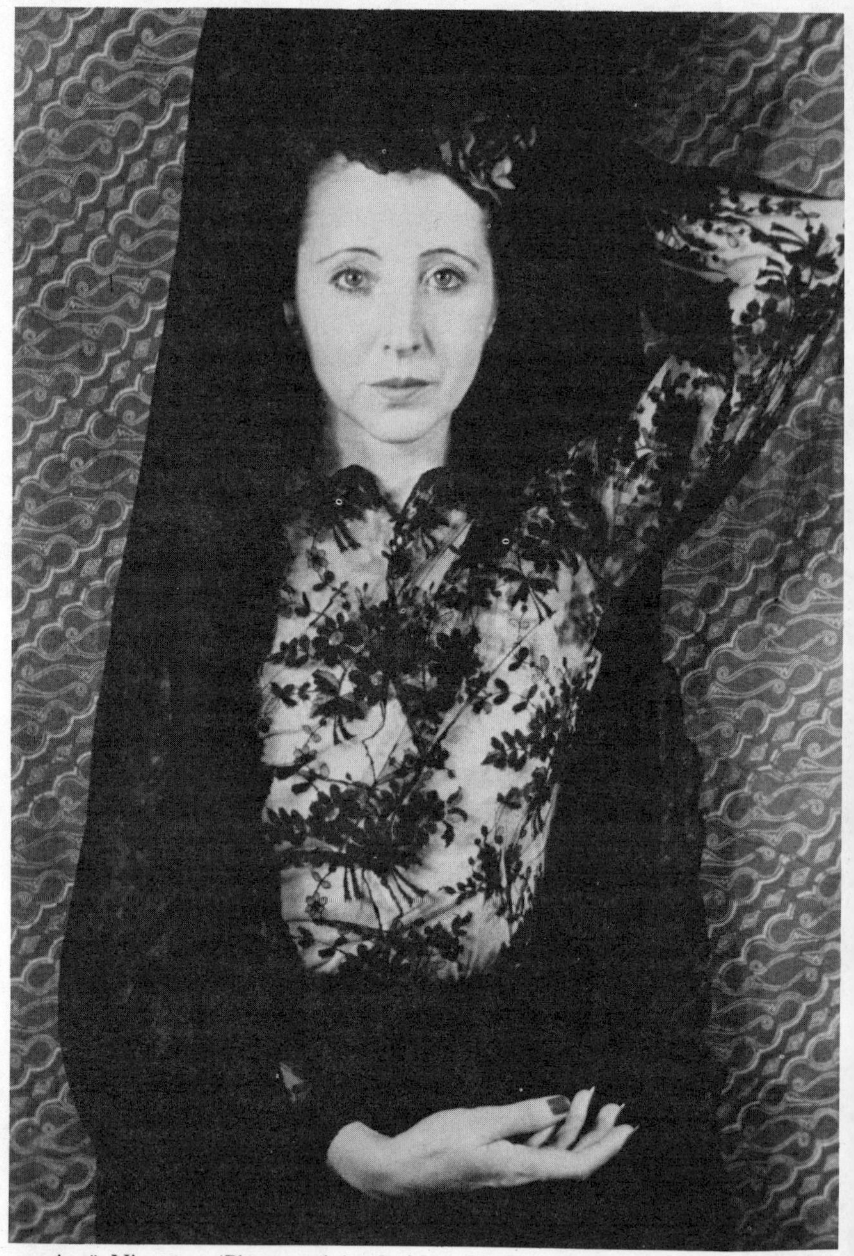

24. Anaïs Nin, 1940. (Photograph by Carl Van Vechten, Courtesy of Yale University Library)

of literary expatriates round Montparnasse," and Cummings in an anonymous satire of "Helen Whiffletree, American Poetess," ridiculed Edna St. Vincent Millay and "the perfect spiritual environment" which she found in Montparnasse, describing her as "the idol of the *Rotonde* and darling of the *Dôme*, to which latter café she dedicated several of her best-known sonnets." Nevertheless, despite their criticism of the dilettantes, serious writers also felt the powerful attraction of Paris, felt instinctively that they had to go there, where important things were happening in the arts.

"Why Do Americans Live in Europe?" was the title of a symposium that appeared in *Transition* in Fall 1928. Gertrude Stein, Hilaire Hiler, Robert McAlmon, George Antheil, Kay Boyle, and Berenice Abbott undertook to answer the question, along with other contributors to *Transition,* all of whom could be described as working seriously in the arts. Their answers vary considerably, but they share a common outlook: they do not generally think of themselves as exiles, however strong their objections to the intellectual, artistic, or "spiritual" (*Transition's* word in its questionnaire) shortcomings of their native land. Furthermore, they do not take themselves too seriously. Here is a typical reaction:

> It is natural for men to travel or to live abroad. They have always done so with profit and pleasure. And since the instinct is natural, I see no reason to defend it beyond this statement. New York, I am told by a friend who has just come from there, is divided into two classes; those who can afford to buy a ticket to Europe and those who cannot.

The answers consider various advantages to living in Europe. Not only is life cheaper, but the compulsion to make money is not so all-consuming. Europe allows leisure and reflection. "What America needs is a gospel of laziness." Europe values the arts and confers self-respect on the artist, while America has no use for him, leaving him with a guilty need to justify himself.

Europe is tolerant, takes a more realistic view of human nature, and leaves a man freer to lead his private life. In short, artists as a group find in Europe the kind of life that is most conducive to creation. And by Europe they usually meant Paris, where most if not all of them were living at the time and where the overwhelming majority of Americans in the twenties preferred to stay. Robert McAlmon speaks for his generation when he says that he prefers France to America, but not England, Italy, or Germany. Ivan Beede states that he lives in France because he has learned to write there. And Harold Salemson, the editor of *Tambour*, sums it all up by saying, "The one reason I prefer living outside of America is that I am able to live in Paris. . . . the center of the world as concerns the things which are of interest to me."

In the twenties Paris was certainly the center of the American literary world. Four of the most important writers of the older generation lived there, and almost all American writers felt compelled to make the pilgrimage, at least. Many went to pay homage to Gertrude Stein, now venerated as a kind of idol in her shrine, with Alice Toklas as chief priestess keeping the wives at bay. Others worshipped James Joyce and purchased *Ulysses* at Sylvia Beach's bookshop. Ezra Pound was on hand during the first half of the decade, the grand strategist of the avant-garde, irascibly and selflessly conducting his campaigns for the arts. Ford Madox Ford joined forces with Pound in 1923 and rallied the young in support of the *Transatlantic Review;* Ford, who had renounced England in favor of France the previous year, preferred the company of Americans to his compatriots. All four of these writers acquired a following of young Americans, and while Gertrude Stein did not get along with Pound and met Joyce but once, their followers were often the same. Of the leaders of the literary avant-garde, only T. S. Eliot was not in Paris, and he came over from London occasionally to solicit a manuscript from Gertrude Stein or attend a performance of Pound's opera.

The young writer who learned most from these elders was

unquestionably Ernest Hemingway. The record of his years in Paris is one of extraordinarily rapid development to full maturity. At the time he arrived he was just another able journalist with literary ambitions, and Paris was full of such writers. But he was disciplined and determined, he worked hard and learned fast, and in Paris, between 1921 and 1927, he found himself as a writer and did a large share of his best work. In retrospect those were his best years, while he was still learning his craft, getting better all the time and knowing it, when hunger was still keen, unspoiled by the surfeit of success. "If you are lucky enough to have lived in Paris as a young man," he quoted himself in the epigraph to his book of Paris reminiscences, "then wherever you go for the rest of your life, it stays with you, for Paris is a moveable feast."

The youthful Hem has been considerably obscured by all the later legendary Hemingways, the tough, self-assured man of the world, the *aficionado*, the war-horse, and especially the grizzled old Papa looking out from the covers of *Life* magazine. When he first arrived in Paris, Hemingway was a diffident young man of twenty-two. He was also precociously knowing and well informed, but he concealed his astuteness in boyish charm. Everyone who knew him then remembers how handsome and ingratiating he was. He arrived in December 1921, bearing letters of introduction to Joyce, Gertrude Stein, and others, written for him by Sherwood Anderson, who had been in Paris the summer before. "Mr. Hemingway is an American writer instinctively in touch with everything worth while going on here," Anderson wrote in his letters of introduction, singling out the perceptive quality that distinguished Hemingway from the start. He lost no time in getting acquainted with Pound, Gertrude Stein, and Sylvia Beach, whose bookstore was the headquarters of many writers. Joyce he always revered as the great writer of his time, and he promptly ordered several copies of *Ulysses*, soon to be published. But his acquaintance with Joyce was purely social; he may have been an occasional drinking companion but never a disciple.

His relationship with Pound and Gertrude Stein was much closer, the relationship of a pupil to his masters. John Peale Bishop, who first met Hemingway in 1922, records his obligation: "In Paris, Hemingway submitted much of his apprentice work in fiction to Pound. It came back to him blue-penciled, most of the adjectives gone. The comments were unsparing. Writing for a newspaper was not at all the same as writing for a poet." Gertrude Stein proved an even more exacting critic and a tough-minded teacher. Bishop quotes Hemingway as saying later, "Ezra was right half the time, and when he was wrong, he was so wrong you were never in doubt about it. Gertrude was always right." Hemingway was an apt pupil, worthy of such discipline. "Toward his craft, he was humble," says Bishop, "and had, moreover, the most complete literary integrity it has ever been my lot to encounter."

His relations with Pound were friendly, then and after. They played tennis and boxed together on an easy man-to-man footing. His relations with Gertrude Stein became more intimate and eventually more troubled. The partisans of each have criticized the other, but there was fault on both sides. In the twenties Gertrude Stein conducted her salon autocratically, surrounding herself with young men who had to please her or be banished from the presence. Hemingway, too, hardened with age and ended up quarreling with most of his old friends. During his first four years in Paris, though, he managed to stay on the good side of Gertrude Stein, and even later, after their falling out, both retained a healthy respect for one another.

They got along famously at the start. Both wrote to Anderson –Gertrude Stein that she found Hemingway "a delightful fellow" and taught him to cut his wife's hair, Hemingway that he and Gertrude Stein were "just like brothers." Between early 1922 and late 1925 they saw a good deal of each other and exchanged postcards and letters when they traveled. Hemingway admired the paintings at the rue de Fleurus and learned about bullfighting there as well as modern art. In the *Autobiography* Alice B. Toklas claims that she first told him about bullfighting, and a letter from Hemingway written in 1923 shows that he had discussed the subject with her and Gertrude Stein and was anxious to discuss it again before going to Pamplona for the first time. The following year Gertrude Stein and Alice Toklas became the godmothers of the Hemingways' child. At the same time Hemingway's letters show that Gertrude Stein was his literary godmother. In August 1924 he wrote from Spain that he was "trying to do the country like Cézanne." Commenting on how hard it was to write, he added, "It used to be easy before I met you. I certainly was bad, gosh, I'm awfully bad now but it's a different kind of bad."

When Gertrude Stein went over the work he had written before coming to Paris, her advice was, according to the *Autobiography*, "Begin again and concentrate." She also advised him to quit journalism if he wanted to become a writer. The *Autobiography* is not to be trusted, but Hemingway's letters to Gertrude Stein echo such advice and show that he valued it highly. It was sound advice. When he lost all but two of his early manuscripts he was forced to begin over again. The story of the suitcase stolen from the Gare de Lyon has as much symbolic as literal truth, signifying that he had shed his juvenilia to start again. He was no doubt better off, as he says himself in *A Moveable Feast*, to leave behind "the lyric facility of boyhood that was as perishable and as deceptive as youth was."

Gertrude Stein was also indebted to Hemingway, as she freely admits in the *Autobiography*. "After all he was the first of the young men to knock at my door and he did make Ford print the first piece of The Making of Americans." After being ignored for so many years, she craved recognition, she needed disciples, and she wanted above all to be published. Hemingway, after trying unsuccessfully to get her published in America, succeeded in Paris when he became an assistant editor of the *Transatlantic Review*. He not only prevailed upon Ford to run *The Making of Americans* in the magazine, he copied the manuscript and corrected the proofs. Thus Gertrude Stein's third book, begun long before in 1906, finally began to appear in excerpts in 1924, and as a result, was published as a book by Robert McAlmon the following year.

In the *Autobiography* Alice B. Toklas says, "In correcting these proofs Hemingway learned a great deal and he admired all that he learned." No doubt about it, Hemingway learned from Gertrude Stein, but he would have been a dull pupil if he had not learned before this. Actually he had already published a Steinian meditation on the Lausanne Peace Conference in *The Little Review* in 1923, which, he explained in a letter to Edmund Wilson, had been written under the influence of Gertrude Stein and a bottle of Beaune. Although he dismissed the parody, Hemingway added seriously, "Her method is invaluable for analysing anything or making notes on a person or a place. She has a wonderful head." He appreciated her writing, imitated it, and made it a part of his own. Here is a paragraph from his story "Soldier's Home," first published in 1925.

> He liked the girls that were walking along the other side of the street. He liked the look of them much better than the French girls or the German girls. But the world they were in was not the world he was in. He would like to have one of them. But it was not worth it. They were such a nice pattern. He liked the pattern. It was exciting. But he would not go through all the talking. He did not want one badly enough. He liked to look at them all, though. It was not worth it. Not now when things were getting good again.

Hemingway's writing contains many such passages written in the style of Gertrude Stein yet unmistakably his own. He was able to perceive what she had discovered and put it to intelligent use. She may have been a more original writer, but she wrote indiscriminately, with no concern for her nonexistent reader, and lazily, never revising. Hemingway, with his rigorous discipline, his painstaking revision, and his determination to convey experience exactly, made his work immediate and lucid as hers was not.

Why they eventually quarreled is not easily explained. He outgrew her, and she was no doubt jealous of his sudden success while she continued to struggle for recognition. She may have taken offense at his parodies. Besides the Peace Conference parody in *The Little Review* he published another in the German magazine *Der Querschnitt* that came closer to home. "The Soul of Spain with McAlmon and Bird the Publishers" makes fun of her repetition and nonsensical nursery rhymes.

> You come to Spain but do not remain. Anna Veronica, Marcial Veronica, Pablo Veronica, Gitanillo Veronica. No they cannot Veronica because because the wind blows. The wind blows and it does not snows look at the bull with his bloody nose.

But they remained friends for a year after that parody appeared. The attack on Hemingway in the *Autobiography* suggests that she was offended more by his parody of her friend Sherwood Anderson in *The Torrents of Spring*. Hemingway confirms this in *A Moveable Feast*, explaining, "I had attacked someone that was a part of her apparatus." *The Torrents of Spring* also made fun of her friend Ford's long-winded and pointless anecdotes and treated Gertrude Stein herself somewhat less than reverently. In a chapter entitled "The Passing of a Great Race and the Making and Marring of Americans," Hemingway mimicked Anderson's maundering reminiscences about Paris:

> There was a street in Paris named after Huysmans. Right around the corner from where Gertrude Stein lived. Ah, there was a woman! Where were her experiments in words leading her? What was at the bottom of it? All that in Paris. Ah, Paris.

The Torrents of Spring was the wild oats of a young writer who had just finished the first draft of *The Sun Also Rises* and who knew that it was good. In his running commentary to the reader Hemingway says that he wrote the parody in ten days and makes jokes about discussing art at the Dôme with Harold Stearns and Sinclair Lewis, sharing a gourmet meal with Dos Passos, and being interrupted in his work by Fitzgerald. His high spirits are evident, and the satire would have been amusing if circulated in manuscript or if excerpts had been published in little magazines. As a book it was objectionable; the humor was sophomoric and the ridicule of a man who had been kind to him callous.

After 1926 Hemingway saw less of Gertrude Stein and less of Paris. He lived there off and on through the twenties, but his orbit had shifted and his world had changed. In the thirties, though he still visited Paris, he returned as an outsider. The change is reflected in "A Paris Letter" he wrote for *Esquire* in the fall of 1933 when he spent three weeks in Paris, depressed by what had happened to his old friends and to the places he had known. Actually, as he realized, he had changed more than Paris, for she was less susceptible to the passage of time. "Paris is very beautiful this fall," he wrote. "It was a fine place to be quite young in and it is a necessary part of a man's education. We all loved it once and we lie if we say we didn't. But she is like a mistress who does not grow old and she has other lovers now. She was old to start with but we did not know it then. We thought she was just older than we were, and that was attractive then. So when we did not love her any more we held it against her. But that was wrong because she is always the same age and she always has new lovers."

From this time forth he began thinking nostalgically of his earlier years in Paris. Just as he had written stories about Michigan in Paris, so now he reminisced about Paris from a distance. In *Green Hills of Africa* he let his mind wander back ten and twelve years to the Boulevard de Sébastopol, the rue Notre-Dame-des-Champs, the fountains in the Place de l'Observatoire, the bust of Flaubert in the Luxenbourg Gardens. In "The Snows of Kilimanjaro" the dying writer remembers his beginnings in the poor neighborhood of the Place de la Contrescarpe before success spoiled everything. "And in that poverty, and in that quarter across the street from a Boucherie Chevaline and a wine co-operative he had written the start of all he was to do. There never was another part of Paris that he loved like that, the sprawling trees, the old white plastered houses painted brown below, the long green of the autobus in that round square, the purple flower dye upon the paving, the sudden drop down the hill of the rue Cardinal Lemoine to the River, and the other way the narrow crowded world of the rue Mouffetard." That writer is Hemingway thinking of all the stories he had not written. "No, he had never written about Paris. Not the Paris that he cared about."

Paris always remained his favorite city, and he finally got around to writing about the Paris he loved in the last years of his life. He was staying at the Ritz in the winter of 1956–57, when the baggagemen demanded that he claim two trunks that had been there since 1927, when he had moved from Paris. Mary Hemingway, who was with him, has written that when the trunks were opened he discovered the notebooks and papers of his early years. During the weeks that followed, he walked the streets of Paris, retracing the steps of his youth, and during the last few years of his life he lingered over those notebooks, collaborating with his younger self, walking around the Left Bank lost in memory, sitting in its cafés, re-creating conversations with people he knew then, reliving the experience of writing his early stories.

Of the many books of reminiscence about Paris in the twenties, only three have any claim to literary merit: *The Autobiography of Alice B. Toklas, Exile's Return*, and *A Moveable Feast.* Most of the others are interesting—often inaccurate—chronicles that tend to disintegrate into fragmentary notes. These three are unified, each in its own way—Gertrude Stein's by the personality and style of her fictional narrator, Cowley's by a coherent view of his generation's collective experience, and Hemingway's by the emergence of the young writer who was himself. Published posthumously thirty years after the other two, *A Moveable Feast* completes the trilogy as a rejoinder to the first and fulfillment of the second—for young Hemingway is Cowley's exemplar.

A Moveable Feast is not autobiography in the usual sense. The story of his five years in Paris is mostly written between the lines, and some of the allusions, as Lewis Galantière noted in reviewing the book, are intended for certain individuals and will only be understood by a few people who were there. The book takes the form of a random collection of brief sketches, held together mainly by the presence of the author. Its model is Turgenev's *A Sportsman's Sketches*, the first book Hemingway borrowed from Sylvia Beach's bookshop and one which he always admired. Hemingway's miscellany of local color, character, and anecdote appears more casual than it is, and his is more a writer's than a sportsman's notebook, although he describes walks in the Latin Quarter, the fishermen along the Seine, the horse races at Enghien, and skiing in the Vorarlberg. Chiefly it is composed of literary anecdote, a genre he ridiculed in *The Torrents of Spring* and *Green Hills of Africa*, but which he cultivates most effectively here. What he ridiculed in those earlier books was the pointless literary anecdote; in *A Moveable Feast* the individual sketches are quite pointed and cumulatively give the book its underlying purpose and sense of direction. They all form a part of the young writer's education, presenting a series of object lessons from which Hemingway learned the principles that he repeated all his life: the writer must work alone, should not talk about his work or—worse yet—read it aloud, should not accept praise, should not pay attention to the critics.

Paris was a city of writers, the ideal place for Hemingway's literary education. There he could meet his elders and measure himself against his contemporaries: Gertrude Stein, Pound, Eliot, Fitzgerald. There he could feel the presence of earlier writers: he rented a room to write in the hotel where Verlaine had died, his favorite café was the Closerie de Lilas where poets had met since the days of Baudelaire, he liked a restaurant down the

Seine that was like the setting of a Maupassant story. In Paris he did most of the serious reading that formed such an important part of his education. His library was Sylvia Beach's bookstore, Shakespeare and Company. "On a cold windswept street, this was a warm, cheerful place with a big stove in winter, tables and shelves of books, new books in the window, and photographs on the wall of famous writers both dead and living." Living or dead they were equally real to him. "The photographs all looked like snapshots and even the dead writers looked as though they had really been alive." He could talk about them with friends like Ezra Pound and Evan Shipman, as he does in one of his most charming anecdotes, "Evan Shipman at the Lilas." (Hemingway dedicated *Men Without Women* to Shipman, an improvident minor poet who, like his friend Harold Stearns, loved the horse races.)

A Moveable Feast tells nothing about the expatriates of Montparnasse. For one thing the subject was stale. For another Hemingway wanted to dissociate himself from the world with which he had been identified. And although he lived in Montparnasse for several years, he made it clear in *A Moveable Feast* that the only way he could work was to stay away from the American cafés. When he tells of writing "The Three-Day Blow" or "Big Two-Hearted River," he is in a quiet café in the company of Frenchmen who do not intrude. Once when he is interrupted in the Closerie des Lilas, he rudely tells his compatriot to clear out of his territory and return to the company of his kind. Writing was a solitary business, and it was impossible to be alone at the Dôme or the Rotonde. *The Sun Also Rises* shows how easy it was to dissipate one's time in Montparnasse and explains why staying away from cafés was part of Hemingway's discipline. Allen Tate, who knew him in the late twenties, remembered that "Ernest Hemingway in those days went to bed at nine o'clock and was up at six to work." Tate shows how well Hemingway had succeeded in educating himself when he describes him as "one of the most intelligent men I know and one of the best-read."

The story of Hemingway's literary apprenticeship gains poignancy from the emotions of his personal life at the time. By the same allusive, indirect method he conveys the story of his first marriage, beginning with innocent young love and ending sadly with its betrayal. Its setting is Bohemia without glamour, the scene of his early struggles amid primitive conditions at 74 rue du Cardinal Lemoine and the flat over the sawmill at 113 rue Notre-Dame-des-Champs. Perhaps he romanticizes when he speaks of going hungry, for he was not exactly a starving artist even after giving up journalism to become a writer. But the feeling is carefully played down, evoked by the physical sensations he renders so exactly, the weather and the time of year, the streets and the sights of Paris. It was his last book and he probably knew it. He wanted to make it as good as his early work and worthy of his best years.

10.

Little Magazines and Other Publishing Ventures

In his various reminiscences about the early twenties Hemingway recalls with grim satisfaction how difficult it was to get his stories accepted. One persistent memory was associated with the rue Notre-Dame-des-Champs, where he lived when he returned to Paris from Canada in 1924 after quitting his newspaper job. In *Green Hills of Africa*, he remembers "*all of the stories back in the mail that came in through a slit in the sawmill door, with notes of rejection that would never call them stories, but always anecdotes, sketches, contes, etc. They did not want them, and we lived on poireaux and drank cahors and water.*" After the success of *The Sun Also Rises* in 1926, his stories were suddenly in demand by *Scribner's*, the *Atlantic*, *New Republic*, and *La Nouvelle Revue Française*. But before that he had his fill of being ignored by commercial publishers and magazines that paid. Edward J. O'Brien had singled him out by dedicating *The Best Short Stories of 1923* to Ernest Hemenway, but he had misspelled his name and reprinted "My Old Man," a story that might have been written by Sherwood Anderson. Scott Fitzgerald had recognized Hemingway's worth and written to Maxwell Perkins at Scribner's, "This is to tell you about a young man named Ernest Hemingway, who lives in Paris (an American), writes for the *Transatlantic Review* and has a brilliant future." He urged Perkins to "look him up right away. He's the real thing." But Perkins was slow to move, and American publishers seemed dishearteningly unresponsive to a young man in a hurry to get his stories published.

Hemingway's experiences were typical. An unknown writer or one who was the slightest bit avant-garde had a hard time catching the eye of the popular magazines and established publishers. His only recourse was to write for literary magazines like those in which Hemingway's early stories first appeared. Hemingway was more fortunate than most. He had the backing of that great apostle of the little magazine, Ezra Pound, the foreign editor of *The Little Review*, a founder of the *Transatlantic Review*, the patron saint of *This Quarter*. When Hemingway returned to Paris, Pound introduced him to Ford Madox Ford, who put him to work as an assistant editor of *Transatlantic*. At that time Paris was the center of the nonprofit publishing industry. Besides the little magazines there was Robert McAlmon's Contact Publishing Company and William Bird's Three Mountains Press, both established in 1922. Between them they published Hemingway's first two books—pamphlets, really—which otherwise would not have appeared in print.

Hemingway had the example of Joyce to show him how fortunate he was and how easily he succeeded. Joyce, the greatest living writer to most Americans of Hemingway's generation, had to struggle all his life to get his works into print and had to be subsidized so that he could go on writing. His cause was taken up by a succession of dedicated women who were not only perceptive enough but determined that Joyce would get published regardless of obstacles. Two of them were Americans—Margaret Anderson who ran *Ulysses* serially in *The Little Review* and as a result had to fight the censors for three years, and Sylvia Beach who became a publisher with the sole purpose of bringing the book into the world. Thus *Ulysses* appeared in Paris under the imprint of Shakespeare and Company a dozen years before it could be published legally in any English-speaking country.

Publishers like Shakespeare and Company were rare, but little magazines were a common phenomenon. Most of them were ephemeral, appearing at irregular intervals for four or five issues until funds ran out. Chronically short of capital, they paid contributors little besides the satisfaction of being displayed before a small, intelligent audience. (*The Transatlantic Review*, *This Quarter*, and *Transition*, which had better financial backing than most, all paid thirty francs a page at a time when the franc was averaging twenty-five to the dollar; many little magazines paid nothing.) They usually published the same authors, and their editors often reappeared on one magazine after another, a circumstance which led William Carlos Williams to say that there was just one continuous little magazine under different names. *The Little Review* was an exception, lasting from 1914 to 1929, but its character changed several times during that period, depending on Margaret Anderson's changing interests as she moved from Chicago to New York to Paris.

In the twenties a number of little magazines were published in Europe, where printing was cheaper, and edited from Montparnasse, where the editors and writers were most likely to meet. Several like *Broom* and *Secession* self-consciously presented the "exile" point of view for a time, until their editors lost interest or quarreled or went home. These two, although published in Rome, Berlin, Vienna, New York—anywhere but Paris—were originally launched from Montparnasse, where their editors consorted during the early twenties: Harold Loeb, Alfred Kreymborg, Slater Brown, Gorham Munson, Matthew Josephson, and Malcolm Cowley.

During the twenties at least eight literary magazines were published by Americans in Paris. Four of them were very little indeed: *Gargoyle* (1921–22) and *The Boulevardier* (1927), both edited by Arthur Moss and Florence Gilliam; *Larus*, edited by Sherry Mangan in America with the collaboration of Virgil Thomson in Paris, 1927–28; and Harold Salemson's bilingual *Tambour*, 1929–30. Three were among the most influential: *The Little Review*, which appeared more and more erratically after 1923, when Margaret Anderson moved to Paris; the *Trans-*

atlantic Review, which lasted only one year, 1924; and *Transition*, which lasted longest in Paris, 1927–38. *This Quarter* (1925–32) was between the largest and the smallest in circulation and published some of the best writing.

The little magazines played an indispensable role in launching new writers and spreading movements like dada and surrealism. None of the editors were infallible, and in their desire to encourage all that was new and experimental they often published inferior work. But they were zealous in the cause of literature and fought the good fight in the avant-garde. Their great hope was always to discover a new genius like Joyce, and they were willing to take chances. On the whole they succeeded, for most important writers of this period first appeared in little magazines.

Hemingway is a good example. His first book published in America was *In Our Time*, a collection of stories set off by short transitional passages of factual reporting. Though it seems highly integrated, *In Our Time* was written and published piecemeal. In fact the book could be called Hemingway's collected works, 1921–25, for it contains nearly all the serious prose he completed during that period. All but four of the thirty-one individual pieces of *In Our Time* first appeared in little magazines or subsidized volumes. Six of the transitional paragraphs were published in the Exiles' Number of *The Little Review* in Spring 1923. Three stories appeared in the *Transatlantic Review* during 1924: "Indian Camp," "The Doctor and the Doctor's Wife," and "Cross Country Snow." "Mr. and Mrs. Elliot," a sarcastic story about an expatriate *ménage à trois*, was published in *The Little Review* for Autumn–Winter 1924–25. And both parts of "Big Two-Hearted River" appeared in the first issue of *This Quarter* in 1925. Five more stories (and a sixth excluded from *In Our Time*, probably because the publisher was afraid it might be considered obscene) were published in Paris by Robert McAlmon and William Bird in *Three Stories & Ten Poems* (1923), *in our time* (1924), and *Contact Collection of Contemporary Writers* (1925). That lower case *in our time* was quite a different book from the American *In Our Time* published the following year. In economy and impact *in our time* was far more effective, containing eighteen "chapters," of which only two were stories and those the shortest, the rest being factual vignettes. But obviously no commercial publisher would consider a book of thirty pages.

Through these early publications Hemingway came to the attention successively of writers, critics, and finally publishers. Influential critics sometimes read the little magazines. Burton Rascoe, literary editor of the *New York Tribune*, first mentioned Hemingway in his column in 1923 and met him when he visited Paris the following year. Edmund Wilson, who had read Hemingway's vignettes in *The Little Review* and brought them to Rascoe's attention, reviewed his first two books in *The Dial* in 1924. Wilson recognized Hemingway's talent from the start and particularly admired *in our time:* "I am inclined to think that his little book has more artistic dignity than anything else about the period of the war that has as yet been written by an American."

Hemingway's work on the *Transatlantic Review* also helped to make his name, for during its brief existence *Transatlantic* was one of the most important literary magazines. Its editor Ford Madox Ford was an old hand, having edited *The English Review* with remarkable success before the war. Well connected in British and French literary circles, he wanted to establish an international review that would represent the best work being produced by young Americans as well, and he chose Paris as the ideal location for such an enterprise. As it turned out, the American contributors outnumbered all the others, a fact which led Ford to ruminate about the great literary movement that was getting under way in the Middle West. To Ford, an amiable mythomaniac, geographical accuracy was less important than dramatic effect, and "Middle Westishness" was a quality that could be found in Parisians or Londoners.

The Paris Review, as *Transatlantic* was originally named, borrowed the city's seal and motto (*Fluctuat nec mergitur*–It bobs up and down but does not sink), prudently limiting itself to the first word of the motto until time should prove the rest. Fluctuate it did from the start, beset by vicissitudes even before the first number appeared in January 1924, and although it managed to keep afloat for twelve monthly issues, it was more than once in danger of going under. Ford, as he readily admitted, was not a businessman, and everything went wrong. His chief backer, John Quinn, the New York lawyer who had defended *The Little Review* against obscenity charges for publishing *Ulysses*, was ailing and died at the end of July. Hemingway, who was left in charge while Ford went to New York to see Quinn, saved the magazine by finding another patron, Krebs Friend, a shell-shocked war veteran who had married a rich woman forty years older than himself. Friend had no talent, but his wife had hopes that writing would rehabilitate him. The three ended up bickering with Ford, who had decided to let the magazine die anyhow at the end of the year.

Hemingway, who presents an uncomplimentary portrait of Ford in *A Moveable Feast*, found him a trying person to deal with; he complained bitterly in letters to Gertrude Stein, and sarcastically challenged the editor's literary tastes in the columns of *Transatlantic*. Hemingway had no patience with Ford's poses and knew he could run the magazine more efficiently himself. McAlmon confirmed this in his memoirs, saying that Ford left the editing to others. But what Hemingway regarded as megalomania was merely Ford's incurable habit of fictionalizing his own past, particularly his collaboration with Joseph Conrad and his war record; and while Ford's past was authentic enough, his embellishments and his personality irritated Hemingway. The difference between them was partly one of temperament, partly one of age, Ford being twice as old as Hemingway and an oversized walrus in appearance. But plenty of other Americans appreciated Ford: Dos Passos admired him greatly, Allen Tate respected him as "the last great European man of letters," and other poets enjoyed Ford's soirées, where they competed in writing limericks and sonnets.

For all his self-glorification, Ford was genuinely devoted to the cause of publishing new talent. Although a poor man, he put more money into *Transatlantic* than anyone else. He bore no grudges and was if anything too patient in the face of adversity. As he wrote to Gertrude Stein when Hemingway threatened to withdraw *The Making of Americans* from *Transatlantic*, claiming that she had been offered "real money" by Eliot's *Criterion*, ". . . I really exist as a sort of half-way house between non-publishable youth and real money—a sort of green baize swing door that everyone kicks both on entering and on leaving." Gertrude Stein, who was a shareholder as well as an author, replied that she was content: "I like the magazine and I like your editing. I am sincerely attached to both so suppose we go on as we are going."

Such squabbles were part of the history of every little magazine. Whatever their differences, Ford commended Hemingway's critical judgment when he entrusted him with the August number and only reproached him with the mildest editorial banter when Hemingway proceeded to eliminate English authors, including Ford, in favor of Americans, and later when Hemingway insulted Eliot gratuitously in the supplement published on the occasion of Conrad's death. (Hemingway wrote: "It is agreed by most of the people I know that Conrad is a bad writer, just as it is agreed that T. S. Eliot is a good writer. If I knew that by grinding Mr. Eliot into a fine dry powder and sprinkling that powder over Mr. Conrad's grave Mr. Conrad would shortly appear, looking very annoyed at the forced return and commence writing I would leave for London early tomorrow morning with a sausage grinder.") In later years Ford always regarded Hemingway with avuncular indulgence—in his introduction to the Modern Library edition of *A Farewell to Arms*, for instance, and in his fictionalized memoirs about the early twenties, *It Was the Nightingale*—and liked to think of Hemingway as one of the authors he had discovered.

Actually the *Transatlantic* could claim no major discoveries, but it did much to further the cause of American writing. The first number opened with four poems by E. E. Cummings and sustained the experimental note with two of Ezra Pound's cantos; later issues included poems by Hilda Doolittle, William Carlos Williams, Natalie Barney (a shareholder, like Gertrude Stein), and Hemingway's friend Evan Shipman. Besides Hemingway, the young fiction writers of the Middle West included Robert McAlmon, Djuna Barnes, John Dos Passos, and Hemingway's friend Donald Ogden Stewart. Most noteworthy was the April number, with the opening chapter of *The Making of Americans* and the first selection to appear in print of a new work by Joyce, christened "Work in Progress" by Ford and destined to bear that title for fifteen years until published as *Finnegans Wake.*

That number also made publishing history with the first story of the Hemingway canon to appear in any magazine and the first review of *in our time*—signed M. R. and presumably written by Marjorie Reid, the magazine's girl Friday. The story, which bore no title in *Transatlantic*, reappeared in *In Our Time* the following year as "Indian Camp." The review, for the most part a summary of the book's contents, made this comment on Hemingway's economy of phrase: "He projects the moments when life is condensed and clean-cut and significant, presenting them in minute narratives that eliminate every useless word. Each tale is much longer than the measure of its lines." Thereafter Hemingway contributed to almost every issue of *Transatlantic.* Apart from two more Nick Adams stories, his contributions were not meant to be taken seriously. He wrote a bantering letter from Paris with social notes on various Americans in Montparnasse and another from Pamplona expressing mainly resentment over the assignment. In addition to his article for the Conrad supplement, he wrote a brief anonymous introduction to a bit of nonsense by Ring Lardner, arguing that it was better dada than anything by Tzara.

Although Ford tried to maintain its international character, *Transatlantic* was dominated by American work, with distinctly less of British, French, and other nationalities. The magazine featured art and music as well as literature, with supplements devoted to Picasso drawings from the Gertrude Stein collection and Ezra Pound's vigorous promotion of George Antheil's musical career. The chief criticism of *Transatlantic* was that it was too heavily freighted with serials. Besides *The Making of Americans*, which ran from April through December, there were always three others running, except in the number edited by Hemingway. Ford used the magazine to serialize his own works in progress: literary criticism under the pseudonym Daniel Chaucer, part of the first volume of his great war novel, and in the later issues selections from his book about Conrad. He was an incredibly prolific writer who could have filled the entire review by himself.

Ford has described the quarters *Transatlantic* shared with the Three Mountains Press at 29 Quai d'Anjou. "We printed and published in a domed wine-vault, exceedingly old and cramped, on the Ile St. Louis with a grey view of the Seine below the Quais." Their host was William Bird, to whom Ford dedicated *No More Parades*, begun during that year. "Publisher Bird printed his books beautifully at a great old seventeenth-century press and we all took hands at pulling its immense levers about. I 'edited' in a gallery like a bird-cage at the top of the vault. It was so low that I could never stand up." Hemingway preferred to read manuscripts out on the quai. Conveniently nearby was Madame Leconte's Rendezvous des Mariniers discovered by Dos Passos during the war, when he rented a room upstairs.

When Ford decided to give Thursday teas for his contributors "after the time-honoured fashion of editors in Paris," the *Transatlantic Review* became a social as well as a literary enterprise. Ford liked parties and fancied himself in the role of host as well as editor encouraging the young. When the teas proved more social than literary and the Americans tended to stretch the French Thursday into an English weekend, Ford decided to change it to a Friday night dance at a *bal musette* in the rue Cardinal Lemoine, where Hemingway had lived when he first came to Paris. Both Madame Leconte's restaurant and the *bal musette* appear in *The Sun Also Rises,* as does the Nègre de Toulouse, the restaurant of Monsieur Lavigne on the Boulevard Montparnasse, where Ford and his friends had reserved tables in the back room. Burton Rascoe, who visited Paris in the latter days of the *Transatlantic*, had dinner with Ford and was taken to the *bal musette* afterward. "Hemingway was there, but he and Ford were not speaking," he reported. "After Ford had asked my wife and me and Mrs. Hemingway to sit at a table with him, Hemingway said to Mrs. Hemingway, 'Pay for your own drinks, do you hear! Don't let him [nodding toward Ford] buy you anything.'" According to Rascoe, Hemingway had angrily resigned from the *Transatlantic* and stopped speaking to Ford over his mild editorial about Hemingway's attack on Eliot.

William Bird's place on the Quai d'Anjou was, as Ford said, the center of the whole Middle Western literary movement. Not only the Three Mountains Press and the *Transatlantic Review* but the Contact Publishing Company used the obliging printer's premises. William Bird was a newspaperman who had come to Paris in 1920 as European manager of his own press service. He combined his two avocations, fine wines and fine printing, in publishing his own book, *A Practical Guide to French Wines.* He had already acquired his ancient hand press on the Ile Saint-Louis in the spring of 1922, when he met Hemingway as a fellow journalist. Bird was looking for books to print, so Hemingway introduced him to Pound, who undertook to commission and edit a series of six contemporary prose works, including Pound's *Indiscretions*, Ford's *Women and Men*, Williams' *The Great American Novel*, and Hemingway's *in our time.* These Bird printed slowly in limited editions—too slowly for Hemingway, who was impatient to appear in print and whose book was the last of the series, announced for 1923, but not published until March 1924. It was Bird's idea to print the title in lower case, Hemingway explained in a letter to Edmund Wilson, and since "that was all the fun he was getting out of it I thought he could go ahead and be a damn fool in his own way if it pleased him." Bird was also responsible for the lower case heading of the *transatlantic review,* but in that instance, Bird has explained, it was necessary to fit the long title on a single line. The practice was later imitated by other little magazines, notably *transition.*

Hemingway also introduced Robert McAlmon to Bird in 1922. McAlmon had married the daughter of one of England's wealthiest shipping magnates the previous year and encouraged his in-laws to distribute their patronage in Montparnasse. His mother-in-law Lady Ellerman presented a bust of Shakespeare to Sylvia Beach's bookshop and subsidized the American composer George Antheil for two years. McAlmon, who had started a little magazine called *Contact* with William Carlos Williams in Greenwich Village, now founded the Contact Publishing Company in Paris. He only published one book in 1922, his own collection of stories, *A Hasty Bunch,* the title suggested by Joyce, who was amused by McAlmon's American idiom. In 1923, when his father-in-law gave him £14,000, McAlmon became the publisher of Montparnasse; he joined forces with Bird, and engaged Darantière of Dijon, who had printed *Ulysses,* to do his Contact Editions.

During the next three years Three Mountains Press and the Contact Publishing Company brought out some thirty English and American books that would not readily have appeared in print. In 1923 McAlmon published Hemingway's first book, *Three Stories & Ten Poems,* and in 1925 "Soldier's Home" made its first appearance in the *Contact Collection of Contemporary Writers* in the company of the best "works in progress" of the time. In addition to works by himself and his wife Bryher, he published poems by Marsden Hartley, William Carlos Williams, and Hilda Doolittle, prose by Ezra Pound, Gertrude Stein, and Robert Coates, not to mention English writers.

Between them McAlmon and Bird published an impressive list, with *in our time, A Draft of XVI Cantos,* and *The Making of Americans* their most important books. Pound, who became very fond of Bird, praised his energy and generosity as well as his craftsmanship and entrusted him with the first book of his cantos, which Bird published "in a dee looks edtn," as Pound wrote in his characteristic orthography, "of UNRIVALLED magnificence." In another letter Pound commented, "My American publishers do not exist. It becomes more and more evident that the American publisher must be left out of one's calculations. Likewise English and henglish publishers. There may some day be a cheaper continental edition. One hopes that the Three Mts. and McAlmon's press in Paris will lead to some more general system of printing over here." What was needed even more was a better system of distribution and advertising in America. Pound, who took to cursing *usura* in his *Cantos*, was thoroughly justified in this instance, for the book business in America depended more on advertising than on literary worth, and booksellers were not overly scrupulous about paying small overseas publishers.

Three Mountains Press and Contact Publishing Company were both short-lived. Bird published his last book in 1926 and sold his press to Nancy Cunard, who then established the Hours Press, publishing among other works *A Draft of XXX Cantos* by Pound. McAlmon lost interest in publishing and was only partly responsible for the last few Contact books that appeared after 1926.

The only other important publisher to appear in Paris was Harry Crosby, who with his wife Caresse established the Black Sun Press in 1927. Crosby, who had been in the ambulance service and later in the French army as a *poilu*, returned to Paris in 1922, but lived in an altogether different world from Montparnasse. Connected through his uncle J. P. Morgan and his cousin Walter Berry with the Morgan Bank and the old Faubourg Saint-Germain of Henry James and Edith Wharton, he found both too confining, quit the bank, and started living the life of sensations celebrated by Huysmans. Crosby committed suicide in 1929, an act which impressed Malcolm Cowley as symbolic, providing a logical conclusion to *Exile's Return*, the story of the generation that was lost at Verdun. Harry and Caresse Crosby both wrote poetry, and in the process of having their books privately printed they developed an interest in fine editions, which led in turn to the publication of contemporary authors when they discovered that writers like Joyce and Lawrence were willing to provide manuscripts. They also published original works by Kay Boyle, Hart Crane, Eugene Jolas, Archibald MacLeish, and letters of James and Proust to Walter Berry. Caresse Crosby continued the Black Sun Press after her husband's death and in 1932 published Crosby Continental Editions, cheap paperback reprints and translations of modern works.

The *Transatlantic Review* had two worthy successors, *This Quarter* and *Transition. This Quarter* led a wandering career, its first three issues appearing in Paris, Milan, and Monte Carlo at the rate of one a year, 1925–27; then after a lapse of two years it returned to Montparnasse for its last three years, 1929–32. *This Quarter* was founded by Ernest Walsh, a consumptive poet who came to Paris to die amid writers he admired and managed to find a sympathetic patroness in Ethel Moorhead, a Scottish woman who had once studied painting with Whistler. The first number was dedicated to Ezra Pound "who by his creative work, his editorship of several magazines, his helpful friendship for young and unknown artists, his many and untiring efforts to win better appreciation of what is first-rate in art comes first to our mind as meriting the gratitude of this generation." Hemingway, who paints an unattractive portrait of Walsh in *A Moveable Feast*, contributed "Homage to Ezra," praising Pound as a major poet who devoted four-fifths of his energies to helping his friends. "And in the end a few of them refrain from knifing him at the first opportunity." Walsh's admiration for Pound was not reciprocated, and when Walsh died, Pound declined to write a tribute for the issue devoted to his memory. Whereupon Ethel Moorhead withdrew the original dedication and reviled Pound.

After commemorating Ernest Walsh she brought out no further issues; eventually *This Quarter* was taken over by Edward Titus, who kept a bookshop in Montparnasse and published books at his Black Manikin Press. Under his direction the magazine appeared regularly every quarter but except for the surrealist number edited by André Breton lacked the flair Walsh had shown in the early numbers. Titus published a story by Hemingway in December 1931, but by that date he probably had to pay a good price for the prestige of publishing Hemingway. The story, "A Sea Change," takes place in a Paris café with a barman called James. Those who knew Montparnasse would immediately think of Jimmie, who was often addressed thus with mock solemnity, and would be tempted to identify the principal characters as certain habitués of the Dingo—located, like *This Quarter*, in the rue Delambre.

Transition was the most ambitious as well as the most durable of the little magazines published abroad. Founded in 1927 by Eugene Jolas and Elliot Paul, it went through the usual metamorphoses, appearing monthly during its first year, quarterly until 1930, then more or less annually until 1938. Its editorial board changed frequently, with Robert Sage, Matthew Josephson, Harry Crosby, and James Johnson Sweeney serving at one time or another; but the driving spirit throughout was Eugene Jolas, and the magazine bore his stamp. Like Elliot Paul and Robert Sage, Jolas was a newspaperman with literary ambitions and a broad interest in the arts. He differed from them in being more European than American, having been born in New Jersey but raised in Lorraine while it was still in German hands. As a result *Transition* was the most international of the little magazines, claiming contributors from seventeen countries during the course of its first year. Some of these were painters; the rest were translated into English, usually by Jolas, who was at home in three languages. The largest number of contributors came from the United States, with France second.

Transition was also the most experimental of the little magazines. The first number opened with a selection from Joyce's "Work in Progress," which *Transition* undertook to serialize and which proved to be its proudest achievement. Eugene and Maria Jolas became loyal disciples of Joyce, and *Transition* assumed some aspects of a house organ, denouncing the piracy of *Ulysses*, celebrating Joyce's fiftieth birthday, publishing exegesis and critical theories inspired by "Work in Progress." The first number also included "An Elucidation" by Gertrude Stein, which had to be reprinted as a supplement when the printer garbled the text. Gertrude Stein contributed frequently to *Transition* until her *Autobiography* precipitated the magazine's only other supplement, *Testimony Against Gertrude Stein.* The foreign contributors were mostly surrealist painters and poets, who had already appeared as dadaists in *The Little Review* when Picabia had a hand in its editing. Surrealism occupied more and more space in *Transition,* finally swamping the magazine in the thirties, when it became "An International Workshop for Orphic Creation" publishing "Anamyths, Psychographs and Other Prose-Texts."

Transition demonstrated that Joyce, Gertrude Stein, and surrealism could have a pernicious effect on the young. "Too much money—and *transition surréalisme*" was the explanation D. H. Lawrence gave for Harry Crosby's suicide; as if to confirm this judgment several excerpts from Crosby's journals appeared in the number published at the time of his suicide, including dreams and reflections on madness. Another writer associated with *Transition,* Abraham Lincoln Gillespie Jr., claimed to be an authority on Joyce and Gertrude Stein and wrote in a style that parodied both and the magazine's jargon as well. Here is one of the more conventional passages from his article entitled "A PastDoggerel Growth of the Literary Vehicle: Language's Relapproach Music and Plastic."

> Indubitably the work of such as Stein, Joyce and Breton show-proves that the Novel (as Literature) is *thru* with feed-my-lambs! concernments. Breton counsels what may be styled the Movie-ThrowBack-Inverse in his recommend-Heroes'-doubleNoseThumbing-Reader-&-Author Suggest. . . . TO WORK THEN, Gang, Miss Stein's & Mr. Joyce's peal clearly that the Vehicle is now The exrudimentablising CreateConcern, a now-yawning DisHibernial plasticklable at

> least. To furth-pursue ThoughtContext at neglexpense of VehiFormConcomitent will be ludisastrous. Already two FormWrights of Skill-freed-to-breathe-Higher-ConschPretense calibre, they, lone Entitles to directly race-pursue BigFishCatchings. Will there be more?

Jolas himself was interested in finding a language to express dreams, feeling that none of his three languages would do, even when used simultaneously. He was also fond of manifestoes proclaiming such apocalyptic events as "The Revolution of the Word" and the "Metanthropological Crisis," and had no trouble finding contributors for long-winded symposia on psychic, mantic, vertigral, and paramythic phenomena. *Transition,* which had never been thin, became thicker and heavier in the thirties, while the proportion of good writing diminished.

Hemingway had left Paris about the time *Transition* came into existence and had little to do with the magazine but was willing to lend his name and growing reputation. He signed the protest against the piracy of *Ulysses* and contributed a story, "Hills Like White Elephants," to one of the early numbers. He appeared in 1928 in a photograph loaned by Sylvia Beach that showed him hunting in Florida—clear evidence that he was already becoming a legendary figure. He did not contribute again until the final number when he responded to Jolas' final questionnaire, which asked, among other questions: "Have you ever felt the need for a new language to express the experiences of your night mind?" Hemingway surely had little interest in Jolas' "Inquiry into the Spirit and Language of Night," but he tried to answer with a straight face. To the question he replied: "I haven't ever felt this as would like to be able to handle day and night with same tools and believe can be done but respect anyone approaching any problem of writing with sincerity and wish them luck." Like his contribution to the obituary number of *The Little Review* nine years before, this was a gesture of fellowship, showing sympathy to little magazines for all the good work they had done.

The most persistent enterprise for the encouragement of writers in Paris was Sylvia Beach's bookshop, Shakespeare and Company. Between 1919 and 1941 it was the American writers' club, where they met fellow writers, received their mail, and cashed their checks, and Sylvia Beach was their best friend, listening sympathetically to their troubles, unfailingly good-tempered and helpful. The writers in turn helped her, particularly during the depression years when there were few Americans to buy books. Then André Gide saved the shop by organizing a series of readings, mostly by French authors, but Eliot also came over from London to read his poetry in 1936, and Hemingway, who shied away from public appearances, read his story "Fathers and Sons" to the Friends of Shakespeare and Company in 1937.

Sylvia Beach remained in Paris through the German occupation and lived there until her death in 1962. She kept the bookstore open until one day in 1941, when a German officer wanted to buy the copy of *Finnegans Wake* on display in the window and, when she refused to sell it, threatened to confiscate all her possessions. In a matter of hours Sylvia Beach and her friends removed the entire contents of the shop and had its name painted over; Shakespeare and Company no longer existed. In 1944 the rue de l'Odéon was liberated by her "best customer," as he regarded himself, Ernest Hemingway. During the liberation of Paris he drove up with his band of irregulars and stopped in front of her house calling "Sylvia!" She tells the story in *Shakespeare and Company:* "I flew downstairs; we met with a crash; he picked me up and swung me around and kissed me while people on the street and in the windows cheered." When Hemingway asked what he could do for her and Adrienne Monnier, they asked him to do something about the German snipers on the rooftops, so Hemingway led his troops up to the roof, and there was no more sniping after that. Sylvia Beach ends her book: "Hemingway and his men came down again and rode off in their jeeps—'to liberate,' according to Hemingway, 'the cellar at the Ritz.'"

MUSICAL SAINTS

CHRONOLOGY V

1913	Stravinsky's *Sacre du Printemps* a riot
1916	Varèse leaves Paris for New York
1917	Satie, *Parade.* Cubist ballet with pop themes, mechanical music, and ragtime
1920	Stravinsky turns neoclassical in *Pulcinella*
1921	Cocteau's ballet *Les Mariés de la Tour Eiffel.* Music by *les Six:* Milhaud, Poulenc, Honegger, Durey, Auric, and Germaine Tailleferre American Conservatory of Music opens its doors at Fontainebleau with Harvard Glee Club on hand Copland and Thomson begin studying with Nadia Boulanger
1924	Antheil, *Ballet Mécanique* Satie's music for *Entr'acte*—"the finest film score ever composed"
1925	La Revue Nègre, starring Josephine Baker
1926	All-American Concert of Chamber Music by students of Nadia Boulanger. "For all of us the concert constituted something of a debut, since all our works were sizeable and I think none of us had ever had works of that seriousness and length performed before"
1926–29	Roy Harris studies with Nadia Boulanger
1927	Isadora Duncan's final appearance on the Paris stage. Buried at Père Lachaise, her funeral attended by 5000 people of all nationalities
1927–28	Gertrude Stein writes libretto of *Four Saints in Three Acts,* Virgil Thomson the music
1928	Gershwin, *An American in Paris,* with genuine klaxons
1934	*Four Saints* sponsored by Friends and Enemies of Modern Music, a hit in Hartford, New York, and Chicago

11.

The Musical Setting

Modern French music developed under the influence of three dominant musical personalities. Claude Debussy set a whole generation experimenting with harmony and form. A foreign composer, Igor Stravinsky, had an influence analogous to that of Picasso in painting; a great revolutionary, forever evolving, he more than anyone else established Paris as a musical capital for the thirty years that his compositions were premiered there. Erik Satie's influence was elusive but ubiquitous. After spending most of his life in obscurity, he emerged as the leader of the avant-garde around whom the young composers rallied to form the group known as *les Six.*

Even more decisive than the composers as a shaping force in French musical life was the great impresario of the Ballet Russe, Sergei Diaghilev. From 1909, when he brought his first troupe of Russian dancers to Paris, until his death in 1929, his ballets were the most exciting events of the Paris theater. Combining the arts of music, painting, and dancing with a perfection that had never been known before, Diaghilev created a new theatrical art. His ballets before the war had a wild Russian brilliance, with spectacular costumes setting off the choreography of Fokine and the incredible dancing of Nijinsky. He discovered Stravinsky, commissioned him to write his first ballet, and brought him to Paris, where he became the principal composer of the Ballet Russe. Stravinsky's first three ballets startled Paris and revolutionized modern music—*L'Oiseau de Feu* in 1910, *Petrouchka* in 1911, and especially, *Le Sacre du Printemps* in 1913. Before the war Diaghilev also presented ballets set to music by Ravel (*Daphnis et Chloé*) and Debussy (*L'Après-Midi d'un Faune* and *Jeux*).

With Diaghilev always in search of new talents the Ballet Russe rapidly became more cosmopolitan and more French. Already before the war Diaghilev had established his headquarters in Monte Carlo. When cut off from Russia by the revolution, he turned to the artists of the School of Paris for his décors. *Parade* in 1917 marked a revolution in the theater, when Cocteau collaborated with Satie and Picasso, both new to the ballet. Picasso produced cubist constructions as costumes, and Satie wrote music to match, using the sounds of modern life, typewriters, airplane propellers, and sirens. It was on this occasion that Apollinaire, writing the program notes, coined the word "sur-realism." In subsequent years Braque, Derain, Dufy, Marie Laurencin, Matisse, and other French artists contributed to the spectacle, while Milhaud, Poulenc, Honegger, and Auric wrote music for the ballet.

Composers, like painters, cast about for fresh sources of inspiration in this most eclectic of centuries. In *Le Sacre du Printemps* Stravinsky had shocked Paris with his primitive rhythms, but all sorts of strange sounds were to follow. Jazz made its appearance in serious music and fascinated composers with its contrapuntal rhythms and the new sonority of the stringless ensemble. Satie, whom Debussy called "a fine medieval musician who has wandered into this century," made a study of Gregorian music, and others, even Debussy and Ravel, wrote in archaic modes. A most important source was eighteenth-century music, and here again Diaghilev played a part, commissioning ballets based on the music of old Italian composers. He presented Stravinsky with some unfinished works of Pergolesi, which Stravinsky proceeded to make his own in

Pulcinella. The result was neoclassicism, the preponderant trend in postwar music.

Apart from jazz America had nothing to contribute to French music and much to learn. But in the dance three American women became celebrities in Paris, each in her own unconventional way. At the International Exposition of 1900 Loie Fuller embodied the perfect expression of *art nouveau* with her long filmy veils rising in the air like butterfly wings under the play of colored lights. Isadora Duncan, who arrived in Paris the following year, was one of the most original figures of her time. A great romantic, she rejected the disciplined movements of the classical ballet in favor of spontaneous self-expression. Her brother Raymond had preceded her in Paris, where he first studied the Greek vases in the Louvre, finding inspiration for costumes and dances. Together the Duncans founded an academy in Paris and a cult that has largely shaped interpretive dancing. For a quarter of a century Isadora was the most famous American in Europe, notorious for her melodramatic life as well as her dancing. After her death the most famous American in Paris was unquestionably Josephine Baker, who had arrived at the age of eighteen, created a sensation in the Revue Nègre in 1925, and stayed on to become an institution. For over twenty years she sang and danced, not only in such spectacles as the Folies Bergère but in operettas and films as well.

In the twenties America produced its first generation of composers, born at the turn of the century or a few years before. Almost all of them felt they had to go to Europe to complete their musical education, and in the postwar decade most of them chose to go to Paris. In America musical training was predominantly Germanic and old-fashioned. As Virgil Thomson remarked, "We all had music teachers who had been formed in Germany or by Germans, and it was time we got out of that." Thomson himself, growing up in Kansas City, had not been able to find a competent teacher until he went to Harvard.

George Antheil, a pupil of Ernest Bloch, wrote of the situation in America the year he went abroad: "In 1922 America did not even yet know whether it could accept as music 'Le Sacre du Printemps.' In 1922 America the prevailing fashion in composition was Debussy-Ravel, plus some Ernest Bloch. . . . Finally, in this 1922–23 America to which I could not return, there was not enough musical activity to satisfy the voracious appetite of the young."

In Europe the new age of Stravinsky and Schoenberg had begun about 1910, but their music was seldom heard in America until the 1920s. It was largely on the initiative of a French composer that modern music got a hearing–Edgard Varèse, who had come to New York in 1916 and organized an orchestra to play new music. In 1921 the International Composers' Guild was founded, with Varèse as its director and the playing of contemporary music as its purpose. This organization led to others which gradually formed a taste for modern music, among them the Copland-Sessions Concerts, organized by two young American composers.

Aaron Copland, in an autobiographical sketch, tells the story of his musical upbringing against all odds. Even in metropolitan New York his conservative teacher was opposed to the "moderns" Scriabin, Debussy, and Ravel, their music was hard to come by, music itself was not taken seriously in school, and there were no music students to consort with. "It was a foregone conclusion," Copland wrote, "that anyone who had serious pretensions as a composer would have to go abroad to finish his studies. Before the war it was taken for granted that 'abroad' for composers meant Germany. But I belonged to the postwar generation, and so for me 'abroad' inevitably meant Paris."

As a direct result of the war the American Conservatory of Music was founded at Fontainebleau, a summer school with French teachers for American students. Walter Damrosch, who had gone over to France in 1918 to train bandmasters for the American army, had proposed such a school, and in 1921 it opened its doors in a wing of the royal palace. Copland was the first to enroll. He went over that summer with the object of acclimating himself to French life while looking for a teacher with whom he could study during the following year. He met that teacher at Fontainebleau. In the fall he, Virgil Thomson, and Melville Smith became the first of a long line of American composers to study under Nadia Boulanger. The list of her pupils between the wars reads like *Who's Who in American Music*.

In a tribute to this great teacher Aaron Copland wrote of her influence on him: "I arrived, fresh out of Brooklyn, aged twenty, and all agog at the prospect of studying composition in the country that had produced Debussy and Ravel." During the three years that he studied with Nadia Boulanger, he acquired not only a thorough training in his craft but a liberal education besides.

> In my own mind she was a continuing link in that long tradition of the French intellectual woman in whose salon philosophy was expounded and political history made. In similar fashion Nadia Boulanger had her own salon where musical aesthetics was argued and the musical future engendered. It was there that I saw, and sometimes even met, the musical great of Paris: Maurice Ravel, Igor Stravinsky, Albert Roussel, Darius Milhaud, Arthur Honegger, Francis Poulenc, Georges Auric. She was the friend of Paul Valéry and Paul Claudel, and liked to discuss the latest works of Thomas Mann, of Proust, and André Gide. Her intellectual interests and wide acquaintanceship among artists in all fields were an important stimulus to her American students: through these interests she whetted and broadened their cultural appetites.

When Copland returned to America Nadia Boulanger helped him to get started in his career. She asked him to write his *Symphony for Organ and Orchestra* for a concert she gave in New York and Boston six months after his return. Virgil Thomson wept when he heard it, overcome with regret that he had not written it himself; in his autobiography he describes it as "exactly the Boulanger piece and exactly the American piece that several of us would have given anything to write." This work brought Copland to the attention of the new conductor of the Boston Symphony, Serge Koussevitzky, who commissioned him to write another work for performance in New York the following season.

In similar fashion Nadia Boulanger helped launch other promising students. Often they were first performed under her aegis. On May 5, 1926, for instance, a concert of chamber music by American composers was given in Paris, with works by Copland, Thomson, Antheil, Herbert Elwell, Theodore Chanler, and Walter Piston. All but Antheil had studied two or three years with Nadia Boulanger. The following spring Roy Harris' *Concerto for Piano, Clarinet, and String Quartet* had its first performance in Paris. This work, written during his first year of study with Nadia Boulanger, won him the Guggenheim fellowship that permitted him to stay on for two more years and, when played in Carnegie Hall the following year, did much to establish his reputation in America.

Harris was older than most students when he began to study with Nadia Boulanger and made of more intransigent stuff. Born on the frontier in Oklahoma and raised in a small California town, he was reluctant about going to France, afraid of becoming alienated from America. Aaron Copland prevailed upon him to go. Now as he reminisces about how it happened, Harris says, "Going to Paris was the best thing I ever did. I was just a truck driver then and had written my first works out of the fullness of my ignorance." In 1926 he left California on his first trip east to hear his work performed by Howard Hanson in Rochester. In the East he was given much encouragement, particularly by Aaron Copland, who talked to him at length about Paris and how necessary it was for any American in the creative arts to go there. Copland suggested that he look up Nadia Boulanger. A patroness who liked Harris' music gave him enough money to get to Europe, and he found a place to live in the village of Juziers outside of Paris for sixty francs a week, *tout compris.*

What he appreciated most about his *pension* was being able to study music full-time. He would go into Paris for a weekly lesson, but he spent the rest of his time in his room studying. He was so single-minded in his determination to become a composer that during his first year he resisted Mademoiselle Boulanger's invitations to meet other musicians at her Friday afternoons. He also resisted her pedagogy. She called him her autodidact and tried to make him submit to her formal discipline. But the frontiersman was not to be tamed. "She wanted me to do what I call Académie Française exercises," Harris explains, "but I wanted something more fluid. What she had in mind was the clipped gardens of Versailles, but I wanted to write big trees. We had an awful row. She was half Russian, you know, and when she saw that her Gallic reasoning didn't work, she used Russian tears. But I couldn't see the point of learning something that wouldn't help me, so I said I was going home. Then she asked me what I wanted to do, and I said, 'You have the most remarkable sense of form of any person I have ever met. You can put your finger on the weak spot of any composition. I want you to go through all the great composers and point out their weaknesses. Not their strengths. I can see those myself.' And that's what we did for three years. And it was wonderful."

Harris also recalls Mlle. Boulanger's energy, her generosity and devotion to her students. "When I started studying with Nadia, she was in the full vigor of her womanhood. Boy, what a powerhouse!" She spent her whole time giving lessons, often to students who could not afford to pay. "She said there were three kinds of music students, the kind who had money and no talent, and those she took; the kind who had talent and no money, and those she took; and the third kind had money and talent, and those she never got." Mlle. Boulanger used to begin her week with her worst students and go on to better and better students as the week advanced; Harris had his lessons on Saturday night. He was invited for dinner before the lesson, and they talked music the whole evening.

Apart from his clash with Mlle. Boulanger, the most nerve-racking experience of his three years in Paris came with the first performance of his *Concerto for Piano, Clarinet, and String Quartet.* Mlle. Boulanger engaged the Roth Quartet and the leading clarinetist in Paris. "She said he was the best clarinet player in the world," and Harris had no doubts about that, "but he couldn't get my rhythms." The clarinetist kept trying, but he intellectualized the music too much and got so upset that he failed to appear at the dress rehearsal. Whereupon Virgil Thomson remarked to Harris, "Well, Roy, if you *will* write masterpieces, you must take the consequences." Harris wanted to take his *Concerto* off the program, but it was the major and concluding work. Mlle. Boulanger decided to play the clarinet part on the piano and did so for the rehearsal. When on the day of the concert the clarinetist turned up, somewhat tipsy, Mlle. Boulanger did not know what to do. She was afraid to let him play and afraid not to let him play because he might make a scene during the performance. Finally he played it—to perfection—and with the other performers on the *qui vive,* the *Concerto,* Harris says, sounded better than it actually was.

After three years Harris experienced the disillusionment of returning to a country that did not care about modern music. "No words can express the nostalgia which oppressed me during my first year of return to America," he wrote a few years later. He was shocked by the noise, the newness, the pragmatic outlook. Europeans understood how artists lived and worked among them, at a different intensity and rhythm; America could not understand the composer. "This society believed and acted on the assumption that all great music had been written; that new mechanical devices for the reproduction of music were really of more significance than new music; that the performances were more important than the music performed; that only *poseurs* and maladjusted eccentrics really stood for the new music, which was a sort of fad; that a musician's business is to teach and perform music, not to create it; that any financial support which might be granted a composer was really in the nature of charity, much like the support given orphan asylums." Ten years later he was still reliving the emotions he felt when he first returned to New York: "I felt a heartache for the sanity and quiet peace of a small French village where respect was shown for the composer who had money to spend."

The American composer whose name is most commonly associated with Paris is of course George Gershwin. He belonged to the same generation as Thomson, Harris, Antheil, and Copland, but he had come to music via Tin Pan Alley. While serious composers were taking up jazz, he was going from jazz to serious composition. He once asked Ravel to teach him composition, but Ravel replied that Gershwin had no need for lessons.

An American in Paris was written in 1928. In the spring of that year Gershwin visited Europe as a tourist and heard his music played wherever he went. He arrived in Paris in time to hear his *Rhapsody in Blue* enthusiastically applauded, and two months later his *Concerto in F* had its European premiere at the Paris Opéra. He had little time to work on the new composition which he had already sketched before leaving New York and which he completed after his return. He did, however, search out the French taxi horns which add an essential note. Although Gershwin never spent any length of time in Paris, the work is clearly inspired by the city and its musical associations, as his program notes indicate: "This new piece, really a rhapsodic ballet, is written very freely and is the most modern music I've yet attempted. The opening part will be developed in typical French style, in the manner of Debussy and the Six, though the themes are all original. My purpose here is to portray the impression of an American visitor in Paris, as he strolls about the city, and listens to various street noises and absorbs the French atmosphere." Gershwin captures the American tourist's Paris with great vivacity, and he catches it at a high moment

–in the springtime, in youth, in high spirits, at the height of success and prosperity. For many who knew it superficially before the crash, Paris is the city of Gershwin's nostalgic impressionism.

12.

Enfant Terrible

One of the most arresting photographs in Man Ray's rogues' gallery is that of a pretty boy with blond bangs named George Antheil. A pianist and composer, Antheil was only twenty-two when he arrived in Paris, but already well established as a prodigy. Short and slight, he tried to make up for his size and youth by his brashness. He carried a revolver in a shoulder holster he had sewn into his evening clothes; when his music created riots, he calmly placed the pistol on the piano before him. Of his genius there could be no doubt.

Antheil had spent the previous year on concert tour in Germany, where he had attracted considerable attention. His success as a pianist had come almost too easily, and he had decided to quit the concert stage in order to make his name as a composer. His own works had been performed in London, Dresden, and Budapest, and his *First Symphony* had been premiered by the Berlin Philharmonic. Apart from the elation of that experience, postwar Berlin had depressed him with its cynicism and misery. In such an atmosphere he could no longer swallow the sentimentality of Richard Strauss or the pretty decadence of Debussy and Ravel. Stravinsky's cold hard brilliance replaced them, an idiom that made more sense to a boy who had grown up in the industrial landscape of Trenton, New Jersey. As luck would have it, Stravinsky spent two months in Berlin just then, befriended Antheil, and arranged a concert for him in Paris. But at the last moment a dark Hungarian girl proved more important to him than any concert, and even worth the risk of losing the great Stravinsky's friendship. Because she was unable to get a French visa, Antheil put off going to Paris for six months.

In his autobiography, *Bad Boy of Music*, he tells of his arrival in Paris with his Hungarian girl Böske on June 13, 1923, a date which they long celebrated as "epochal." After the depressing gray of Berlin, Paris seemed full of brightness and color. More important still, he adds in italics, "*This was the city of Stravinsky's music!*" In response to the composer's invitation, he had timed his arrival for the premiere of Stravinsky's *Les Noces* at the Ballet Russe. He found it resembled the percussive music he had written in Berlin, compositions he called *Death of the Machines*, *Mechanisms*, and *Sonata Sauvage*, inspired by wars, factories, and his girl Böske respectively. Antheil was more affected by Stravinsky's music for *Pulcinella* performed on the same program. This was his introduction to neoclassicism, which was to have a pernicious effect on his own composition.

In Paris he and Böske found a tiny one-room apartment in the *entresol* above Sylvia Beach's bookshop. Eventually the apartment expanded into an adjoining room and then another. At first it was too small to accommodate a piano, so Adrienne Monnier invited him to use the one in her apartment. In *Shakespeare and Company* Sylvia Beach proudly claims, "Adrienne and I were in on the *Ballet Mécanique* from the beginning," and remembers how it sounded. "The piano is a percussion instrument, and that was the impression you got when George played it, or, rather, punched it. A woman who swept Adrienne's rooms used to listen, leaning on her broom, to what she called 'The Fireman.' She found it curious but stirring."

The *Ballet Mécanique*, which is what everyone remembers about Antheil, was mostly written during his first winter in Paris and completed by the end of 1924. Before this Antheil produced several other, less notorious works. First he wrote a little quintet celebrating his joy at having found a home in Paris with Böske. "It is full of little themes heard on our own street corner, the cry of our old-clothes man; it is Paris in our summer of 1923." Then at the urging of Ezra Pound he composed two violin sonatas for a protégée of Pound's, the violinist Olga Rudge. Pound proceeded to take Antheil's career in hand, promoting him as America's most promising composer. Pound was then going through a period of musical enthusiasm, but his faith in Antheil appeared quite reasonable at the time. In the mid-twenties Virgil Thomson and Aaron Copland both regarded Antheil as the leading American composer of their generation.

Pound, who played the bassoon, fancied himself a composer and music critic. He had long been interested in the troubadours and in early music generally; he believed as a matter of principle that poets should cultivate music and was himself composing an opera on a libretto drawn from François Villon. He was above all fond of expounding his musical theories, such as the notion he shared with Antheil that rhythm was the all-important element in music. William Carlos Williams, who came to Paris at this time, listened with a certain measure of skepticism; he had known Pound and his enthusiasms in college. And while he admired his remarkable sense of time, he considered it Nature's compensation for the regrettable fact that Ezra was tone-deaf. Even the tenor who sang one of the two voices in *Villon* said that Pound had no ear, though the opera showed a certain flair. Virgil Thomson remembers it favorably on the whole: "The music was not quite a musician's music, though it may well be the finest poet's music since Thomas Campion." Williams surmised that Antheil had helped with the notation. Antheil also played the clavichord accompaniment; during rehearsals he used to play jazz "heavily" on this delicate instrument.

Pound was primarily an impresario. He took up Antheil much as he had taken up the French sculptor Gaudier-Brzeska before the war—took him up as a cause, publicized him in the *Transatlantic Review*, borrowed his writings on music, incorporated them into his own, and presented their dialogue in *Antheil and the Treatise on Harmony*, published by the Three Mountains Press in 1924. In his autobiography Antheil professes to be embarrassed by the book and dismisses Pound as "a ridiculous Don Quixote" fighting the cubist-vorticist-abstractionist campaign ten years after it had been won. But Antheil was never known to shun publicity, and Pound was an extremely useful friend, with all sorts of connections. He introduced him to Jean Cocteau, "the most powerful Parisian talent scout," as Antheil describes him in his autobiography. Cocteau had the power to launch a composer, for he ruled over the fashionable musical salons where new works were often tried out. Among the wealthy and noble patrons of music was a remarkable American woman, Natalie Barney, the friend of French writers, to whom Remy de Gourmont had addressed his *Lettres à l'Amazone*, and a writer herself, chiefly in French. Antheil's *First String Quartet* was premiered in her salon.

Others took an interest in Antheil, mostly members of the English-speaking literary colony like Joyce, McAlmon, and Margaret Anderson, but also the French composer Jacques Benoist-Mechin, who performed Antheil's music and wrote a book about him. Antheil's most fervent admirer was his pupil Bravig Imbs, who arrived in Paris at the age of nineteen with two ambitions, "one to become a great composer and the other to write the great American novel." Although he achieved neither ambition, he produced one of the earliest and most readable books about Paris in the twenties, *Confessions of Another Young Man.* Its first half was devoted to "The Sweet and Violent George Antheil." Only Hemingway seems to have expressed doubts about Antheil's genius, defiantly publishing his dissenting opinion in the *Transatlantic Review:* ". . . I preferred my Stravinsky straight."

Antheil was well known to readers of the little magazines through his own contributions as well as Pound's. *Transatlantic* published the score of his *Sonata 3* and two of his critical articles as well as his marginalia to Pound's music criticism.

This Quarter published an "Antheil Musical Supplement" entirely devoted to his work, with the score of his *Airplane Sonata* and extracts from six other works, including "Mr. Bloom and the Cyclops" from an opera he was writing based on a libretto from Joyce's *Ulysses*. Antheil never finished this opera or his "Anna Livia" Symphony, though some years later he was one of the thirteen composers who set Joyce's *Pomes Penyeach* to music. He also wrote music for a play by Yeats, *Fighting the Waves*.

Antheil created his first sensation in Paris in October 1923, when he played three short piano sonatas at the Théâtre des Champs-Elysées. His performance was meant to be the curtain raiser for the opening night of the Ballets Suédois. Since this was the most important musical event of the season after the Ballet Russe, the audience was distinguished and expectant. "They had not come to hear me," Antheil explains, "but to see the opening of the ballets." He later learned that he had been chosen to start the program because of his reputation for creating riots; the Ballets Suédois wanted publicity. By his own amusing account Antheil succeeded admirably, giving Paris such entertainment as it had not had since the premiere of Stravinsky's *Sacre du Printemps* in the same theater ten years before. "My piano was wheeled out on the front of the stage, before the huge Léger cubist curtain, and I commenced playing. Rioting broke out almost immediately. I remember Man Ray punching somebody in the nose in the front row. Marcel Duchamp was arguing loudly with somebody else in the second row. In a box nearby Erik Satie was shouting, 'What precision! What precision!' and applauding. The spotlight was turned on the audience by some wag upstairs. It struck James Joyce full in the face, hurting his sensitive eyes. A big burly poet got up in one of the boxes and yelled, 'You are all pigs!' In the gallery the police came in and arrested the surrealists who, liking the music, were punching everybody who objected." The riot was premeditated, not only as a publicity stunt but as a film sequence. Antheil, who played his role without ever suspecting it, wondered why the stage was floodlit but never realized there were cameras in the audience until the following year when he saw the riot he had created in a film starring Margaret Anderson's friend Georgette Leblanc. It was Margaret Anderson who had asked Antheil to play his most radical compositions to produce the desired effect.

This debut had many repercussions. Antheil became a celebrity overnight, with a reputation that was to stamp him for life. "The French called him *sauvage*," Bravig Imbs remarked, "for that was the side of his character he showed at the piano." Antheil was all that Paris loved, the last word in fashion, a brilliant, iconoclastic youth who seemed destined to revolutionize music. Nor was this mere notoriety, for Satie and Milhaud had applauded his *Airplane Sonata* and *Mechanisms;* and according to Antheil, Satie, Honegger, and Prokofiev followed his lead in composing mechanical ballets. When interviewed by the press Antheil announced that he was composing a *Ballet Mécanique*. The title immediately caught on. In French it is particularly apt, a clever bit of dada combining the fantastic with the banal, suggesting not only the dance of the machines but a common housekeeping appliance, the lowly carpet sweeper or *balai mécanique*.

In 1924 *Ballet Mécanique* was made into a film by an American cameraman and a French artist, Dudley Murphy and Fernand Léger. With Antheil's music they combined abstract designs, mass-produced objects, and human beings moving mechanically, to create one of the important experimental films of the time. Neither the artist nor the composer had ever worked in the cinema before, but their talents complemented each other in this modernistic ballet of pots and pans, abstractions and washerwomen.

In 1925 the *Ballet Mécanique* was performed privately at the old Pleyel studios, where Chopin had once played. This was merely a trial run of the pianola part without the drums and other sound effects. Since the music had been registered on mechanical piano rolls, the composer-virtuoso was not required, so he chose this moment to go off on vacation in Tunis. He left Bravig Imbs in charge, instructing him to send out invitations to a dozen or so friends and members of the press. *Confessions of Another Young Man* gives an account of that first performance:

> The terrific thumping—it was a new idea then to employ the piano as a percussive instrument—and wild chords which seemed to be torn alive and bleeding from the maws of machines, electrified the audience. Joyce seemed gripped in spite of himself, Fraser was suffering from unpleasant shock, Elliot Paul was deeply absorbed, Sylvia enthralled. The relentless outpouring of the composer's tumultuous emotion, accompanied by a fundamental rhythm which had the harrowing persistence of a tom-tom, was overwhelming. I had heard snatches of the *Ballet* before, but now that coherence was established its force was centupled. Time and again the music would surge to an impossible peak, and then break with a despairing cry, falling to a turgid swirl of muttering bass notes. The *Ballet* was so intense and concentrated, so strange and even irritating to the ear, that there was a gasp of audible relief when the first roll abruptly finished.

When the three rolls had been played, Joyce asked to hear part of the second roll again and commented, "That's like Mozart."

Antheil's absence at such a time seems strange, for he never missed an opportunity to demonstrate or discuss his accomplishments. Actually his departure for Tunis was part of a campaign to stir up greater publicity. Before leaving he had explained his scheme to Imbs, who worked on the Paris edition of the *Chicago Tribune*, and who was to release the story that Antheil had gone to Africa "in the search of new rhythms" and disappeared. From Tunis Antheil wrote letters which Imbs showed to reporters, indicating that Antheil had been deserted by his guides but was pushing on into the interior, where the music was "just sticks." Thus a few days after the press notices of the *Ballet Mécanique*, the Paris papers carried a sensational story that the young composer had been lost in the desert. The story was cabled to Chicago, widely circulated, and progressively exaggerated. In *Bad Boy of Music* Antheil quotes the headline: "Composer Eaten Alive by Lions in the Sahara!" He also reflects ruefully that his publicity-seeking antagonized the press.

Ezra Pound probably did as much damage to Antheil's reputation when he continued to champion his music in extravagant articles: "Three years ago Antheil was talking vaguely of 'tuning up' whole cities, of 'silences twenty minutes long *in the form*,' etc. . . . Now, after the three years, I do not in the least regret any then seeming hyperbole, or any comparison of Antheil and Stravinsky that I then made in the former's favour." Such grandiose and invidious claims were bound to arouse more hostility than admiration.

Pound's statement was published in 1926, the year in which Antheil reached his zenith. The year began well with a performance of his *First String Quartet* at Natalie Barney's salon on New Year's Day. This performance resulted in a commission to write his *Second Symphony*, which received its premiere at the Théâtre des Champs-Elysées on June 19 under the direction of Vladimir Golschmann. At the same time the *Ballet Mécanique* was finally given its first public performance. Everyone who was there remembers this concert as a historic occasion. Accounts vary, but all agree that the hall was crowded and the concert a riotous success. Bravig Imbs provides the liveliest report, describing the Montparnasse characters in the audience and their reactions. The *Second Symphony* went quietly enough, but with the *Ballet Mécanique* all bedlam broke loose. The work was scored for eight pianos, a player piano, percussion, xylophones, airplane propellers, and other mechanical appliances. "Above the mighty noise of the pianos and drums arose cat-calls and booing, shrieking and whistling, shouts of 'thief' mixed with 'bravo.' People began to call each other names and to forget that there was any music going on at all."

Since the *Ballet* was notorious long before the concert, one can only conclude that the audience came in order to have a riot.

In his autobiography Antheil does not mention this performance of the *Ballet Mécanique*, but he gives an equally improbable account of a salon performance one hot summer day a few weeks later with eight grand pianos crowding two hundred guests, and Golschmann standing on a piano to conduct. Despite the incongruous social setting, the guests must have felt very much like Ezra Pound's utopian audience of factory workers: "With the performance of the Ballet Mecanique one can conceive the possibility of organising the sounds of a factory, let us say of boiler-plate, or any other clangorous noisiness, the actual sounds of the labour, the various tones of the grindings; according to the needs of the work, and yet, with such pauses and durées, that at the end of the eight hours, the men go out not with frayed nerves, but elated—fatigued, yes, but elated."

In concert or in salon Paris heard almost all of Antheil's music during that spring and summer of 1926. As he turned twenty-six, his career looked more promising than ever. At that moment Aaron Copland commented, alluding to the claque of literary expatriates, "Potentially speaking, Antheil is all they claim and more; one needn't be particularly astute to realize that he possesses the greatest gifts of any young American now writing." But Antheil had gone as far as he would go. The following year in New York, the *Ballet Mécanique*, with twice the original number of pianos and a real airplane propeller, was a flop. Ten years later Copland noted that Antheil's promise had yet to be fulfilled.

His greatest triumph should have come in April 1927, with an all-Antheil concert in Carnegie Hall and the premiere of his new piano concerto in Paris. But publicity and fashion, which had made him famous, caused his downfall. Skeptical New York had heard too much about this young sensation. When his concert was publicized as a circus, the critics reviewed it as such, ignoring the merits of his *Jazz Symphony* and quieter works to ridicule his *Ballet Mécanique.* Paris lost interest in Antheil when his new concerto proved to be derivative. For three years he had enjoyed a reputation for iconoclasm, but now he no longer represented the music of the future. By his own admission Antheil had allowed himself to be corrupted: "I had become a mere imitator of the latest and most elegant Parisian (and also most decadent), the most recent neoclassicism of Stravinsky."

Paris was his undoing. In later years he reflected a good deal on what had happened to him between the ages of twenty-three and twenty-six. "Paris, although more sympathetic to new art than any other city, was a difficult one in which to hold one's artistic integrity." Summing up its musical fashion, he wrote, "The neoclassicism of Paris was preoccupied with style, chic, pretty new sound, quick musical wit, everything but new expression of form, of the greater abstract meaning of music. Paris liked extraordinary and new contortions of the old classic sounds—much in the way that a modern dressmaker takes an old painting and fabricates a new style from the costumes of Rembrandt, or Leonardo da Vinci." Of its effect on him he confessed, "How effete my tastes had become in Paris! How effete still were the tastes of my colleagues who had dragged too much of their Paris studies and tastes home with them!"

The rest of his life was anticlimax. After his New York fiasco he went back to Paris, but he did not remain long. He spent six more years in Europe, then returned to New York to work for George Balanchine, who considered him the ideal American composer for Parisian ballets. But Antheil was disgusted with this work after a few years: "I did not wish to be a Parisian in New York." He moved on to Hollywood and wrote music for the movies until he was able to earn his independence and compose seriously again in his forties and fifties. Before his death he achieved some measure of success as a composer. But he never succeeded in living down his past. The *Ballet Mécanique* remains his definitive composition in the machine style that has typed him ever since.

13.

The Trade of Being a Saint

Of all the American composers who went to Paris, none stayed so long or became so thoroughly Gallicized as Virgil Thomson. He lived in Paris off and on during most of the period between the wars, and to this day he calls 17 Quai Voltaire his residence. Although he has lived in New York since 1940, he continues to visit Paris once or twice a year, though not for long: "I regard Paris as my home town," he says, "and you never want to stay in your home town, though it's always pleasant to visit."

Virgil Thomson first arrived in Paris in June 1921 as a member of the Harvard Glee Club, which made a tour of France and other European countries that summer. In his autobiography he lists the activities of the busy two weeks the Glee Club spent in Paris: "lunching with Maréchal Foch, a tea with Joffre, elegant parties at private establishments and a shocking push at the presidential palace, a masked ball at the Opéra, ballets by Milhaud and Cocteau and all six of Les Six at the Théâtre des Champs-Elysées, singing three packed-house concerts in the Salle Gaveau and conducting at High Mass in Saint-Eustache." When the Glee Club went home, Thomson stayed on in Paris. He had a traveling fellowship from Harvard, and he wanted to spend the year studying with a French teacher. Through Melville Smith, a Harvard graduate who was also studying music in Paris, he met Nadia Boulanger and began taking private lessons in counterpoint, harmony, and composition. He also took organ lessons with her at the Ecole Normale de Musique.

Mlle. Boulanger lived off the Place Clichy not too far from the Paris Conservatory, so Thomson looked for lodging in the same neighborhood. He found one at 20 rue de Berne, back of the Gare Saint-Lazare, in a residential hotel which Roy Harris describes simply as "a whorehouse." Thomson's room was just large enough for a grand piano, and no one complained when he played at night. Nearby was a Swedish church where he was able to practice the organ. And not too far away was a bar that was just then becoming a favorite resort of French composers and artists, Le Boeuf sur le Toit, named after the ballet produced by Cocteau and Milhaud. Thomson became acquainted with them and with other French composers of his generation during his first year in Paris. He also met Satie several times but was reticent in his company, not wishing to force his acquaintance on a composer he admired so much until he had thoroughly mastered his work.

From the start Thomson was attracted to French life and culture. At Harvard he had been thoroughly grounded in the music of Debussy and Ravel and had his musical outlook oriented toward France. In Paris he found the advanced teaching he needed, a much more active musical life, and a good place to work. Temperamentally he was much in sympathy with the French. He had the same kind of witty, skeptical, perceptive mind and appreciated the pleasures of Paris as well. "I felt at home with France, its music, its food, its people, its reading and writing." He also felt the need to get away from America in order to be himself. He quotes Gertrude Stein as saying that "it wasn't so much what France gave you as what she did not take away. America's always trying to lecture you for your own good and all that kind of thing, and to make you afraid of yourself."

His first year in Paris did much to determine his later

development. He learned much from the instruction of Nadia Boulanger and from the new music that was being composed and performed in Paris. The music of Satie in particular he felt as "an extraordinary influence," dominating his own work. For in Paris he began to compose in earnest. Another influence that affected his composition was the Catholic liturgy. Thomson, who had been a church organist since boyhood, had evolved musically from his Baptist origins but was always to show a predilection for church music. Both Mlle. Boulanger and Erik Satie were particularly interested in medieval modes, so it is not surprising that Thomson now began to compose works for organ and chorus in the same tradition: a *Sanctus*, a *Pastorale on a Christmas Plainsong*, an *Antiphonal Psalm*. During the next few years his *Sanctus* grew into two Masses, and he developed a facility at setting words to music which has always been his forte.

At the end of his year in Paris Thomson tried to get his fellowship extended for another year, but Harvard required him to return and take his degree. He spent the next three years in Boston and New York studying and teaching, though he had a persistent urge to return to Paris, finish his studies with Nadia Boulanger, and start composing full-time. In 1923 he bought a steamship ticket, only to decide that it would be wiser to study in New York on his Juilliard fellowship; finally in 1925 he turned down several tempting offers and sailed for France. He had managed to save up some money, and if necessary he knew he could support himself by writing music criticism. During his first sojourn in Paris he had begun writing articles on musical events for the *Boston Transcript*, and after his return to the United States he had written regularly for *Vanity Fair*, a magazine that was not only fashionable but paid well. But Thomson regarded writing as a last resort. "I didn't want to teach, I didn't want to write articles, I didn't want to get myself that involved any more with other people's music. I just wanted to sit down and write my own."

Paris was a good place because there he was removed from

such temptations and because the living was cheap. He arrived with five hundred dollars that lasted him for seven months, and during the years that followed he "sort of lived around on more or less nothing." He gave piano lessons; occasionally he wrote articles; he had a patroness for several years; once in a while he had commissions. Twice he received a veteran's bonus, but each time he spent the money giving a concert of his own music. He was as resourceful and frugal as a Frenchman, and he even managed to live with a certain amount of style.

When he returned to Paris in September 1925, he went back to the rue de Berne and to Mlle. Boulanger. She had been critical of the *Missa Brevis* he had submitted to her the previous year, and he felt he had to prove himself to her. Early in 1926 he completed his first important work, the *Sonata da Chiesa*, and emancipated himself from her guidance. Written for clarinet, trumpet, viola, horn, and trombone, this unorthodox piece of church music progresses from a Negro chorale to a tango movement to a baroque fugue. In these incongruous elements and in its neoclassical dissonance the sonata recapitulates Thomson's musical education and forecasts a versatile career full of witty parodies. The *Sonata da Chiesa* received its first performance at the Société Musicale Indépendante in a concert of chamber music by American students of Nadia Boulanger. Some of Thomson's work had already been performed during his first year in Paris, but he was still a student then; now he made his debut as a mature composer. "There were lots of people present," Thomson writes in his autobiography, "lots of laudatory reviews later, along with some shocked ones, the latter mostly with regard to my Church Sonata, which . . . made funny noises."

In 1926 he and George Antheil became close friends and allies. Though not a student of Nadia Boulanger, Antheil appeared on the all-American program, possibly because his name was the only one then known in Paris. In June Antheil dedicated his *Second Symphony* to Thomson, who had shown greater appreciation of the work than anyone else. Then on three successive Friday afternoons Antheil and Thomson performed their works in the salon of Mrs. Christian Gross. This wealthy American dipolmat's wife wanted to launch herself in Parisian society, and the two young composers were equally ambitious to launch themselves musically. Together they plotted a series of concerts at the height of the social season, to which they invited Parisian composers and their patrons. Naturally such works as the *Ballet Mécanique* and the *Sonata da Chiesa* appeared on the program, and it was thus that Thomson's *Five Phrases from the Song of Solomon* had its premiere. This work for the soprano voice has an accompaniment worthy of Antheil: tom-tom, cymbals, gong, and woodblock.

In 1926 Thomson met Gertrude Stein. She had invited Antheil to call on her, and he extended the invitation to Thomson for moral support. Bravig Imbs was present on this occasion; in fact he may have suggested that Antheil be invited. At that time Imbs was the major-domo of the little court at 27 rue de Fleurus, observing its ceremonies and intrigues with fascination. He describes Alice Toklas' "sieve and buckler" technique of sifting out and warding off candidates. She happened to interview Antheil first while Thomson was ingratiating himself with Gertrude Stein; otherwise she would never have allowed him to pass. Thomson was a formidable rival, with a quick verbal intelligence and a cutting wit as sharp as her own. For years she resented his friendship with Gertrude Stein. In the *Autobiography* she is forced to admit, "Gertrude Stein had not found George Antheil particularly interesting although she liked him, but Virgil Thomson she found very interesting although I did not like him."

Antheil was never invited again, but Thomson became a regular caller. Gertrude Stein was pleased to discover that he had read *Tender Buttons* as an undergraduate and flattered when he set some of her short pieces to music. Although her musical appreciation was limited, she was interested enough to go to the rue de Berne to hear him sing and play Satie's *Socrate*, an austere, undramatic rendering of several Platonic dialogues about the death of Socrates. In the *Autobiography* she comments, "He had understood Satie undoubtedly and he had a comprehension quite his own of prosody. He understood a great deal of Gertrude Stein's work, he used to dream at night that there was something there that he did not understand, but on the whole he was very well content with that which he did understand. She delighted in listening to her words framed by his music. They saw a great deal of each other."

Thomson was no flatterer. Far from being a hanger-on, he had his own circle of acquaintance and enhanced Gertrude Stein's salon by introducing such friends as the poet Georges Hugnet, who later translated Gertrude Stein, and the painter Christian Bérard, who did her portrait. Thomson even had his own small painting collection, which she examined with curiosity, though not with complete approval. Through all the years of their friendship he maintained his independence yet managed ultimately to survive the inevitable broils. When a telephone was installed at 27 rue de Fleurus and Alice Toklas banished all the favorites by *coups de téléphone*, he was the only one of the young men to ingratiate himself again. On another occasion Gertrude Stein suspected him of intriguing against her; when he attempted to make peace by sending her the program of a concert at which he was playing some of her works, she sent back her calling card with a note to read, "Miss Stein declines further acquaintance with Mr. Thomson." They were not reconciled for several years, during the very period when he was preparing the production of their opera, *Four Saints in Three Acts*.

If he set her words to music, it was not only out of friendship and esteem but in response to the musical possibilities of her writing. He began with two short poems that were by their nature tuneful. Gertrude Stein herself spoke of their melody, an element she usually tried to suppress in her writing.

The opening and refrain of "Susie Asado" sounds like pure bird song:

> Sweet sweet sweet sweet sweet tea.
> Susie Asado.

"Preciosilla" closes with similar iterations, capped by a jazzy conclusion:

> guest, go go go go go go, go. Go go. Not guessed. Go go.
> Toasted susie is my ice-cream.

Virgil Thomson says, "Gertrude Stein was a very classical English poet. She followed the genius of the language." What he presumably means is that her writing is lyrical and her syntax falls into familiar patterns, whether or not the sense is clear. To take a typical example, her remark about Chaucer's poetry, "It sounds as sounds that is to say as birds as well as words," brings out the play on sounds she delighted in. Thomson naturally was more interested in sound than sense and did not care that her writing had no form beyond the individual line. For that matter rather little of it could be classed as poetry. When confronted by the long, formless passages of "Capital, Capitals," Thomson had to devise new musical solutions. He decided to bring out the static character of the writing by vocalizing the monotone. The piece is scored for four men and a piano, each voice representing one of the four ancient capitals of Provence. When alternating in the short lines of dialogue, the different voices lend variety; but in the long wordy speeches they all sound equally monotonous, chanting endlessly on one note.

At about the same time Thomson experimented with a variety of genres that were to find their way into *Four Saints*. Mrs. Gross had given him a commission out of gratitude for his concerts at her salon. With this he began writing his *Symphony on a Hymn Tune* and diverting himself with his *Variations on*

Sunday-School Tunes, parodies of all the inept organ playing he had ever heard, from banal foursquare hymns to misguided improvisation. He made his first attempt at setting French texts and began composing "portraits," musical meditations on his friends. Like Gertrude Stein's literary portraits, these present a record of his acquaintance and activities over the years. He wrote over a hundred and fifty in all, many of them with fanciful titles like *Bugles and Birds* (Pablo Picasso), *Parades* (Florine Stettheimer), and *Portrait of a Young Man in Good Health* (Maurice Grosser with a bad cold).

During the next few years his works were performed on both sides of the Atlantic and began to attract some attention. In 1927 the Duchesse de Clermont-Tonnerre asked him to put on a performance of *Capital, Capitals* in her salon. In 1928 he presented a concert of his own works and another in collaboration with the French composer Henri Cliquet-Pleyel. In 1931 he had another one-man concert with an entire program of new compositions, including musical settings of Racine, Bossuet, and Max Jacob. On this occasion a veteran's bonus permitted him to engage a distinguished quartet and singers from the Opéra and the Opéra-Comique.

Meanwhile in America *Five Phrases from the Song of Solomon* and *Capital, Capitals* were performed at the Copland-Sessions Concerts, and Thomson was invited to conduct his *Sonata da Chiesa* in Boston. He spent the winter of 1928–29 in America enjoying his success. "I have been interviewed, caricatured, written about, talked about, and entertained," he wrote in a letter to Gertrude Stein. But he had no thought of staying. "I shall be glad to get back to Paris where I am not a public character." In the spring he went home to Paris.

Home was now 17 Quai Voltaire. His orbit had shifted when he stopped taking lessons with Nadia Boulanger, and he had moved to his new address on November 1 (All Saints' Day), 1927. There on the left bank of the Seine across from the Louvre he had a tall studio apartment in a handsome eighteenth-century building. Bravig Imbs has described his quarters and the décor provided by artist friends. "There was a great expanse of yellow curtained glass but the panes were too high up on the wall to look out of. Below them was a little door, about a foot square, which when opened, showed just a glimpse of the great grey Louvre, a portal or two, like a picture. It was quite a lovely room with a magnificent Bérard hanging over the piano and some of Maurice Grosser's sensitive still lifes on the opposite wall; at the head of the balcony stairs, two of Tonny's fantastic spirited drawings and in the alcove below, one of Hans Arp's amusing bas-reliefs."

The day after he moved to the Quai Voltaire, Thomson began work on *Four Saints in Three Acts.* He had gone from short songs to extended recitative, and confident he could handle any text Gertrude Stein could provide, he had asked her to write an opera. He proposed a mythological work based on the Italian baroque *opera seria,* and they began to consider possible subjects. "We thought we wouldn't deal with Greek mythology or Swedish or anything Scandinavian because that had been handsomely done by Wagner. And so we thought, well, history can be considered as a form of mythology, and we looked around history. Gertrude wanted to do something about George Washington and American history, but I said I didn't like eighteenth-century costumes because everybody looks alike; you can't tell one character from another when they get wigs on. So we said, well, after all there are the lives of the saints, that's mythology too. And we started looking around for saints that we liked."

Gertrude Stein had always liked saints in general and certain saints in particular. "And so it was natural that when I wanted saints that they should be Spanish Saints," she wrote in *Everybody's Autobiography.* "There are saints everywhere there have been saints in Italy and in France and even in Germany and I suppose in Austria, I do not know anything about them, but the important saints have been Spanish and Italian and that is natural enough, there must be really weather in which to wander in order to be a saint." Her particular favorites were

Saint Francis of Assisi and Saint Teresa of Ávila, but Saint Francis and other Italian saints had received too much attention from the nineteenth-century Anglo-Florentines, so she chose Saint Ignatius Loyola to go with Saint Teresa. These two great contemporaries, the mystic of Ávila and the militant of Barcelona, together epitomized the Spanish landscape and character, and to Gertrude Stein an opera or a play was simply a portrait in a landscape. She did not care for emotion on stage or dramatic events. "A saint a real saint never does anything, a martyr does something but a really good saint does nothing, and so I wanted to have Four Saints who did nothing and I wrote the Four Saints In Three Acts and they did nothing and that was everything." In Gertrude Stein's opinion, "Generally speaking anybody is more interesting doing nothing than doing something." In other words, character is more interesting than action. And to her character meant charisma.

Saint Teresa and Saint Ignatius had both organized religious orders, and this permitted Gertrude Stein to group other saints around them, most of them unhistorical, some forty in all, men saints and women saints. The result is a series of static tableaux composing the disciples around the two principal saints. Eventually in Maurice Grosser's scenario these became scenes from the saints' lives, but in Gertrude Stein's text they are simply group portraits in which nothing happens. Virgil Thomson has provided a delightful contemporary interpretation of Saint Teresa and Saint Ignatius, "each surrounded by younger saints learning the trade of being a saint at the feet of the living consecrated masters, very much as the young American writers were clustered around Gertrude Stein and James Joyce." The implied subject of *Four Saints in Three Acts* is "the artist's life in Paris," he says, "people living near one another often collaborating on artistic projects, all of them devoting their lives to the disinterested effort of being better artists and making good art. We couldn't write about art that way, but we could write about saints with the understanding between ourselves that it was artists we were writing about, and were treating the saints as if they were artists and viewing artists as if they were possibly saints."

Thomson has remarked that Gertrude Stein approached a subject as a composer would, choosing a theme and letting it develop itself. In *Four Saints* she meditates on Spain as well as the saints themselves, her memories of visits there and other private associations. (She had always loved Spain and Alice Toklas had loved it even more; one of the critical moments in their life together had occurred at Ávila in 1912, when Alice Toklas wanted to stay there forever.) As she meditates on her theme Gertrude Stein also lets her attention drift to her surroundings at the moment. She readily returns from sixteenth-century Spain to the present in which she is writing, to a croquet scene and a walk in the country ("What happened to-day, a narrative"). She also proceeds by verbal associations, putting down whatever comes into her head and letting the rhythm or sound lead her on, as in the counting rhymes that occur from time to time: "A saint is one to be for two when three and you make five and two and cover." The text is full of verbal games, riddles and rhymes, puns and paradoxes, clichés and nonsense. Apart from the vast store of childish jingles and ancient charms, Gertrude Stein had her own repertory to draw on: "Bee time vine," "When this you see remember me," and her favorite bit of dialogue, "How do you do. Very well I thank you." All these she wove into a playful lilting text, with no concern for relevance.

Her libretto is a collage, with all sorts of miscellaneous matter stuck together. It has no plot, for plot meant development in time, and Gertrude Stein was not interested, preferring to dwell in the static present. Nor did she care about dialogue or any of the conventions of the drama. In fact she made fun of them, running stage directions into dialogue indiscriminately, constantly announcing a new act or scene, and hopelessly jumbling the sequence. The title *Four Saints in Three Acts* pleased her ear, but she deliberately left the number of divisions as indeterminate as the number of saints. Her whole attitude is best summed up in Act IV.

> How many acts are there in it.
> How many saints in all.
> How many acts are there in it.
> Ring around a rosey.

She called the work "an opera to be sung," probably to distinguish it from all the unsung operas she had written. Virgil Thomson calls it "an oratorio about an opera," thus indicating something of his interpretation.

The text she provided makes difficult reading, but when brought to life by his music, all difficulties vanish. The words and music together justify themselves as the listener enjoys the sound of individual phrases without worrying about overall meaning or plot; he listens as he would listen to an opera in a familiar foreign language or for that matter an oratorio in English. On the printed page the words of Handel's *Messiah* read very much like Gertrude Stein, especially when unpunctuated: "The Lord is His name is His name is His name. The Lord the Lord the Lord the Lord is His name." And the phrasing of the *Messiah* sometimes produces Steinian effects: "All we like sheep," if one listens for meaning, sounds more gastronomic than moral. But of course no one listens primarily for meaning; what Thomson says about the Latin used in church music is equally true of English. In church music, he points out, Latin is not a dead language, but it conveys more aesthetic emotion than content. Thomson cites the Kyrie and the Alleluia as parts of the Mass that can be handled as syllables of sound rather than meaning; neither the Kyrie nor the Alleluia happens to be Latin, but then neither is Gertrude Stein's writing the same as English. The obscurity of her text, far from imposing a limitation, left him freer to deal with the sound and weight of the words. He followed the line of her syntax, often clarifying and punctuating as well as musically expressing the sense.

His music brings out all the miscellaneous character of the libretto. Thomson kept his model in mind, the Italian baroque opera about a mythological subject. The formula called for a tragic ending, and there was nothing tragic about Gertrude Stein's saints; otherwise his treatment was fundamentally religious. He drew on all varieties of church singing for his recitative and for most of the set pieces. "Pigeons on the grass alas" is treated with the gentle reverence befitting a vision of the Holy Ghost, and the "magpie in the sky," another sacred emblem, trumpets seraphically. These passages, followed by his Hallelujah chorus ("Let Lucy Lily Lily Lucy Lucy . . ."), give the work a spiritual climax. But the opera is not entirely solemn. After all, gaiety is a natural part of the saintly life; beatific means happy. So Thomson has mixed in plenty of jollity and introduced a number of musical jokes, from the opening oompah-pah on. The basically devout style is merrily profaned by snatches of Stephen Foster steamboat and banjo music, military marches, drunken tangos, and sour waltzes. The instrumentation is comic too, particularly in the final interlude, when the music runs down as the air is let out of one instrument after another. In its discontinuity, Thomson's score is like the libretto, a collage. He does exactly what Gertrude Stein did when she introduced in the midst of her Spanish baroque saints such a line as "My country 'tis of thee sweet land of liberty of thee I sing."

Thomson finished *Four Saints* in July 1928, and it was not produced until February 1934. Meanwhile he performed it privately to anyone who would listen, playing the piano and singing all the parts himself. When he went to America, Carl Van Vechten asked him to give a performance in his apartment and invited a group of friends. This led to other closet performances, and gradually the work acquired a reputation in New York and Paris. Thomson saw its possibilities when he wrote to Gertrude Stein about the New York audience's response to *Capital, Capitals:* "Capitals swell success. N. Y. talks of nothing else since three days. Audience roared with laughter during and bravos afterwards. Critics charmingly confused. Some thought it a good joke, some a bad joke and one or so got quite angry. . . . the poets were all disgusted with the words and the composers thought the music too low for anything. But the audience's way of taking it proved to me the possibility of having a regular boob success with the opera, at least it might run long enough to pay its expenses and it might just might (and without surprising me at all) make a little money."

In 1929 the text was published in *Transition*, and the opera was seriously considered for performance by the Darmstadt Opera, but finally turned down—on account of the music, Thomson says. Eventually A. Everett Austin, a museum director who had known Thomson at Harvard and who was the founder and president of an organization called the Friends and Enemies of Modern Music, decided to inaugurate a new wing of his museum with a performance of *Four Saints* in the theater. Thus it happened that the opera had its premiere in Hartford, Connecticut, in the altogether appropriate company of a big Picasso retrospective and an exhibition of sets from the Ballet Russe.

The stage production united all the arts in a collaboration worthy of the late Diaghilev. In preparing *Four Saints* for its premiere Virgil Thomson became its impresario. Gertrude Stein had originally suggested Picasso as a stage designer, but Thomson preferred an artist of his own generation. He had met in New York the painter Florine Stettheimer, a kind of American Dufy who was unknown to the public because she never exhibited her work, but who had a touch of fantasy and a fondness for fragile materials that Thomson wanted for his décor. He discovered John Houseman and started him on his career in the theater by placing him in charge of the production. He imported Frederick Ashton from London to do the choreography. He picked and trained the cast himself, making the most successful innovation of all when he decided to have

Negro singers. He had been impressed by their stage presence and beautiful diction as well as the quality of their voices. He discovered further advantages in rehearsal. "They move so beautifully. And they understood Gertrude Stein. And they can act out a religious subject without embarrassment. Everything was wonderful about them. But the original impulse was to have their extreme clarity of singing speech on the principle that if the meaning of the text is obscure you don't want to add any further obscurity through mumbling pronunciation. That which is hard to understand must be very, very clearly pronounced. And Negroes pronounce more clearly than anybody else does."

Gertrude Stein had told Thomson to make whatever changes in the libretto he wished. Originally he had put everything to music, but for the stage production he cut the text down to manageable size and used the scenario prepared by his artist friend Maurice Grosser in collaboration with Gertrude Stein. She had also made suggestions for the ballets, which together with the scenario enhanced the spectacle, giving the opera a more visible form. Thomson had made some changes in the cast, dividing Saint Teresa into two parts and adding a *compère* and *commère*, a man and a woman who serve as commentators, reading or singing the stage directions that form a large portion of the text. In the stage production the two Saint Teresas were dressed as cardinals, while the *commère* and *compère*, representing the laity, wore modern evening dress. Saint Ignatius was dressed like a proper saint in a baroque painting, and the other saints were dressed as choral singers, in robes and surplices. The sets were mostly of cellophane, with lace, feathers, glass beads, and other delicate materials–suggested perhaps by the *bal des matières* given in Paris by the Vicomte de Noailles a few years before. "Miss Stettheimer's sets are of a beauty incredible," Virgil Thomson reported in a letter to Gertrude Stein, "with trees made out of feathers and a sea-wall at Barcelona made out of shells and for the procession a baldachino of black chiffon & bunches of black ostrich plumes just like a Spanish funeral. Saint Teresa comes to the picnic in the 2nd Act in a cart drawn by a real white donkey & brings her tent with her and sets it up & sits in the door-way of it. It is made of white gauze with gold fringe and has a most elegant shape."

The spectacle and the music performed a marriage of the arts in the best Parisian tradition, and the audience was worthy of the occasion. In addition to the Friends and Enemies of Modern Music who subsidized the production, the enlightened and fashionable of New York were on hand, among them many friends of Gertrude Stein who cabled and wrote enthusiastically. Van Vechten, who in 1913 had gone to the Ballet Russe on the same night as Gertrude Stein, reported, "I haven't seen a crowd more excited since Sacre du Printemps. The difference was that they were pleasurably excited. The Negroes are divine, like El Grecos, more Spanish, more Saints, more opera singers in their dignity and *simplicity* and extraordinary plastic line than *any* white singers could ever be. And they enunciated the text so clearly you could understand every word. Frederick Ashton's rhythmic staging was inspired and so were Florine's costumes and sets. Imagine a crinkled sky-blue cellophane background, set in white lace borders, like a valentine against which were placed the rich and royal costumes of the saints in red velvets, etc. and the dark Spanish skins." Some members of the avant-garde criticized Thomson for turning his back on modern music, but *Four Saints* was generally praised. It literally made theatrical history, for America had few operas of its own and no theater like this. *Four Saints* also made history by becoming a popular success on Broadway and later in Chicago, for a total of sixty performances. "Pigeons on the grass alas" became a household expression.

Thomson, who had come to America in 1932 and 1933 to plan the production and rehearse the performance, found himself spending more time in New York during the next few years. He returned to Paris in the spring of 1934, but was called back by John Houseman to collaborate in the newly founded Phoenix Theater and later in the WPA Theater Project. As the idea of collective endeavor in the arts began to spread in America, Thomson was much in demand. He wrote symphonic accompaniments for films, the first serious American composer to do so; his orchestral suites for *The Plow that Broke the Plains* and *The River* have led an independent life, but they were originally written to accompany the beautiful documentaries of Pare Lorentz. Thomson also provided the music for Lincoln Kirstein's ballet *Filling Station*, which had its first performance in the same Avery Memorial Theater in Hartford where *Four Saints* had inaugurated a trend four years before. In that brief span of the middle thirties, modern music had finally found a place in the American theater, thanks partly to Virgil Thomson and the example of Paris.

While he was busy writing music in America, he kept in touch with Paris by making occasional visits and continued to think of 17 Quai Voltaire as the place where he lived. Despite his success, he was dissatisfied with America, where he found himself on a treadmill, caught up in the process of earning money without earning freedom, working under pressure instead of producing his best work spontaneously. For such reasons his friend Maurice Grosser concluded that "France is a rich country and America a poor one," and Virgil Thomson, quoting that remark in his autobiography, added, "In terms of just plain feeling good, France was in those days, even for the poor, the richest life an artist ever knew." He managed to return to Paris in 1938 with an advance from a publisher to write a book. *The State of Music*, published the following year, was hailed by Aaron Copland as "the most original book on music America has produced." But France deserves part of the credit, for only in Paris would an American composer live in such proximity to painters and poets as to include a chapter on each in a book anatomizing the musical profession. Thomson explains that he feels at home in Paris because of the company of sixty thousand painters; and he is conversant with poetry, photography, cinema, ballet, and theater as only a Parisian is likely to be. Music, he points out, can only be written in a musical metropolis, and only in Paris was music in such close touch with all the other arts. He describes the composer, in what appears to be a self-portrait, as a social animal:

> Living in hotels and temporary lodgings, and frequently being unmarried, your composer is a great diner-out. Of all the artist-workers, he is the most consistently social. Those painters who live in touch with the world of decorating and mode and fashion are not infrequently snobs, horrid little snobs, for all their camaraderie and democratic ways. The composer is not a snob at all. He is simply a man of the world who dresses well, converses with some brilliance, and has completely charming manners. He is gracious in any house, however humble or grand; and he rarely makes love to the hostess. He eats and drinks everything but is pretty careful about alcohol as sedentary workers have to be.

Much of the book is about the economics and politics of his profession, with chapters entitled "How Composers Eat" or subtitled "The Economic Determinism of Musical Style." As a writer Thomson is unfailingly entertaining, informative, and perspicacious.

Thomson stayed on in Paris until June 8, 1940, six days before the Germans occupied the city. Even then he lingered in France, near the Spanish border, until his money ran out. Finally in October he returned to America on the same ship as Man Ray. Back in New York he began writing for the *Herald Tribune* and for the next fourteen years was acknowledged as America's leading music critic, though often criticized for his modern and French bias. He was highly provocative, and he meant to be, whether in his criticism of musical establishments, such as the established repertory of Romantic symphonic works, or in his praise of contemporaries. He made no secret of his partiality for

French composers, writing tributes to Debussy, Ravel, and Satie. He compared Debussy to Beethoven as a founding father and placed Satie above Stravinsky and Schoenberg.

Three months after leaving France he wrote an article on Satie and French music that best defines his position: "The Satie musical aesthetic is the only twentieth-century musical aesthetic in the Western world." Dismissing Schoenberg, Hindemith, and Stravinsky as backward-looking composers, he finds that "Satie is the only one whose works can be enjoyed and appreciated without any knowledge of the history of music." Though they lack prestige, these works exemplify the qualities that Thomson admires. "They are as simple, as straightforward, as devastating as the remarks of a child. To the uninitiated they sound trifling. To those who love them they are fresh and beautiful and firmly right. And that freshness and rightness have long dominated the musical thought of France." This leads him to expatiate on the special quality of French music, its avoidance of "the impressive, the heroic, the oratorical, everything that is aimed at moving mass audiences," in favor of "quietude, precision, acuteness of auditory observation, gentleness, sincerity and directness of statement." In his peroration Thomson seems to have his own music in mind as well as that of France. "It wears no priestly robes; it mumbles no incantations; it is not painted up by Max Factor to terrify elderly ladies or to give little girls a thrill. Neither is it designed to impress orchestral conductors or to get anybody a job teaching school. It has literally no devious motivation. It is as simple as a friendly conversation and in its better moments exactly as poetic and as profound."

Thomson has sometimes been called an American Satie. He resembles the French composer more in his outlook than in his music. Satie was an ironist born in an age of watery sentiments. There was nothing revolutionary about his iconoclasm; he was simply opposed to all that was pompous and romantic. Hence his satire; hence the simple, classic austerity of his music. Thomson shares many of Satie's principles. He feels that modern music has become needlessly complicated and pretentious. After writing in the dissonant style of Stravinsky for a time, he reacted against it, turning to a simpler, more direct expression. He is not afraid of the commonplace. He is not embarrassed to communicate with his audience, just as Satie was not ashamed to play the piano and write songs for a Montmartre cabaret. "Satie did not work at a piano," he remarks of the composer's habits, "he worked at a café." Thomson's wit is often like Satie's and used for the same purpose—to deflate. Both have a highly developed awareness of the absurd and a fondness for parody. Thomson likes incongruous mixtures of elegance and homespun; he describes *Four Saints in Three Acts* as "modern, baroque, pop art." Satie was much given to comical titles and remarks; the best known is his composition in seven movements entitled *Three Pieces in the Shape of a Pear with a Way of Beginning, a Continuation of the Same, and Some More Followed by a Repetition.* Thomson has sometimes emulated him, as in "*Le Berceau de Gertrude Stein*" *ou* "*Le Mystère de la rue de Fleurus,*" *Huit poèmes de Georges Hugnet to which have been added a Musical Composition by Virgil Thomson entitled* "*Lady Godiva's Waltzes.*" (Lady Godiva was Gertrude Stein's Ford.) He also wrote a piano sonata "for Gertrude Stein to improvise at the pianoforte," using only the white keys; Gertrude Stein did not play the piano and did not read music readily, but she sometimes improvised "sonatinas" on the piano, always avoiding the black keys. Such musical jokes were very much in the spirit of Satie.

Aesthetically, intellectually, gastronomically, and otherwise, Virgil Thomson often seems more French than American. He even looks like a Frenchman, with his small, neat, well-fed figure, complete to the rosette of his Legion of Honor. Quick and self-possessed in speech and movement, he is also lucid and precise in his writing, with that *clarté* the French so much admire. "On my arrival in 1921 I had become a Parisian instantaneously," he writes in *Virgil Thomson.* "Paris was where I felt most at home." His autobiography is full of such remarks indicating that he was happier, more comfortable, more at ease, and hence better able to compose in Paris than anywhere else. Paris provided not only the ideal musical setting but a way of life that cushioned him against the nervous anxieties of America and the political anxieties of the rest of Europe. There he found all the comforts he liked, the best food in the world, and no end of social stimulation. Always extremely gregarious, Thomson knew everyone who was fashionable, intellectual, or creative in that brilliant international society.

When cut off by the war he became a New Yorker in fact without ceasing to be a Parisian in spirit. His feelings about Paris later found musical expression in *The Seine at Night*, dedicated to Kansas City, where he was born and raised, with a backward look at his twenty years spent in Paris: "And so I offer to the other city I love, and the only other where I have ever felt at home, a sketch, a souvenir, a postcard of the Seine, as seen from in front of my own house, a view as deeply a part of my life and thought as Wabash Avenue, where I spent my first twenty years." His program notes sound the theme of nostalgia that runs through all American reminiscences about Paris: "*The Seine at Night* is a landscape piece, a memory of Paris and its river, as viewed nocturnally from one of the bridges to the Louvre—the Pont des Saints-Pères, the Pont des Arts, or the Pont Royal. The stream is so deep and its face so quiet that it scarcely seems to flow. Unexpectedly, inexplicably, a ripple will lap the masonry of its banks. In the distance, over Notre Dame or from the top of faraway Montmartre, fireworks, casual rockets, flare and expire. Later in the night, between a furry sky and the Seine's watery surface, fine rain hangs in the air."

DOWN AND OUT IN PARIS

CHRONOLOGY VI

1931	Miller's first published story, "Mademoiselle Claude," appears in *New Review* Miller forms avant-garde of death with Fraenkel and Lowenfels, meets Anaïs Nin
1932	Céline, *Voyage au Bout de la Nuit*, "the best book out of France since Proust" Surrealist number of *This Quarter.* "The Dadaists were more entertaining"
1932–34	Quiet days in Clichy with Alf Perlès
1934	Cowley, *Exile's Return* Miller, *Tropic of Cancer*
1935	Miller begins *Hamlet* correspondence with Fraenkel; they agree to stop at one thousand pages Miller plans book of short stories on Paris, including "Max," the story of a tragicomic Jewish refugee
1936	Beginning of Spanish Civil War Anaïs Nin, *House of Incest,* a surrealistic prose poem begun in 1932 Miller, *Black Spring,* also begun in 1932
1937	Perlès becomes editor of *The Booster*, "a contraceptive against the self-destructive spirit of our age," with boosts for all and sundry
1938	Booster Publications produces Miller's *Money and How It Gets That Way* International Surrealist Exhibition Munich Crisis. "Peace in our time" *Booster* becomes *Delta,* publishes "Special Peace and Dismemberment Number with Jitterbug-Shag Requiem"
1939	*Tropic of Capricorn* Jack Kahane, Miller's publisher, dies the day after war begins

14.

Cancer and Delirium

On March 4, 1930, a slight, bald, middle-aged American arrived in Paris. Mild-mannered and bespectacled, he had the air of a college professor. Café waiters often took him for a German or a Scandinavian. "I lack that carefree, audacious air of the average American," he wrote in a letter at the time. "Even the Americans ignore me. They talk English at my elbow with that freedom which one employs only when he is certain his neighbor does not understand." Like so many Americans during the previous decade he had come to write, but his circumstances were altogether different. They came mostly from families which could afford to support their idleness. They usually sowed a very small crop of unpublishable literary oats and indulged in mild libertinage with their own kind along the Boulevard Montparnasse: got drunk in the American cafés for a season or two, mastered a few dozen French clichés, read a little, wrote a little, then went home to bourgeois respectability. They were the university wits of their day, following the pleasant fashion of their class, but their creative impulses were largely wishful and soon dissipated.

Henry Miller came from another world. An outcast from the lower middle class, a dropout after two months of college twenty years before, an outsider in his native land, he had worked at a succession of odd jobs and seen more of life than most men. He had no desire to associate with his compatriots in Montparnasse when he first arrived, referring to them scornfully as "the insufferable idiots at the Dôme and the Coupole." And this was more than the usual reflex of the American abroad, to whom all other Americans were a source of embarrassment. Miller had a deep-seated hatred of all things American. For him the United States represented "the air-conditioned nightmare" of technology without a soul. He had come to Europe to get away from America and to find a way of life that would answer to his psychic needs. Like most Montparnasse Americans he was a sentimental expatriate. Unlike them he found what he wanted and succeeded as a writer.

Miller had been to London and was on his way to Madrid, according to his later accounts, when he ran out of money. But the letters he wrote at the time reveal no intention to travel any farther. On his first Sunday in Paris he wondered, "Will I ever get to really understand the true spirit of this people?"—not a question asked by the casual transient. A few weeks later he wrote, "I love it here, I want to stay forever." Paris was the destination toward which he had been moving for years, ever since his friend Emil Schnellock had described it to him. Schnellock, whom Miller had known as a schoolboy, had lived abroad and become a painter. To Miller it was incredible that his friend, "just a Brooklyn boy" like himself, should have been magically transformed into an artist and cosmopolite. No doubt his example more than anything else affected Miller's decision to become a writer at all costs. Years later in *Tropic of Capricorn* Miller was to write: "Even now, years and years since, even now, when I know Paris like a book, his picture of Paris is still before my eyes, still vivid, still real. Sometimes, after a rain, riding swiftly through the city in a taxi, I catch fleeting glimpses of this Paris he described; just momentary snatches, as in passing the Tuileries, perhaps, or a glimpse of Montmartre, of the Sacré Coeur, through the Rue Laffitte, in the last flush of twilight. . . . Those nights in Prospect Park with my old friend Ulric are responsible, more than anything else, for my being here today."

Miller's wife June also played a crucial role. As Mona or Mara she appears in *Tropic of Capricorn* and other autobiographical romances, an enigmatic figure who entered his life in the early twenties, a Broadway taxi dancer with literary aspirations. Their love was often tempestuous, but through it all she was determined that he would become a writer. She persuaded him to quit his job at Western Union, she worked so that he could write, she found patrons for his work among her admirers by passing herself off as the author. Thus she raised money for a trip to Europe, convinced that he would be able to write there. They went together in 1928, but only on a tour. In 1930 she found the money to send him alone, intending to join him when she had more. As she knew better than Miller, he had reached a dead end in New York.

In one of his first letters from Paris in 1930 he voiced his deep sense of frustration: "I can't understand my failure. . . . Why does nobody want what I write? Jesus, when I think of being 38, and poor, and unknown, I get furious." By the time he landed in Paris he had been writing for eight years. He had completed four books and countless stories and articles. Only three articles had ever been published. Discouraged by poverty, debts, and the fact that his wife had to work so that he could lead "the true life of the artist," he still yearned for the comforts of bourgeois life. These contradictory feelings of guilt and self-pity, the compulsion to succeed and the interpretation of success as money, were all neuroses of Protestant America, with its gospel of work and wealth. In Paris Miller was never troubled by such worries. Though he lived more parasitically and marginally than ever, he was psychologically liberated as he had never been in New York. Hence the euphoric mood that marks all his writing during the decade he spent in Paris. There at last he was able to write, on the first page of *Tropic of Cancer:* "I have no money, no resources, no hopes. I am the happiest man alive. A year ago, six months ago, I thought that I was an artist. I no longer think about it, I *am*."

Miller's first impressions of Paris—and the most reliable account of his first eighteen months there—are to be found in the letters he wrote to Emil Schnellock at the time. His first letter, written three days after his arrival, announces: "I will write here. I will live quietly and quite alone. And each day I will see a little more of Paris, study it, learn it as I would a book. It is worth the effort. To know Paris is to know a great deal. How vastly different from New York! What eloquent surprises at every turn of the street. To get lost here is the adventure extraordinary. The streets sing, the stones talk. The houses drip history, glory, romance." From the start he liked everything about the city, its cosmopolitan atmosphere, the variety of people, their nonconformity. "Here is the greatest congregation of bizarre types. People do dress as they please, wear beards if they like, and shave if they choose. You don't feel that lifeless pressure of dull regimentation as in N. Y. and London."

The letters written within a month of his arrival are full of wonder and delight. Everything is new and charming, the language, the way of counting, the procedure in the restaurants, the tipping. The police are allowed to smoke on duty. Gourmet meals are cheap. The writing in the newspapers and magazines is intelligent and sophisticated. Miller was prepared to see good in everything, from the fifty thousand artists of Paris selling their work to an appreciative public to the custodian in the underground toilet writing a love letter, happy with her lot, unlike the silly stenographer in a New York skyscraper. As on his previous visit he was overcome by the setting, particularly at night. "I am on the verge of tears. The beauty of it all is suffocating me. . . . I am fairly intoxicated with the glamour of the city." His second letter, sixteen pages long, describes that emotion peculiar to the place, *la nostalgie de Paris,* nostalgia that can be experienced at the moment itself.

At the same time Paris gave him an inexhaustible supply of material and the urge to write. Within three weeks of his arrival he reported, "I have added a hundred pages to my book and done excellent revision work also. No water colors. I am overwhelmed yet by the multifarious, quotidien, anonymous, communal, etc. etc. *life!*" The program announced in his first letter of exploring the city and writing about it was carried out in a number of long letters written during his first two months or so. Actually these were not letters at all, but feature articles for circulation to magazine editors and for eventual use in a book on Paris Miller planned to write. Bearing such titles as "Spring on the Trottoirs" and "With the Wine Merchants," they usually described itineraries in quest of local color.

Paris was always a great city for walkers, and Miller was one of its most tireless pedestrians, covering enormous distances in his search for the picturesque. The paintings he had seen colored his vision so that wherever he went he found scenes from Monet, Pissarro, Seurat. In painting even more than literature Paris has always drawn its lovers back toward the past. Miller was particularly susceptible to this nostalgia for a city he had never known, regretting that he had been born too late. Many years later, in *Big Sur and the Oranges of Hieronymus Bosch,* he was still wishing he had been there as a young man: "What would I not give to have been the comrade or bosom friend of such figures as Apollinaire, Douanier Rousseau, George Moore, Max Jacob, Vlaminck, Utrillo, Derain, Cendrars, Gauguin, Modigliani, Cingria, Picabia, Maurice Magre, Léon Daudet, and such like. How much greater would have been the thrill to cycle along the Seine, cross and recross her bridges, race through towns like Bougival, Châtou, Argenteuil, Marly-le-roi, Puteaux, Rambouillet, Issy-les-Moulineaux and similar environs circa 1910 rather than the year 1932 or 1933!" Actually the world he yearned for was older than 1910; it was the impressionists' Arcadia painted in that string of sparkling villages along the Seine before they were industrialized into grimy suburbs.

Although somewhat self-conscious as literary compositions, the Paris letters marked an important stage in Miller's writing. They were good exercises, and they provided him with plenty of material that he was soon to use in his own way. Miller thought he was writing a book on Paris to match Paul Morand's slick guided tour of New York, which he had been reading with considerable envy at its success. He hoped his impressions might amount to "something popular, saleable, palatable." Unwittingly he was already at work on *Tropic of Cancer.* The letters contain the earliest writing that was to go into that book. One of them in particular, entitled "Bistre and Pigeon Dung," contains several passages that Miller saved and later wove into the fabric of his book. Here is one that reappears on one of the opening pages of *Tropic of Cancer*, only slightly revised:

> Twilight hour, Indian blue, water of glass, trees glistening and liquescent. Juares station itself gives me a kick. The rails fall away into the canal, the long caterpillar with sides lacquered in Chinese red dips like a roller-coaster. It is not Paris, it is not Coney Island—it is crepuscular melange of all the cities of Europe and Central America. Railroad yards spread out below me, the tracks looking black, webby, not ordered by engineers but cataclysmic in design, like those gaunt fissures in the Polar ice which the camera registers in degrees of black.

Another passage in the same letter describes a nude by Dufresne with "all the secondary characteristics and a few of the primary," likening it to a thirteenth-century *déjeuner intime*, a vibrant still life, the table so heavy with food that it is sliding out of its frame—exactly as it appears at the beginning of the second chapter of *Tropic of Cancer.* Still another passage describes the animated street market in the rue de Buci on a Sunday morning, then moves on to the quiet Square de Furstenberg nearby, providing a page at the beginning of the third chapter of the book. Here is Miller's original description of the Square de Furstenberg, a spot that particularly appealed to him:

> A deserted spot, bleak, spectral at night, containing in the center four black trees which have not yet begun to blossom. These four bare trees have the poetry of T. S. Eliot. They are intellectual trees, nourished by the stones,

> swaying with a rhythm cerebral, the lines punctuated by dots and dashes, by asterisks and exclamation points. Here, if Marie Laurencin ever brought her Lesbians out into the open, would be the place for them to commune. It is very, very Lesbienne here, very sterile, hybrid, full of forbidden longings.

When he incorporated this passage into *Tropic of Cancer,* Miller revised for economy and sharpness of outline, but kept the imagery unchanged. The original, written in April 1930, shows his particular vision of the city; he had yet to discover how to use it.

"Bistre and Pigeon Dung" was probably rattled off in one day, like other fifteen- or twenty-page letters. Under the stimulation of Paris Miller was indefatigable: "I feel that I could turn out a book a month here. If I could get a stenographer to go to bed with me I could carry on twenty-four hours a day." Walking in the city was a creative act in itself. He was forever composing in his head as he walked, the writing as vivid to him as if he had put it down on paper. Sometimes he could not remember what he had actually written and had to ask Schnellock. His books of the thirties were all to be written in this state of exaltation, as he walked around Paris in the present tense.

Other letters anticipate *Tropic of Cancer* even more in spirit. Miller lost no time in getting acquainted with the most squalid sights. He had always been attracted to the ghetto and the slums; now he often painted the ugliest street scenes.

> I looked around and there stood a brazen wench, leaning against her door like a lazy slut, cigarette between her lips, sadly rouged and frizzled, old, seamed, scarred, cracked, evil greedy eyes. She jerked her head a few times inviting me to come back and inspect her place, but my eyes were set on a strange figure tugging away at some bales. An old man with enormous goitres completely circling his neck, standing out below the hairline like huge

> polyps, from under his chin hanging loosely, joggling, purplish, veined, like gourds of wine—transparent gourds. Here the breed is degenerate and diseased. Old women with white hair, mangy, red lips, demented, prowl about in carpet slippers, their clothes in tatters, soiled with garbage and filth of the gutters.

This was Quasimodo's Paris, he pointed out, visible from the towers of Notre Dame, the inhabitants no different from those in the Middle Ages. But there was nothing romantic about the way he saw them. "They have bed-bugs, cockroaches and fleas running all over them, they are syphilitic, cancerous, dropsical, they are halt and blind, paralyzed, and their brains are soft."

Picturesque and sordid, this is Miller's Paris. Here even more than in the passages he actually used can *Tropic of Cancer* be anticipated. Again and again he dwelt with relish on the cancerous street scenes he found in the old quarters. He also explored the uglier regions of the modern industrial city, walking through endless dead stretches of suburb, bleak neighborhoods like those of his native Yorkville or Brooklyn. Paris provided local color of the particular kind that appealed to his imagination. Some six or seven weeks after his arrival he listed the topics he wanted to write about, including in addition to such standard items as the flea market, the six-day bicycle races, and the Grand Guignol, some that appealed to his rather special tastes: the slaughterhouses, the mummies at the Trocadéro, the Moslem cemetery, sexual perversions, the pissoirs, a comparative study of toilets on the Left Bank and toilets on the Right Bank. As this list suggests, Miller took particular delight in all that was unappetizing and macabre.

Miller's accounts of his first two months in Paris are full of enthusiasm. His feelings never changed, but the idyll soon ended. The troubles recorded in *Tropic of Cancer* were just beginning: the long walks to American Express for the check that never arrived, the constant change of address, the search for cheap hotels, soon followed by homelessness and hunger.

He had arrived with enough money to last him till the middle of April and with expectations that his wife would send more. By the latter part of April his money had run out, and he had to go without food for five days. Then he received a small amount, not enough to last long, for in early May he was penniless again and desperate enough to think of looking for a job. A week later he was solvent again, quoting prices and urging Schnellock to come to Paris where he would show him how to live on less than twenty-five dollars a week. Miller's standards were still fairly grand.

As his circumstances grew progressively worse, his notions of poverty became more realistic. In August he was living with Monsieur Nanavati, the Hindu he calls Mr. Nonentity in *Tropic of Cancer*, and complaining of his lot as a servant: "Life is very hard for me—very. I live with bed-bugs and cockroaches. I sweep the dirty carpets, wash the dishes, eat stale bread without butter. Terrible life. Honest!" After that his friend Alfred Perlès took care of Miller off and on, sneaking him past his concierge and hiding him in his hotel room; Perlès worked at night, so Miller could sleep in his bed then.

He became well acquainted with hunger and vagrancy and discovered that the climate was miserable most of the year. October was rainy and cold. June came for a visit, but she brought no money and stayed only three weeks under wretched circumstances. Miller began to realize that he could not live on hopes indefinitely and resigned himself to leaving before long. Several letters mentioned plans to return to New York. But he managed to hang on till December, when he found a friend who took him in for the winter. Then his constant obsession was food: "What we artists need is food—and lots more of it. No art without food." Phagomania, his chronic complaint, is as prominent as lust in *Tropic of Cancer*.

He spent the winter months in a studio with a view of the Eiffel Tower. Ten years later he dedicated *The Wisdom of the Heart* to the man who took him in, Richard Galen Osborn, "who rescued me from starvation in Paris and set my feet in the right direction." Osborn was a Connecticut Yankee who worked in a bank by day and indulged his fondness for French culture in all its forms by night. He liked to talk with Miller about modern French writers, he liked to drink Anjou, and he had a weakness for the ladies. One day he added a third member to the household, the Russian princess who appears in *Tropic of Cancer* as Masha. The book presents a fairly faithful portrait of their absurd *ménage à trois* based on a letter Miller wrote to Schnellock at the time: "Irene has the clap, Osborn has bronchitis, and I have the piles." The letter records Irene's dialogue for four pages, later reproduced almost verbatim when the episode was expanded into half a chapter. Osborn wrote his own story about their life together, "No. 2 Rue Auguste Bartholdi," presenting the same basic circumstances from another point of view and rather unexpectedly portraying Miller as a man who worked all the time.

In the same letter Miller described the full beard he grew that winter, a shaggy, dark red beard that would soon make him look like Dostoevsky. According to *Tropic of Cancer*, he grew the beard at the request of a painter, who then did his portrait with his typewriter in the foreground and the Eiffel Tower in the background. The painter was John Nichols, a great talker who regaled Miller with anecdotes about the artists he knew and who accompanied him to that favorite resort of painters, the Cirque Médrano, where they had "a fine Seurat night." Miller, who always sought the company of painters, acquired many artist friends in Paris. When Osborn had to give up the studio, Miller went off to stay with a sculptor, Fred Kann, who lived near the Montparnasse cemetery.

Nichols' portrait has vanished along with the beard, but a verbal portrait survives from about the same period in an article that appeared in the Paris edition of the *Chicago Tribune* with a caricature of Miller by the Hungarian artist Brassaï. The writer was an American newspaperman with the unlikely name of Wambly Bald who wrote a weekly column called "*La Vie de Bohème*." What he had to say was not particularly memorable, except as evidence that Miller was already a notorious character who in his daily life enacted the role he was about to turn into literature. The role came to him naturally; he was simply acting himself as a *clochard*, a Paris bum. He was of course fully aware of the impression he created and capable of exploiting it. He could even have ghost-written the article himself, for he often wrote Bald's weekly column; and certainly the man who wrote *Tropic of Cancer* was not above self-portraiture. Miller returned the compliment by depicting Bald—probably without the least malice—as his most scabrous character.

After a year in Paris Miller calculated that he could live on six dollars a week, if only he had it, but actually he was living on nothing at all. How he managed is explained by Alfred Perlès in *My Friend Henry Miller:* "Henry was always to be seen at one or the other of the terraces, the Dôme or the Coupole, surrounded by people he had just met or was just meeting. Impossible to say how he picked them up and where and why." After his first few months in Paris Miller had overcome his prejudices against the Montparnasse cafés, finding them good places to cadge food and drink. He had a great talent for making friends, and as he explains in *Tropic of Cancer*, "It's not hard to make friends when you squat on a *terrasse* twelve hours a day. You get to know every sot in Montparnasse. They cling to you like lice, even if you have nothing to offer them but your ears." Eventually he worked out a rotating dinner schedule with his friends, dining with a different friend every evening of the week. Sometimes he performed small services in exchange, giving English lessons or walking a child in the Luxembourg Gardens. But usually his friends were only too willing to feed him for the pleasure of his company. He was a most ingratiating person, a spellbinding talker, and a man of completely unaffected charm. Perlès observed that people loved to watch him eat and drink.

Miller did not begin writing *Tropic of Cancer* until the end of August 1931, but everything he experienced during that first year and a half in Paris went into the book as substance or style, the world's rottenness or his crazy hallucinated vision of it, that particular combination of "cancer and delirium" which gives the book its own very special atmosphere. By the time he began writing the book he had thoroughly explored the lower depths. What he had seen and heard would have depressed any other man beyond words; Miller was fully alive to it but buoyed up by his sense of humor, and because he had gone to rock bottom himself, elated that he had survived, more alive than ever. Then at last he succeeded in writing what had been bottled up inside him for so many years.

Toward the end of his first year in Paris he took stock of himself and his writing. To Schnellock he reported the opinions of friends who urged him to stay on: "I'm supposed to be a guy with promise. Besides that, I'm supposed to be a *romantic*. People wonder and shake their heads. How is it that things happen to that guy the way they do? Always in the midst of exciting things, adventures, confessions, etc. But the question in my mind is: what am I doing for literature?" He was still trying to finish the manuscript he had brought with him from New York, probably the novel called "Crazy Cock," but was disgusted with it, unable to express his true feelings, boxed in by too much careful plotting and form. When he finished he wanted to burst through all such barriers. "I will explode in the Paris book. The hell with form, style, expression and all those pseudo-paramount things which beguile the critics. I want to get myself across this time—and direct as a knife thrust." In another letter written about the same time he gloried in the life he was leading: "Great days—full of missing meals—but rich in paint, verbiage and local scenery. Getting into such a bummy condition that people everywhere nudge one another and point me out." Despite hunger and hardship he felt he had lived more richly during one year in Paris than in all the rest of his life. Here is the protagonist of *Tropic of Cancer:* "I feel now exactly as all the great vagabond artists must have felt—absolutely reckless, childish, irresponsible, unscrupulous, and overflowing with carnal vitality, vigor, ginger, etc. Always on the border of insanity, due to worry, hunger, etc. But shoving along, day after day."

Finally on August 24, 1931, having finished his novel at last, he announced that he was ready to go to work on the book he had been wanting to write: "I start tomorrow on the Paris book: first person, uncensored, formless–fuck everything!"

At the end of his second summer in Paris, Miller worked for a time as a proofreader for the Paris edition of the *Chicago Tribune*. His friend Perlès, who earned his small income as a proofreader, got him the job. Miller disapproved of jobs on principle but liked this one. He enjoyed the atmosphere of the newspaper office, the noise of the machinery, and the company of his fellow workers, especially the typesetters who were all like characters out of a French novel. Working at night had a charm all its own. Every evening he, Perlès, and Wambly Bald would make their long walk across Paris to the newspaper office. After work they would eat in a nearby bistro, the favorite haunt of pimps, whores, newspapermen, and others who worked by night. Then in the early morning hours, when all Paris was deserted, they would walk home again. Though Miller worked only a short time for the newspaper, the impressions of that time remained among the most vivid of his Paris years. Of the many writers and would-be writers who worked on the *Tribune* or the Paris edition of the *New York Herald*, only Miller and Bravig Imbs have given any sense of the atmosphere. Most of the journalists' accounts are full of sophomoric clichés.

Although Miller preferred the subterranean drudgery of proofreading to the more exalted editorial work upstairs, he was only too willing to be published in a newspaper, even anonymously or pseudonymously. Long before he was employed by the *Tribune* he wrote feature articles for that paper's Sunday edition. Only employees were supposed to contribute such articles, so Perlès submitted them as his own. In his biography Perlès reprints one of these articles, "Rue Lourmel in Fog," which is very much like the impressionistic compositions Miller had sent to Schnellock when he first arrived in Paris. Other articles appeared in the *Tribune* or in the *Herald* during his first year in Paris: "The Cirque Médrano," "The Six-Day Bike

Race," "Paris in *Ut Mineur.*" The usual rate was fifty francs, and once Miller received three hundred and fifty francs, but the important thing was that he was getting his work published readily for the first time in his life. He had tried to write for newspapers and popular magazines in the past, but with no success.

During his second year in Paris Miller's work also appeared in a literary magazine for the first time, Samuel Putnam's recently founded *New Review*. Putnam was a scholarly newspaper correspondent who had come to Paris in 1926 to translate Rabelais. Besides the standard modern translation of that difficult author, he produced translations of contemporary authors ranging from François Mauriac to Kiki. For all his mastery of the written language, Putnam spoke French with such an abominable accent as to be almost unintelligible. He was a steady customer of the Montparnasse bars, where Miller probably met him about the time he quit as associate editor of *This Quarter* and decided to found his own quarterly. Miller appeared twice in the *New Review* and edited one issue with Perlès. Putnam made the mistake of asking them to see the magazine through the press when he had to go to America for a visit. They promptly threw out some of the contents they found boring, including a long article by Putnam, and put in material they thought livelier, including a story by Miller. They also decided to add a supplement, a bawdy, vituperative, nonsensical parody of all manifestoes called "The New Instinctivism," denouncing everything: "A proclamation of rebellion against the puerilities of art and literature, a manifesto of disgust, a gob of spit in the cuspidor of post-war conceits, a healthy crap in the cradle of still-born deities." When the printers sent proofs to Putnam, he quashed the supplement, but the review appeared with the contents Miller and Perlès had chosen.

Miller first appeared in the *New Review* as a film critic. The second number, which came out in the summer of 1931, included his review entitled "Buñuel or Thus Cometh to an End Everywhere the Golden Age." Miller, who had been a cineast since childhood, was delighted to be in Paris where he could see avant-garde films that were never shown in New York. On the first Sunday after his arrival he had made a pilgrimage to Studio 28 in Montmartre to see one of the great surrealist films, *Un Chien Andalou,* made by Buñuel in collaboration with Dali the previous year. A week or so later he went to a ciné club meeting and was impressed by the brilliant discussion. By October 1930 he had made friends with the film maker Germaine Dulac, who promised June an important role in a talkie that was to be made in two or three months; nothing ever came of this proposal, and Madame Dulac, whom Miller described as "one of the celebrated Lesbiennes of Paris and all Europe," may have had only a passing interest in June. Toward the end of October he saw the new Buñuel-Dali film, *L'Age d'Or,* and in December he sent Schnellock a draft of his article for the *New Review.* His admiration for Buñuel never diminished. In the mid-thirties he paid tribute to him again in a long article on the cinematic art entitled "The Golden Age." Less explicit but even more pervasive is the influence of Buñuel's films on certain surrealist sequences in Miller's writing, particularly "Into the Night Life" in *Black Spring.*

Miller's first published story, "Mademoiselle Claude," appeared in the third number of the *New Review* in the fall of 1931. That story marks the actual beginning of his literary career, announcing all the characteristics of the *Tropics*—the first person monologue, the progressive narrative moving into the present tense, with events happening and time passing as the story unfurls. Here too are the tropical moral values—the generous whore who is almost an angel, the narrator-*maquereau* who wants to be a saint. He finds her customers to keep her from being sad, and they end up going to the clinic together every day, more in love than ever. Even the imagery is here: "Paris looks to me like a big, ugly chancre. The streets are gangrened. Everybody has it—if it isn't clap it's syphilis. All Europe is diseased, and it's France who's made it diseased."

The style anticipates *Tropic of Cancer* with its flowing

rhythms: "The idea, though, of waking up in the morning, the sun streaming in the windows and a good, faithful whore beside you who loves you, who loves the guts out of you, the birds singing and the table all spread, and while she's washing up and combing her hair, all the men she's been with and now you, just you, and barges going by, masts and hulls, the whole damned current of life flowing through you, through her, through all the guys before you and maybe after, the flowers and the birds and the sun streaming in and the fragrance of it choking you, annihilating you. O Christ! Give me a whore always, all the time!" Miller liked that long sentence well enough to quote part of it in *Tropic of Cancer.*

Miller was fascinated by the Paris whores. On his first Sunday in Paris he had noted with surprise: "Montmartre is simply lousy with whores. Little bars, hardly bigger than a coffin, are jammed with them." The imagery is typical, if not the reaction. "Wow! they make you shiver those dolled-up spectres. They sit in the cafés and beckon to you from the window, or bunk smack up against you on the street, and invite you to come along." By May he had found his first girl friend, a whore named Germaine. In December he wrote, "And who is Mlle. Claude? Ah, the prettiest, juiciest, cleverest little cocotte in Montparnasse. Osborn and I share her once in a while. Such taste, such discretion, such politesse." He found her intelligent, well-read, animated, and refined. He recommended her to Schnellock, who could address her in care of the Coupole. Though the letter ends half-humorously, sounding like an advertisement, Claude is described in similar terms in *Tropic of Cancer,* but compared unfavorably with that ordinary hustler Germaine, who according to the book, served as the real model for the story. "She was a whore all the way through," Miller concludes, "and that was her virtue!"

By the time "Mademoiselle Claude" appeared in print Miller had started writing *Tropic of Cancer.* He had already met most of the characters and had most of the experiences that went into the narrative. But there is more to that book than mere storytelling; *Tropic of Cancer* dramatizes a particular outlook, a satiric blend of humor and iconoclasm, a fiercely critical view of the world. In the fall of 1931 Miller was being exposed to some of the ideas that gave the book its philosophical bias. He then lived for a time with Michael Fraenkel, a prophet of doom whose theories appear in the first two chapters and elsewhere. On the opening page Miller summarizes Fraenkel's death philosophy, complete with Fraenkel's favorite weather metaphor.

> Boris has just given me a summary of his views. He is a weather prophet. The weather will continue bad, he says. There will be more calamities, more death, more despair. Not the slightest indication of a change anywhere. The cancer of time is eating us away. Our heroes have killed themselves, or are killing themselves. The hero, then, is not Time, but Timelessness. We must get in step, a lock step, toward the prison of death. There is no escape. The weather will not change.

There is usually a note of ridicule in Miller's treatment of Fraenkel's ideas, but he also admits that Fraenkel is one of the two writers he respects, the other being Perlès. The reason he takes them seriously is that, unlike other writers he knows, these two have fervor. "They are possessed. They glow inwardly with a white flame. They are mad and tone deaf. They are sufferers."

Fraenkel was a small intense man with a goatee who bore a marked resemblance to Trotsky. Born in Russia and brought to the United States as a boy, he became the greatest book salesman in America and saved enough money to retire at the age of thirty in 1926. He had always wanted to write, and Paris seemed the best place for a writer to go. His writing was the product of a philosophical mind obsessed with one subject, the spiritual death of modern man as symbolized by the millions of deaths of the Great War. His friend Walter Lowenfels plays upon the central paradox of Fraenkel's life in an unpublished biographical sketch, "The Life of Fraenkel's Death," pointing out that Fraenkel earned his living in America so that he could retire in Europe to write about death.

Lowenfels himself followed a similar pattern. He too had been in business in America, the family butter business which he later treated as something of a joke, contrasting butter with poetry, and which he quit at the age of twenty-nine, having decided to go to Europe to write. His ideas were akin to Fraenkel's, though not nearly so extreme. At the time they became friends he had just finished an elegy on Apollinaire. Under the influence of Fraenkel he then took death as his central theme and wrote a sequence of elegies called *Some Deaths*, lamenting the suicides of poets such as Hart Crane and Harry Crosby, René Crevel and Jacques Rigaut. Fraenkel and Lowenfels also formed what they called an anonymous school, writing books together anonymously in the spirit of French writers and painters before them. In *Tropic of Cancer* Miller jokes about an anonymous collaboration proposed by Fraenkel, to be called "The Last Book," and some years later Miller and Fraenkel actually did collaborate on a book, the *Hamlet* correspondence, which was published by Fraenkel's Carrefour Press.

Miller became acquainted with Fraenkel about the time he started writing *Tropic of Cancer*. Lowenfels and Fraenkel had already been in league for two years or more. Now the three of them formed what Lowenfels calls "the avant-garde of death." Neither he nor Miller took Fraenkel's monomania altogether seriously. "Henry and I really joked about Fraenkel's death business—turning it into something else, something we could use in our business, which was, say what you like, writing." Fraenkel was useful to Miller in more immediate ways, for he owned an apartment building at 18 Villa Seurat and was better off than Miller's other friends. A number of people have claimed an influence on Miller when he was still unknown, but their most important contribution at this time was keeping him alive. This was Lowenfels' motive in bringing Miller and Fraenkel together, this and Fraenkel's need for an intelligent audience, which was as great as Miller's need for bed and board.

The Miller-Fraenkel relationship was a strange and amusing one, founded on phagomania and the death obsession and kept alive by talk. Both men were prodigious talkers. Miller remembers that Fraenkel used to drop in at breakfast time, stay through lunch, through dinner, and far into the evening, talking, talking all the time, leaving Miller exhausted. Fraenkel in turn was overwhelmed by Miller's talk. "It was extraordinary, amazing, incredible. A compulsion mechanism, a kind of sickness, if you like, something pathological." But he also adds, "It was talk of the highest order I ever heard." Though by nature stingy and indifferent to food, Fraenkel would occasionally buy Miller a meal just to be able to keep talking. In *Tropic of Cancer* Miller complains that there is not a scrap of food in the house. He also registers a feeling of impermanence, fearing his chair will be pulled out from under him as he types. Fraenkel, ever the businessman, rented out apartments and soon evicted Miller by renting the room he occupied. Miller liked the Villa Seurat and returned there to live three years later; meanwhile his discussions with Fraenkel continued and turned into correspondence when Fraenkel traveled about the world.

Years later, in an article entitled "The Genesis of the *Tropic of Cancer*," Fraenkel reminisced about the beginning of their acquaintance: "And then one day Walter told me about a strange man he had run across in Montparnasse, a fellow called Miller. He was described as one of tremendous vitality, zest, enthusiasm, an amazing talker, without visible means of support, a kind of derelict, but gay and happy withal, alive. 'Not alive exactly,' he said, 'but certainly not dead. Alive in a kind of confused, old-fashioned way. An interesting chap. Why not drop him a line, a *pneu?* He is down and out and maybe he can do some typing for you.' And then with a twinkle in his eye: 'Take him on. Just your meat.' Did he perhaps see a possible disciple in him?" According to Fraenkel there were no preliminaries between them, no reservations; they immediately talked to each other like old friends. Fraenkel gave Miller his book *Werther's Younger Brother*, a self-portrait ending in suicide. Miller responded with a long enthusiastic fan letter which Fraenkel quotes: "You say things that no one in America is saying—that I would dearly love to say myself." Miller, who had been told that Fraenkel's book was pessimistic and confused, "found everything touched with a wild beauty, and if there were disorder, then it was, as Bergson said, an order of disorder which is another order."

Though Fraenkel claims too much credit for his influence on *Tropic of Cancer*, he gives the best explanation on record of Miller's state of mind at the time. And though he was only the latest in a series of friends to advise Miller to write spontaneously, his insight may have been the clearest. Certainly his advice was most timely. Beneath Miller's restless confusion Fraenkel detected a determination to be himself. Miller had come to Paris to make a new start but had not yet found himself. When Fraenkel read Miller's novel in manuscript, "Crazy Cock," he immediately saw that Miller was trying to write for the publishers, not for himself. "By this time I knew the sort of person he was, impulsive, erratic, anarchic, a mass of contradictory moods, ideas, feelings, and I told him to sit down before the machine and white paper and write anything and everything that came to his mind, as it came, red-hot, and to hell with the editors and the public. Write as you talk, I told him. Write as you live. Write as you feel and think. Just sit down before the machine and let go—tell everything you are going through now; you've got all the material you want right in this, in what you are thinking and feeling and going through *now*."

As they talked endlessly of death, Miller found the theme that could integrate his creative impulses and give him the direction he lacked. His obscenity, his violence, his inner chaos, and love of corruption are all expressions of "The Death Theme." So Fraenkel thought at any rate, though at times his disciples may have had their little joke at his expense. Lowenfels wonders whether the Fraenkel they remember is not a creature of their imagination. He feels that Fraenkel did not come through very well in his own writing. A greater thinker than writer, he left more of himself in the writings of others, in Miller's early work and Lowenfels' poems written between 1929 and 1934. Lowenfels also remarks that Fraenkel was at his best when writing under the stimulus of Miller. No doubt they inspired each other, but long before he met Fraenkel, Miller was steeped in the thinking of Oswald Spengler, whose apocalyptic view he had taken as his own. Miller had in fact reread the first volume of *The Decline of the West* since coming to Paris and in doing so had concluded that Spengler was the greatest of contemporary writers, greater than Joyce, Mann, or even Proust. "There is great music, great literature, great ideas." Surely his thinking in *Tropic of Cancer* was fired by Spengler, though Fraenkel undoubtedly fanned the flames.

The book that most immediately anticipated *Tropic of Cancer* was Louis-Ferdinand Céline's first novel, *Voyage au Bout de la Nuit*. Not only the Spenglerian sense of doom is there, but the very idiom and tone, the picaresque narrative and the gallows humor that Miller adopted. Céline's *Voyage* is another episodic autobiographical novel that dwells on all that is vicious, treacherous, sadistic, obscene, diseased, and repulsive in human nature. The central character is an underdog adventurer who lives by luck and by his wits. Céline's favorite setting is the ugly, working-class Paris where he was born and where he practiced medicine, though he also traveled about the world like Candide, finding inhumanity wherever he went. His experience eventually drove him to bitter misanthropy, but his first book achieved a balance between laughter and pessimism that is much the same as Miller's comic treatment of inherently tragic matter. After reading *Voyage au Bout de la Nuit* it is easier to understand *Tropic of Cancer*, for Céline's war experience exposes the "civilization" that both writers attacked. Céline lost his innocence in the Great War, suffered shell shock, was cured of his illusions, learned to distrust all ideals and to place the law of self-preservation above all others. Miller, despite his imagery of trench warfare and poison gas, had no direct experience to compare with Céline's, yet he had gone through the same process of disenchantment, emerging with even fewer scruples. He too had become a militant anarchist, declaring war on society.

Despite the many striking parallels between the two books, Céline and Miller produced their works quite independently. Miller had finished the first draft of *Tropic of Cancer* before the publication of *Voyage au Bout de la Nuit* in November 1932. He read the book soon after it appeared and was overwhelmed, although he found it difficult reading and had to spend a week isolated in a hotel room with a dictionary to decipher its colloquial French. During the next two years he was to revise his own book three times before it appeared in print, so conceivably Céline could have influenced the rewriting. But the letters to Schnellock reveal that Miller had found his style and subject matter before he had ever heard of Céline. It was simply another case of two writers responding to their time and place with the same perceptions.

Like Céline's novel, *Tropic of Cancer* is autobiographical, but it is not to be taken as documentary. Although Miller protests that he is writing the plain unvarnished truth, this gambit is one of the oldest in fiction. He is closer to fact than most novelists, but his method is theirs, his powerful imagination producing a metamorphosis as it colors and heightens the original circumstances. Miller has confessed that he has difficulty remembering what he imagined and what actually happened.

Tropic of Cancer gives a more or less fictionalized account, then, of the adventures of a character named Henry Miller who explored the lower depths in Paris during the depression. The book is a jumble of sensations, reflections, conversations, encounters, and hallucinations, all filtered through the consciousness of its narrator in the first person, present tense. The chaos is deliberate, for Miller wanted to put down impressions and thoughts as they occurred to him, to depict a man "in the grip of delirium." He also wanted "to get off the gold standard of literature," to write without revising, and to record "all that which is omitted in books."

Tropic of Cancer is sometimes compared to *The Sun Also Rises*, not for the similarities but for the differences between them. The comparison is absurd yet apt, for it shows how much the world had changed between the mid-twenties and the early thirties. Henry Miller's adventures in Paris present a burlesque of the expatriate romance. Instead of a potentially tragic hero, the protagonist is a clown whose escapades mock all sense of human dignity. Instead of investing his characters with a glamour that excuses their faults, Miller caricatures his friends, bringing out all that is grotesque, ludicrous, or contemptible in their private lives. He also sees his surroundings in a jaundiced light and thereby makes more meaningful use of his Paris scenery. For Hemingway Montparnasse provided an appropriate backdrop, a likely setting for the lost generation, but his characters stayed on the surface and could just as well have dissipated elsewhere. Miller penetrated far deeper into Paris than any other American writer and projected a vision of the city that was altogether different. He succeeded only as Céline had done in making its ugliness symbolic of private and universal anguish, a sordid modern-day inferno, a labyrinth of cancer and despair.

15.

Epitaph for a Generation

Much of *Tropic of Cancer* is lived in cafés and hotels, the usual setting of the expatriate life. But the book also has a more permanent background in certain neighborhoods. During his first year in Paris Miller found his natural habitat in the Fourteenth *Arrondissement*, the district back of the Boulevard Montparnasse where many artists lived. The location was handy to the American cafés when he had to scout for meals and small loans; Perlès, who was always ready to put him up, lived in a hotel there; Fraenkel and Lowenfels also lived in the vicinity, as did others who fed him regularly. Miller often went to other sections of Paris for food and lodging, but he always returned to the *Quatorzième*.

This lower middle class quarter was the Parisian equivalent of the Fourteenth Ward of Brooklyn, where he had lived as a boy. Completely off the beaten track, it has none of the glamour usually associated with Paris, though most of the city is in fact like the Fourteenth *Arrondissement*, commonplace, monotonous, rather ugly. To Miller it was "an awfully genuine, homely neighborhood," as he wrote to Schnellock during his first year in Paris, and he felt at ease among its inhabitants. "Everyone knows me, likes me, treats me like a Prince. Drinks are cheap, life flows leisurely, no intellectual slush, just kind honest folk." This was always to be the Paris of Miller and his friends, a provincial backwater somewhat removed from Montparnasse and the bright lights. Better than any other Americans, they knew the everyday life of the petit bourgeois and the proletariat. Being poor themselves, they wanted a cheap place to live and a quiet place to work.

Actually Miller's first real home in Paris was across the city at the foot of Montmartre. During his first two years he had no fixed abode but lived with one friend after another. He spent the first two months of 1932 in Dijon as an English teacher at the Lycée Carnot. The job provided room and board but no salary and no comforts; in *Tropic of Cancer* Miller describes the institution in terms that suggest Cummings' Enormous Room rather than a boarding school. Once again Perlès bailed him out, finding him another job at the *Tribune*, and in March 1932, shortly after Miller's return to Paris both moved into a small apartment at 4 Avenue Anatole France in Clichy. Perlès evidently paid the rent, for Miller's job at the *Tribune* did not last long. Anaïs Nin, who visited them when they had just moved in, described the apartment in her diary: "A few pans, unmatched dishes from the flea market, old shirts for kitchen towels. Tacked on the walls, a list of books to get, a list of menus to eat in the future, clippings, reproductions, and water colors of Henry's. Henry keeps house like a Dutch housekeeper. He is very neat and clean. No dirty dishes about. It is all monastic, really, with no trimmings, no decorations." The apartment was plain and bare, but it was home. The neighborhood was a grimmer version of the Fourteenth *Arrondissement*, a working-class quarter with plenty of sordid bars, yet it suited them perfectly.

Miller still remembers the two years he lived in Clichy as the best in his life. "When I think about this period," he wrote in *Quiet Days in Clichy*, "it seems like a stretch in Paradise. . . . even though the world was busy digging its grave, there was still time to enjoy life, to be merry, carefree, to work or not to work." With his living problem solved, he was free to write, and he went at it with prodigious energy. Perlès remembers the clatter he made, typing at high speed, and Miller himself recalls that one day he turned out forty-five pages. In a furious creative outburst he began working on four or five books at once, finishing *Tropic of Cancer*, beginning *Black Spring*, *Tropic of Capricorn*, a book on Lawrence that he never completed, and enough shorter pieces to fill at least one volume. At the same time he was painting water colors to illustrate his writings. These and other activities are outlined in his wall charts for the period. Miller liked to pin lists and memoranda on the walls: "Get old manifestoes of Dada and Surrealism, Steal Good Books from American Library, Write Automatically." His charts outlined works in progress, enumerating themes and topics to be written about and further research to be done. They admonished him to follow a daily work schedule and to carry out his projects in a disciplined way. Some of his eleven commandments seem rather contradictory:

> 3. Don't be nervous. Work calmly, joyously, recklessly on whatever is in hand.
> 4. Work according to Program and not according to mood. Stop at the appointed time!
> 7. Keep human! See people, go places, drink if you feel like it.
> 11. Write first and always. Painting, music, friends, cinema, all these come afterwards.

Miller's wall charts suggest that he worked all the time, while his writings create the impression that he did nothing but play. In Clichy he was somehow able to do both.

Those who claim to have influenced Miller in the thirties tend to speak slightingly of Alfred Perlès, dismissing him as a hanger-on. Miller himself has always given Perlès a central role in his Paris years. Perlès was not only his benefactor, sharing whatever he had, and his greatest friend, with whom he found most in common, but also an insidious influence. "He is right under my skin," Miller wrote many years later in his notes to

The Henry Miller Reader, and elsewhere in the same collection he commented that Perlès "had quite a hand" in the final draft of *Tropic of Cancer*. In the book itself he went even further, stating on one of its opening pages, "I am writing this for my friend Carl," that being the name he gave Perlès in his fictionalized narratives.

As a writer no one could have been further removed from Miller. "Fred has a finesse which I lack, the quality of an Anatole France," Miller once remarked to Anaïs Nin, who understood Miller's gifts better than he did at the time, and who contrasted the two writers in her diary. Perlès was a subtle ironist who wrote in three languages, but it was not his writing that influenced Miller. Rather it was his character that provided Miller with a point of view that he could use in his writings, a mixture of cynicism, bravado, and buffoonery. Perlès was born to be a Miller character, a rogue and clown who lived marginally by his wits. A castaway of the Austro-Hungarian Empire, the bearer of a Czechoslovakian passport, he had managed to save his skin during the war—evidently by some discreditable ruse—and afterward had gravitated to Paris via all the capitals of Europe. In his portrait of Perlès in "Remember to Remember" Miller notes that his friend seldom talked about his past. Nevertheless the sense of futility engendered by the war played a large part in his outlook. Fundamentally Perlès was a dadaist.

Another writer who played a major role in Miller's life at this time was Anaïs Nin. Like Perlès she came from another world. A cultivated cosmopolite, she had much to teach him but much to learn as well. They met through Richard Osborn in the fall of 1931, began by exchanging works in manuscript, soon became more involved when Miller's histrionic wife June appeared on the scene, entangling them in a feverish romance *à trois*, and started corresponding intensively when Miller went to Dijon. In the opening pages of her published diary, which begins that winter, Anaïs Nin presents herself as a kind of Emma Bovary living in a romantic village outside of Paris. Fond of role-playing, she led a triple life as the gracious lady of Louveciennes, the Bohemian writer, and the psychoanalyst's apprentice. Fond of intrigue, she was fascinated by June, whom she found "the most beautiful woman on earth," but in the long run found more to admire in Miller. In December 1932, when June returned to Paris, rendering Miller's life impossible, it was Anaïs Nin who provided him with the money to make his escape to England, an experience he recounted in one of his funniest narratives, "Via Dieppe-Newhaven."

Married to an American banker, Anaïs Nin could afford to be Miller's patroness. She frequently helped him out with small gifts, later underwrote the publication of *Tropic of Cancer*, and eventually rented an apartment for him in the Villa Seurat. Miller admired her as a writer and as a clairvoyante—"*un être étoilique*," as he called her in an article about her voluminous diary, using her own word, coined by analogy to "*lunatique*." He was enormously impressed by her diary, an endless labyrinth which he compared to the writings of Proust, and he regarded the diary as a form that would replace the novel—like his own autobiographical narratives. Miller's letters to Anaïs Nin also show how much he relied on her for advice and criticism. Humble and anxious to learn, he turned to her as his chief literary mentor.

Better than any other source, his letters to her record the everyday facts about the most creative period of his life. His letters from Dijon, for example, not only describe the circumstances behind two chapters in *Tropic of Cancer* but register his response to French culture. Miller had long been in love with the language, but this was the first time he had lived completely in French. At the same time he was reading Proust, which she had lent him, and falling under the spell of the written language. "Proust is going to my head," he wrote. "I am nearing the end of the first volume and have deliberately stopped reading because I want to ration my enjoyment and my suffering." He was reading in a big café with an orchestra playing and people talking all around him, yet he had no trouble concentrating on the involuted style. Proust was one of the authors he absorbed with the sense that the writing was addressed directly to him. "The man seems to take the words out of my mouth, to rob me of my very own experiences, sensations, reflections, introspections, suspicions, sadness, torture, etc. etc. etc."

After Miller's return from Dijon, Anaïs Nin noted in her diary, "With me he explores the symphonies of Proust, the intelligence of Gide, Cocteau's fantasies, Valéry's silences, the illuminations of Rimbaud." With the exception of Rimbaud, Miller was already acquainted with these writers, for he had introduced Osborn to them the year before. But it was one thing to read French authors in translation, as Miller had done in New York during the twenties, and another to examine their subtleties with a woman who was thoroughly at home with the language and culture. For an autodidact who read avidly but erratically, such a teacher could fill in the gaps from her more sophisticated background. Under her tutelage he deepened his understanding of French literature. It was already broad, and critics have cited Rabelais, Villon, Rousseau, Sade, Restif de la Bretonne, Rimbaud, Lautréamont, and others as sources for *Tropic of Cancer*. Disconcertingly, Miller has announced that he had not read most of his sources before writing the book, but the critics could reply that he wrote in the tradition of the *poètes maudits*, whether he had read them or not. Miller's reading remains full of surprises. In the fifties he confessed that he had not yet read Restif de la Bretonne or managed to "wade through" Rousseau's *Confessions*, though he had tried several times. He feels a particular affinity for Balzac, Rimbaud, Cendrars, and Giono, none of whom had any significant influence on his own writing. To this day he admits that he cannot read the Marquis de Sade.

Apart from Céline and Proust, the French writers Miller most resembles are the dadaists and surrealists. But here again influence appears dubious. "I was writing Surrealistically in

America before I had ever heard the word," Miller declares in "An Open Letter to Surrealists Everywhere," and in *Tropic of Capricorn*, which chronicles his life in the early twenties, he states, "I was perhaps the unique Dadaist in America, and I didn't know it." Nevertheless he became more immediately aware of surrealism upon his arrival in Paris, and more susceptible in the presence of Anaïs Nin. Her diary reflects a preoccupation with dreams and fantasies, analyzed in the light of surrealism, psychoanalysis, and astrology—the kind of thinking that increasingly fascinated Miller. An entry for April 1932 records that she has begun writing surrealistically under the influence of *Transition*, Breton, and Rimbaud. The work she wrote was her autobiographical *House of Incest*, which "directly inspired" Miller's "Scenario," according to his own prefatory acknowledgment. The resemblance is hard to find, but both writers were concerned with the problem of adapting film techniques in writing dream scenarios, and both works present a sequence of surrealistic visions.

Although Anaïs Nin frequently contrasted her dreams and illusions with Miller's harshly realistic writing, she also saw that he had a great deal in common with the surrealists. In her diary she observed that like Breton he believed in freedom from all restraints, "to write as one thinks, in the order and disorder in which one feels and thinks, to follow sensations and absurd correlations of events and images." He too believed in the cult of the marvelous, of mystery, of the unconscious, in "an effort to transcend the rigidities and patterns made by the rational mind." Along with her he was attracted to the improvisation, madness, and chaos of the dadaists and surrealists. At the same time he was living on an all too realistic plane. He took her out of her enchanted garden down into the streets, introducing her to a life which she had only read about in *Bubu de Montparnasse*. While she never escaped from her introspection, Miller made the best of both worlds in his writing, allowing his imagination to rampage, yet remaining firmly anchored in reality.

Black Spring, dedicated to Anaïs Nin and datelined "Louveciennes;–Clichy;–Villa Seurat. 1934–1935," was his major work of the Clichy period. While obviously written by the same hand, this book is quite different from *Tropic of Cancer*, less violent and obscene, more euphoric. Though the materials are basically autobiographical, the method is not narrative; instead of character and episode, Miller presents a series of monologues, meditations, reminiscences, dreams, and visions, shifting back and forth from his Paris surroundings to his early years in Brooklyn and New York. Composed in ten independent sections, the book was nonetheless conceived as a whole and developed through a process of organic growth. Underlying its chaotic variety in style and technique is a coherence of theme and symbol. Organization, structure, discipline was always Miller's biggest problem. His wall charts for the early thirties show how he labored to organize his materials; most of his "Major Program" is a detailed outline of the multifarious elements that went into *Black Spring*.

Miller began writing that book about the beginning of May 1932 and was absorbed in it during the next two years. He may have originally thought of it as an autobiography, for its title was to be "Self-Portrait." In June 1933 he decided to incorporate a "dream book" he had been keeping, and in February 1934 he decided to make this section the climax of the entire work, using the dreams to recapitulate its major themes. By April 1934 he had finished a version of the book, still called "Self-Portrait," which Anaïs Nin took to London when she went in search of a publisher for his books. But he went on adding, rearranging, and revising long after. During the thirties he was forever rewriting and reorganizing, never satisfied with his work.

Black Spring reveals none of his labor. The writing seems completely spontaneous, the language prodigal and exuberant, the imagination rampant, giving the impression that Miller was elated all the time he worked. This euphoria seems to be the mood of Clichy, and the book is full of local scenery: Sacré

Coeur up on the hill, the Gare Saint-Lazare, the cemetery, the red-light district. Clichy is Céline country, but the book has none of Céline's ferocity or disgust. Miller lists plenty of horrors, only to forget them immediately, so that the theme of impending doom in the title is never taken seriously. Miller is in a mellow mood, sitting in the Place Clichy in the sunshine or cycling along the Seine on the outskirts of Paris. He is closer to Proust in his vivid recollections of childhood and to the surrealists in his dreams and "grand obsessional walks" around Montmartre.

Two sections of the book are particularly surrealistic, "The Angel Is My Watermark" and "Into the Night Life." The first begins with "the dictation," a demonic seizure that possesses Miller so that he becomes merely a passive instrument, a hand that writes down what is transmitted. Like the surrealists Miller believes that the best writing comes from such subconscious outpouring, the source of his most inspired virtuoso passages. In painting too he demonstrates the role of improvisation, retracing the steps in producing a water color. The process illustrates surrealist theory and practice: creation on impulse, the element of chance, the proximity between art and madness. "Into the Night Life" deals with the dream world. Miller had been recording his dreams for some time when he realized that he could use them in *Black Spring*. In this instance he made a deliberate decision to write surrealistically, as the subject demanded, and to produce a scenario, since the cinema was the best medium for surrealism.

Miller was really a self-made surrealist, a primitive who had been working in the same vein before he came upon Breton's movement. In "An Open Letter to Surrealists Everywhere," he wrote, "Scarcely anything has been as stimulating to me as the theories and the products of the surrealists." Yet he instinctively distrusted the sterile dogmatism of the surrealist movement and always showed a marked preference for dada. *Black Spring* is full of parodies and puns, zany free associations and digressions, anarchy and irreverence. Miller in a comic mood is constantly running off the rails.

> To prognosticate this reality is to be off either by a millimeter or by a million light years. The difference is a quantum formed by the intersection of streets. A quantum is a functional disorder created by trying to squeeze oneself into a frame of reference. A reference is a discharge from an old employer, that is to say, a mucopus from an old disease.

"Jabberwhorl Cronstadt" is dadaistic from start to drunken finish, a parody of nonsensical language that begins: "He lives in the back of a sunken garden, a sort of bosky glade shaded by whiffletrees and spinozas, by deodars and baobabs, a sort of queasy Buxtehude diapered with elytras and feluccas." "Burlesk" is a ragout of phrases and styles taken from a sign in a bar, a Dutchman's letter, a Negro church service, the pitchman's spiel at Minsky's, and all kinds of learned jargon. Miller's gift for pedantic nonsense later reached its highest expression in *Money and How It Gets That Way*, a treatise written in such impeccable jargon that economists have been known to take it seriously. This dada masterpiece was dedicated to Ezra Pound, who in the thirties became obsessed with economic theories. In a postcard commending *Tropic of Cancer* Pound had remarked that Miller had not pondered the question: "What IS money? who makes it/ how does it get that way?///"

Miller left Clichy early in February 1934 and spent the next seven months at various addresses. Then on September 1, 1934, he moved into an apartment at 18 Villa Seurat that was to be his home for the remainder of his stay in Paris. Though surrounded by a rather slummy neighborhood, the Villa Seurat was more like a prosperous suburban street, a quiet impasse with plenty of light and air between the houses. The residents were mostly successful artists who liked their comfort. Anaïs

Nin rented a top-floor studio apartment for Miller in Fraenkel's old house at the end of the street.

Here, she remarked, he had begun writing *Tropic of Cancer*, and now at last, four years later, the book appeared in print on the day he returned. During the next few months Miller kept busy sending the book around to various writers, nervously awaiting their response, watching for reviews, checking the bookstores to see how it was selling. On the whole the writers received it favorably, the book sold slowly but steadily, and Miller gradually became known. The most gratifying response came from Blaise Cendrars, who not only gave the book its first review but came to call, treated Miller to a feast, and praised him publicly, insisting that the book must be translated into French since it belonged to the great Catholic and Rabelaisian tradition of France. Miller was speechless for once in his life, embarrassed in the presence of this writer he so admired. Cendrars's review, written about Christmas, begins, "Unto us is born an American writer," shows a hearty appreciation of Miller's Paris, and concludes that "this book springs from our soil, and Henry Miller is one of us, in spirit, in style, in his power and in his gifts, a universal writer like all those who have been able to put into a book their own vision of Paris."

The Villa Seurat became the headquarters for a circle of friends who gathered around Miller, most of them writers or painters. Besides Fraenkel, Perlès, and Anaïs Nin, the group included Betty Ryan, an American painter who lived downstairs; David Edgar, "the most lovable neurotic America ever produced," who specialized in a mixture of psychology and theosophy; the German painter Hans Reichel, described in "The Cosmological Eye" as a mad visionary; and Conrad Moricand, an impoverished Swiss astrologer. Another friend was the Hungarian photographer Brassaï, who appears anonymously in *Tropic of Cancer* as Miller's guide to some of the most sordid neighborhoods, and whom Miller celebrated in "The Eye of Paris." Lawrence Durrell, the English writer living in Greece, had begun an enormous correspondence with Miller in 1935 and became a member of the circle in 1937. All in all, they represented an odd assortment, the flotsam and jetsam of international society, with neither a true Frenchman nor an orthodox American among them.

During the later thirties the Villa Seurat became the headquarters for several publishing ventures. Perlès, who had been editing a monthly bulletin called *The Booster* for the American Country Club of Paris, found himself out of a job and in possession of the magazine one day. Without changing its name he altered its character entirely by recruiting Miller and Durrell as associate editors and chief contributors along with himself. The result was the zaniest of all little magazines, with dada manifestoes and mastheads, "boosts" for all and sundry, some serious writing, but mostly bawdy nonsense. The president of the country club soon disassociated himself from the magazine, but the editors managed to keep it going for six issues between September 1937 and Easter 1939, the last three appearing as *Delta.* A more serious venture was the Villa Seurat Library, a series of books edited by Miller. Only three titles were published: Durrell's *Black Book*, Miller's *Max and the White Phagocytes*, and Anaïs Nin's *Winter of Artifice.*

During the latter thirties Miller began to discover that his work as editor and literary agent could be a full-time job. As he became better known, the demands on his time increased, and much of his energy went into correspondence about various schemes, often to help others. His life was more stable now than it had been during his earlier years in Paris, and he had the satisfaction of being a writer at last, but he found that he had far less time for writing. His major project during these years was *Tropic of Capricorn,* a book he had been struggling with since 1932. In his letters to Durrell he frequently mentioned it but only to say it was not yet finished. Finally in August 1938 he announced that he had reached the end, though the revising remained to be done. Miller was always a digressive writer, but *Tropic of Capicorn* is more disconnected than most of his books, creating the impression that he was constantly distracted during the writing. The book contains some brilliant passages, which by their discontinuity indicate where he sat down to write and where he left off. In *Big Sur and the Oranges of Hieronymus Bosch* he gives an amusing account of "the dictation" of *Tropic of Capricorn*, protesting that the most obscene passages were not his idea at all, that he had no choice but to set them down as dictated. "I didn't have to think up so much as a comma or a semicolon; it was all given, straight from the celestial recording room. Weary, I would beg for a break, an intermission, time enough, let's say, to go to the toilet or take a breath of fresh air on the balcony. Nothing doing! I had to take it in one fell swoop or risk the penalty: excommunication."

Memories of those years in the Villa Seurat are scattered throughout *Big Sur and the Oranges of Hieronymus Bosch*. Written twenty lears later, this is in part an account of Conrad Moricand's disastrous visit to Big Sur, an event which naturally reminded Miller of their earlier encounters. He looked back on his years in Paris as the best of his life and those in the Villa Seurat as the most serene. Under Moricand's influence perhaps, he dwelt on the astrologic side of experience, his dreams, his chance encounters, his horoscope, his nature as a Capricorn. Among other things, the Capricorn is an ambulatory paranoiac, as Miller demonstrates once again in describing his walks around the outlying regions beyond the Fourteenth *Arrondissement*. These morning constitutionals, which were supposed to relax him for the long hours of typing, usually stimulated him to the point that he saw hallucinatory sights. "Goats from the *banlieue*, gangplanks, douche bags, safety belts, iron trusses, *passerelles* and *sauterelles* floated before my glazed eyeballs, together with headless fowl, beribboned antlers, rusty sewing machines, dripping ikons and other unbelievable phenomena." Apart from the modern junk this could be the surrealistic world of Hieronymus Bosch.

Big Sur and the Oranges of Hieronymus Bosch also tells of his last evening in Paris, his farewell dinner with Moricand

and his final, solitary visit to Montparnasse. In the drizzling rain he stopped off for a drink, alone again as he had been so many years before when he first arrived. His departure seems an anticlimax, but he intended to return. He was going off to Greece to visit Durrell, who had been inviting him for two years, but Miller had constantly postponed the trip, content with his routine in the Villa Seurat and determined to finish *Tropic of Capricorn.* When it was published at last, in May 1939, he felt free to take a "sabbatical year," left Paris the following month, and sailed from Marseilles on July 14, 1939. When the war broke out, he was forced to return to America.

As Perlès says in his biography, "Paris never wore off." Back in his native land Miller became a permanent expatriate. Not only did he loathe America as much as ever, but wherever he went, whatever he saw and did, reminded him of Paris and left him terribly homesick. Memories of France turn up constantly in his later writings. In 1946, with the war over but the postwar prospect none too bright, he sat down to write "Remember to Remember," a long evocative essay about the French provinces and their capital. Here he dwells lovingly on the flavor, the ambiance, the wealth and variety of the garden of France, and the inexhaustible charm of the city.

In 1946 he saw clearly what he had not seen at the time, how much those first two years there had meant to him. "I was so desperately hungry not only for the physical and the sensual, for human warmth and understanding, but also for inspiration and illumination. During the dark years in Paris all these needs were answered. I was never lonely, no matter how miserable my condition. To be a prisoner of the streets, as I was for a long time, was a perpetual recreation. I did not need an address as long as the streets were there free to be roamed. There are scarcely any streets in Paris I did not get to know. On every one of them I could erect a tablet commemorating in letters of gold some rich new experience, some deep realization, some moment of illumination."

He remembered the little everyday details, the look of an

ordinary street in the morning, the faded façades of houses, the sparrows chirping, the smell of fresh bread. Most of the time during "those ten glorious years" was spent in unexciting ways, yet he found an extraordinary satisfaction in the commonplace. "I treasured the little menus written out by hand each day. I liked the waitresses even though they were slatternly often and bad tempered. To see the bicycle cops patrolling in pairs at night always gave me a thrill. I adored the patches in the old carpets which covered the worn stairs in the cheap hotels. The way the street cleaner went about his task fascinated me. The faces of the people in the Metro never ceased to intrigue me, as did also their gestures, their conversation."

Above all Paris was a city of writers and artists. Bookshops, art galleries, the very streets told of a creative past and present. "One needs no artificial stimulation, in Paris, to create. The atmosphere is saturated with creation. One has to make an effort to avoid being over-stimulated." The Villa Seurat, where he lived for almost five years, was named after an artist of the past and provided an ideal setting for those of the present. "The whole street is given up to quiet, joyous work. Every house contains a writer, painter, musician, sculptor, dancer, or actor. It is such a quiet street and yet there is such activity going on, silently, becomingly, should I not say reverently too? This is how it is on my street, but there are hundreds of such streets in Paris. There is a constant army of artists at work, the largest of any city in the world. This is what makes Paris, this vast group of men and women devoted to the things of the spirit. This is what animates the city, makes it the magnet of the cultural world."

ACKNOWLEDGMENTS

Much information has come from manuscript sources and from interviews, notably of Alice Toklas, Slater Brown, Man Ray, Virgil Thomson, Roy Harris, Henry Miller, and Walter Lowenfels. For permission to quote unpublished materials I am indebted to Marion Morehouse Cummings, John Dos Passos, Virgil Thomson, Henry Miller, and the Gertrude Stein Collection, Yale University Library. Mrs. J. Sibley Watson Jr. graciously invited me to see her collection of paintings by E. E. Cummings. George Stade and F. W. Dupee kindly allowed me free use of the letters of E. E. Cummings which they were editing for publication. Among librarians Donald Gallup of the Yale Collection of American Literature, Howard C. Rice Jr. of the Princeton University Library, and Brooke Whiting of the University of California at Los Angeles were particularly helpful. Gertrude Rosenthal literally opened the doors of the Baltimore Museum of Art to me. My friend Bernard Sinsheimer faithfully did research for me in Paris.

To preserve me from error the following read portions of this book in manuscript: Slater Brown, Nicolai Cikovsky Jr., S. Foster Damon, John Dos Passos, Donald Gallup, Robert U. Nelson, David Sanders, Virgil Thomson, and Annette Smith. Daniel Aaron and Esther Wagner read the entire manuscript, offered indispensable advice, and sustained my morale.

For their assistance with this new edition I am indebted to Robert Bertholf, Margot Cutter, Elizabeth H. Dos Passos, James

D. Hart, Lois Sprigg Hazell, A. Walton Litz, Townsend Ludington, Richard M. Ludwig, Juliet Man Ray, and Robert Potter.

To all of these and to all others who contributed to this book by their assistance, cooperation, and encouragement I give warm thanks.

I also wish to thank the following for permission to quote or reproduce materials which they control:

The Cone Collection, The Baltimore Museum of Art, for photographs of Gertrude, Leo, and Michael Stein, for the portraits of Gertrude Stein by Lipchitz and Vallotton, and the portrait of Leo Stein by Picasso.

The Metropolitan Museum of Art, Bequest of Gertrude Stein, 1946, for the portrait of Gertrude Stein by Picasso.

The San Francisco Museum of Art for the photograph of Matisse painting Michael Stein.

The Yale University Library for Picabia's portrait of Gertrude Stein and Carl Van Vechten's photograph of Anaïs Nin.

Man Ray for his *Self-Portrait*, *Object of Destruction*, *Clock Wheels*, and for photographs of himself, George Antheil, Gertrude Stein, and Alice Toklas.

The Yale University Art Gallery, Collection Société Anonyme, for a copy of Man Ray's *Clock Wheels*.

The Sylvia Beach Collection, Princeton University Library, for photographs of Sylvia Beach, Ernest Hemingway, John Dos Passos, and George Antheil.

The James Joyce Collection, Lockwood Memorial Library, the State University of New York at Buffalo, for the photograph of Ezra Pound, John Quinn, Ford Madox Ford, and James Joyce.

Miss Therese Bonney for the photographs of Virgil Thomson with Gertrude Stein and Virgil Thomson with Herbert Elwell, Walter Piston, and Aaron Copland.

Virgil Thomson for the photograph of a scene from *Four Saints in Three Acts*.

Brassaï for the photograph of Henry Miller.

BIBLIOGRAPHY

I. GERTRUDE STEIN

Barr, Alfred H., Jr. *Matisse, His Art and His Public.* New York: Museum of Modern Art, 1951.

Picasso, Fifty Years of His Art. New York: Museum of Modern Art, 1956.

Brinnin, John Malcolm. *The Third Rose: Gertrude Stein and Her World.* Boston: Atlantic, Little, Brown, 1959.

Brooks, Van Wyck. *Opinions of Oliver Allston.* New York: Dutton, 1941.

The Confident Years: 1881–1915. New York: Dutton, 1952.

Flanner, Janet (Genêt). *Men and Monuments.* New York: Harper, 1957.

Paris Journal: 1944–1965. Edited by William Shawn. New York: Atheneum, 1965.

Flaubert, Gustave. *Trois Contes.* Garden City, N.Y.: Doubleday, 1962. *Three Tales.* Translated by Walter F. Cobb. New York: New American Library, 1964.

Gallup, Donald, editor. *The Flowers of Friendship: Letters Written to Gertrude Stein.* New York: Knopf, 1953.

Haas, Robert B., and Donald C. Gallup. *A Catalogue of the Published and Unpublished Writings of Gertrude Stein.* New Haven: Yale University Library, 1941.

Haas, Robert Bartlett. "Gertrude Stein Talking–a Transatlantic Interview," *Uclan Review* (Summer 1962), pp. 3–11.

Hapgood, Hutchins. *A Victorian in the Modern World.* New York: Harcourt, Brace, 1939.

Jolas, Eugene, *et al. Testimony against Gertrude Stein.* Transition Pamphlet No. 1 (February 1935).

Kahnweiler, Daniel-Henry. *Juan Gris, His Life and Work.* London: Lund Humphries, 1947.

Introduction to *Painted Lace and Other Pieces* by Gertrude Stein. New Haven: Yale University Press, 1955.

Luhan, Mabel Dodge. *European Experiences.* New York: Harcourt, Brace, 1935. *Movers and Shakers.* New York: Harcourt, Brace, 1936.

Olivier, Fernande. *Picasso et Ses Amis.* Paris: Stock, 1933. *Picasso and His Friends.* Translated by Jane Miller. New York: Appleton-Century, 1965.

Pollack, Barbara. *The Collectors: Dr. Claribel and Miss Etta Cone.* Indianapolis: Bobbs-Merrill, 1962.

Raynal, Maurice. "*Le Banquet Rousseau,*" *Les Soirées de Paris* (Jan. 15, 1914), pp. 69–72.

Reid, B. L. *Art by Subtraction: A Dissenting Opinion of Gertrude Stein.* Norman: University of Oklahoma Press, 1958.

Saarinen, Aline B. *The Proud Possessors.* New York: Random House, 1958.

Sawyer, Julian. *Gertrude Stein: A Bibliography.* New York: Arrow Editions, 1940.

Sprigge, Elizabeth. *Gertrude Stein: Her Life and Her Work.* New York: Harper, 1957.

Stein, Gertrude. *Three Lives.* New York: Grafton Press, 1909.

Tender Buttons. New York: Claire Marie, 1914.

Geography and Plays. Boston: The Four Seas, 1922.

The Making of Americans. Paris: Contact Editions, 1925.

Composition as Explanation. London: Hogarth Press, 1926.

The Autobiography of Alice B. Toklas. New York: Harcourt, Brace, 1933.

Portraits and Prayers. New York: Random House, 1934.

Lectures in America. New York: Random House, 1935.

Picasso. New York: Scribner's, 1939.

Paris France. New York: Scribner's, 1940.

What Are Masterpieces. Los Angeles: Conference Press, 1940.

Things as They Are. Pawlet, Vt.: Banyan Press, 1951.

Stein, Leo. *Appreciation: Painting, Poetry and Prose.* New York: Crown, 1947.

Journey Into the Self: Being the Letters, Papers & Journals of Leo Stein. Edited by Edmund Fuller. New York: Crown, 1950.

Sutherland, Donald. *Gertrude Stein: A Biography of Her Work.* New Haven: Yale University Press, 1951.

Sypher, Wylie. *Rococo to Cubism in Art and Literature.* New York: Random House, 1960.

Toklas, Alice B. *The Alice B. Toklas Cook Book.* New York: Harper, 1954.

What is Remembered. New York: Holt, Rinehart and Winston, 1963.

Van Vechten, Carl. Introduction and Notes, *Selected Writings of Gertrude Stein.* New York: Random House, 1946.

Fragments From an Unwritten Autobiography. 2 vols. New Haven: Yale University Library, 1955.

Vollard, Ambroise. *Recollections of a Picture Dealer.* London: Constable, 1936.

Williams, William Carlos. *Selected Essays of William Carlos Williams.* New York: Random House, 1954.

Wilson, Edmund. *Axel's Castle.* New York: Scribner's, 1931.

II. E. E. CUMMINGS AND JOHN DOS PASSOS

"Announcement," *The Dial* (January 1926), pp. 84–88.

Apollinaire, Guillaume. *Oeuvres Complètes.* Edited by Michel Decaudin. Paris: André Balland et Jacques Lecat, 1966.

Astre, Georges-Albert. *Thèmes et Structures dans l'Oeuvre de John Dos Passos.* 2 vols. Paris: Lettres Modernes, 1956.

Barbusse, Henri. *Le Feu.* Paris: Flammarion, 1916. *Under Fire: The Story of a Squad.* Translated by Fitzwater Wray. New York: Dutton, 1917.

Baum, S. V. *EΣTI: E. E. Cummings and the Critics.* East Lansing: Michigan State University Press, 1962.

Cendrars, Blaise. *Panama, or The Adventures of My Seven Uncles.* Translated and illustrated by John Dos Passos. New York: Harper, 1931.

Selected Writings of Blaise Cendrars. Edited with a critical introduction by Walter Albert. New York: New Directions, 1966.

Cowley, Malcolm. *Blue Juniata.* New York: Jonathan Cape & Harrison Smith, 1921.

Exile's Return. New York: Viking, 1951. [Originally published 1934.]

Cummings, E. Estlin, *et al. Eight Harvard Poets.* New York: Lawrence J. Gomme, 1917.

Cummings, E. E. *The Enormous Room.* New York: Modern Library, 1934. [Originally published 1922.]

CIOPW. New York: Covici, Friede, 1931.

i: Six Non-Lectures. Cambridge: Harvard University Press, 1953.

Poems: 1923–1954. New York: Harcourt, Brace, 1954.

A Miscellany Revised. Edited by George J. Firmage. New York: October House, 1965.

Damon, S. Foster. *Amy Lowell.* Boston: Houghton Mifflin, 1935.

Dos Passos, John. *One Man's Initiation—1917.* London: Allen & Unwin, 1920. Reprinted as *First Encounter.* New York: Philosophical Library, 1945.

Three Soldiers. New York: Doran, 1921.

A Pushcart at the Curb. New York: Doran, 1922.

Orient Express. New York: Harper, 1927.

1919. New York: Harcourt, Brace, 1932.

U.S.A. New York: Harcourt, Brace, 1938.

The Theme Is Freedom. New York: Dodd, Mead, 1956.

Mr. Wilson's War. Garden City, N.Y.: Doubleday, 1962.

Occasions and Protests. Regnery, 1964.

The Best Times: An Informal Memoir. New York: New American Library, 1966.

Fenton, Charles A. "Ambulance Drivers in France and Italy: 1914–1918," *American Quarterly* (Winter 1951), pp. 326–343.

Firmage, George J. *E. E. Cummings: A Bibliography.* Middletown, Conn.: Wesleyan University Press, 1960.

Grossman, D. Jon. *E. E. Cummings.* Paris: Pierre Seghers, 1966.

Hall, Donald. "T. S. Eliot: The Art of Poetry I," *Paris Review* (Spring–Summer 1959), pp. 46–70.

Hemingway, Ernest. Introduction to *Men at War: The Best War Stories of All Time.* New York: Crown, 1942.

Holder, Alan. *Three Voyagers in Search of Europe: A Study of Henry James, Ezra Pound, and T. S. Eliot.* Philadelphia: University of Pennsylvania Press, 1966.

Howarth, Herbert. *Notes on Some Figures Behind T. S. Eliot.* Boston: Houghton Mifflin, 1964.

Lowell, Amy. "The New Manner in Modern Poetry," *New Republic* (March 4, 1916), pp. 124–125.

Norman, Charles. *The Magic-Maker: E. E. Cummings.* New York: Macmillan, 1958.

Ezra Pound. New York: Macmillan, 1960.

E. E. Cummings: The Magic Maker. New York: Duell, Sloan & Pearce, 1964.

Peeters, Georges. "How Cocteau Managed a Champion," *Sports Illustrated* (March 2, 1964), pp. 66–72.

Potter, Jack. *A Bibliography of John Dos Passos.* Chicago: Normandie House, 1950.

Pound, Ezra. *Instigations of Ezra Pound.* New York: Boni and Liveright, 1920.

The Letters of Ezra Pound, 1907–1941. Edited by D. D. Paige. New York: Harcourt, Brace, 1950.

Shattuck, Roger. *The Banquet Years: The Arts in France, 1885–1918.* Garden City, N.Y.: Doubleday, 1961.

Steegmuller, Francis. *Apollinaire: Poet Among the Painters.* New York: Farrar, Straus, 1963.

Tate, Allen. "Random Thoughts on the 1920's," *Minnesota Review* (Fall 1960), pp. 46–56.

Taupin, René. *L'Influence du Symbolisme sur la Poésie Américaine (de 1910 à 1920).* Paris: Champion, 1929.

Williams, William Carlos. *The Autobiography of William Carlos Williams.* New York: Random House, 1951.

Wrenn, John H. *John Dos Passos.* New York: Twayne, 1961.

III. MAN RAY

Balakian, Anna. *Surrealism: the Road to the Absolute.* New York: Noonday Press, 1951.

Barr, Alfred H., Jr., editor. *Fantastic Art, Dada, Surrealism.* New York: Museum of Modern Art, 1936.

Baur, John I. H. *Revolution and Tradition in Modern American Art.* Cambridge: Harvard University Press, 1951.

Belz, Carl I. "Man Ray and New York Dada," *The Art Journal* (Spring 1964), pp. 207–213.

Brown, Milton W. *American Painting from the Armory Show to the Depression.* Princeton: Princeton University Press, 1955.

The Story of the Armory Show. New York: Joseph H. Hirshhorn Foundation, 1963.

Collection of the Société Anonyme: Museum of Modern Art 1920. New Haven: Yale University Art Gallery, 1950.

Cubism: Its Impact in the USA, 1910–1930. Albuquerque: University of New Mexico, 1967.

Jean, Marcel. *The History of Surrealist Painting.* Translated by Simon Watson Taylor. New York: Grove Press, 1960.

Josephson, Matthew. *Life Among the Surrealists.* New York: Holt, Rinehart and Winston, Inc., 1962.

Knight, Arthur. *The Liveliest Art.* New York: Macmillan, 1957.

Lebel, Robert. *Marcel Duchamp.* Translated by George Heard Hamilton. New York: Grove Press, 1959.

Levy, Julien. *Surrealism.* New York: Black Sun Press, 1936.

Man Ray. Los Angeles: Los Angeles County Museum of Art, 1966.

Motherwell, Robert, editor. *The Dada Painters and Poets.* New York: Wittenborn, Schultz, 1951.

Nadeau, Maurice. *The History of Surrealism.* Translated by Richard Howard with an introduction by Roger Shattuck. New York: Macmillan, 1965.

Newhall, Beaumont. *The History of Photography.* New York: Museum of Modern Art, 1949.

Norton, Louise. "The Richard Mutt Case," *The Blind Man* (May 1917), pp. 5–6.

[Prin, Alice.] *Les Souvenirs de Kiki.* Paris: Henri Broca, 1929.

Kiki's Memoirs. Translated by Samuel Putnam with an introduction by Ernest Hemingway. Paris: Black Manikin Press, 1930.

Ray, Man. *Les Champs Délicieux.* Paris: Société Générale d'Imprimerie et d'Edition, 1922.

Revolving Doors, 1916–1917. Paris: Editions Surréalistes, 1926.

Photographs, 1920–1934, Paris. Hartford, Conn.: James Thrall Soby, 1934.

Self Portrait. Boston: Atlantic, Little, Brown, 1963.

Richter, Hans. *Dada: Art and Anti-Art.* New York: McGraw-Hill, 1965.

Rosenblum, Robert. *Cubism and Twentieth-Century Art.* New York: Abrams, 1961.

Sanouillet, Michel. *Dada à Paris.* Paris: Jean-Jacques Pauvert, 1965.

391: Revue Publiée de 1917 à 1924 par Francis Picabia. Edited by Michel Sanouillet. Paris: Le Terrain Vague, 1960.

Verkauf, Willy, editor. *Dada: Monograph of a Movement.* New York: George Wittenborn, 1957.

Waldberg, Patrick. "Bonjour Monsieur Man Ray!" *Quadrum* (1959), pp. 91–102.

Surrealism. New York: McGraw-Hill, 1965.

Weitz, William C. *The Art of Assemblage*. New York: Museum of Modern Art, 1961.

IV. ERNEST HEMINGWAY

Anderson, Margaret. *My Thirty Years' War*. New York: Covici, Friede, 1930.

Les Années Vingt: Les Ecrivains Américains à Paris et Leurs Amis 1920–1930. Paris: Centre Culturel Américain, 1959.

Baker, Carlos. *Hemingway: The Writer as Artist*. Princeton: Princeton University Press, 1963.

Beach, Sylvia. *Shakespeare and Company*. New York: Harcourt, Brace, 1959.

Bell, Millicent. "The Black Sun Press: 1927 to the Present," *Books at Brown* (January 1955), pp. 2–24.

Bishop, John Peale. *The Collected Essays of John Peale Bishop*. Edited with an introduction by Edmund Wilson. New York: Scribner's, 1948.

[Charters, James.] Jimmie the Barman. *This Must Be the Place: Memoirs of Montparnasse*. Edited by Morrill Cody with an introduction by Ernest Hemingway. London: Herbert Joseph, 1934.

Cohn, Louis Henry. *A Bibliography of the Works of Ernest Hemingway*. New York: Random House, 1931.

Crosby, Caresse. *The Passionate Years*. New York: Dial Press, 1953.

Dahlberg, Edward. "Beautiful Failures," *New York Times Book Review* (Jan. 15, 1967), pp. 4, 36, 38–40.

Ellmann, Richard. *James Joyce*. New York: Oxford University Press, 1959.

Fenton, Charles A. *The Apprenticeship of Ernest Hemingway: The Early Years*. New York: Farrar, Straus and Cudahy, 1954.

Fitzgerald, F. Scott. *The Letters of F. Scott Fitzgerald*. Edited by Andrew Turnbull. New York: Scribner's, 1963.

Ford, Ford Madox. Introduction to *A Farewell to Arms* by Ernest Hemingway. New York: Modern Library, 1932.

Introduction to *Transatlantic Stories*. New York: Dial Press, 1926.

It Was the Nightingale. Philadelphia: Lippincott, 1933.

Letters of Ford Madox Ford. Edited by Richard M. Ludwig. Princeton: Princeton University Press, 1965.

Galantière, Lewis. "There Is Never Any End to Paris," *New York Times Book Review* (May 10, 1964), pp. 1, 26.

Gallup, Donald C. "The Making of the Making of Americans," *The New Colophon* (1950), pp. 54–74.

Goldring, Douglas. *The Last Pre-Raphaelite: A Record of the Life and Writings of Ford Madox Ford*. London: Macdonald, 1948.

Hanneman, Audre. *Ernest Hemingway: A Comprehensive Bibliography*. Princeton: Princeton University Press, 1967.

Hemingway, Ernest. *Three Stories & Ten Poems.* Paris: Contact Publishing Company, 1923.

in our time. Paris: Three Mountains Press, 1924.

"The Soul of Spain with McAlmon and Bird the Publishers," *Der Querschnitt* (November 1924), p. 278.

In Our Time. New York: Boni and Liveright, 1925.

The Torrents of Spring. New York: Scribner's, 1926.

The Sun Also Rises. New York: Scribner's, 1926.

Men Without Women. New York: Scribner's, 1927.

Green Hills of Africa. New York: Scribner's, 1935.

The Fifth Column and the First Forty-Nine Stories. New York: Scribner's, 1938.

A Moveable Feast. New York: Scribner's, 1964.

By-Line: Ernest Hemingway: Selected Articles and Dispatches of Four Decades. Edited by William White. New York: Scribner's, 1967.

Hemingway, Mary. "The Making of the Book: A Chronicle and a Memoir," *New York Times Book Review* (May 10, 1964), pp. 26–27.

Hoffman, Frederick J., Charles Allen, and Carolyn F. Ulrich. *The Little Magazine: A History and a Bibliography.* Princeton: Princeton University Press, 1946.

Hoffman, Frederick J. *The Twenties: American Writing in the Postwar Decade.* New York: The Free Press, 1962.

Huddleston, Sisley. *Paris Salons, Cafés, Studios.* Philadelphia: Lippincott, 1928.

Jolas, Eugene. *I Have Seen Monsters and Angels.* Paris: Transition Press, 1938.

Knoll, Robert E. *Robert McAlmon: Expatriate Publisher and Writer. University of Nebraska Studies,* New Series, No. 18 (August 1957).

Laney, Al. *Paris Herald: The Incredible Newspaper.* New York: Appleton-Century, 1947.

Lawrence, D. H. *The Collected Letters of D. H. Lawrence.* Vol. II. Edited with an introduction by Harry T. Moore. New York: Viking, 1962.

Lewis, Sinclair. "Self-Conscious America," *The American Mercury* (October 1925), pp. 129–139.

The Little Review (March 1914–May 1929).

Loeb, Harold. *The Way It Was.* New York: Criterion Books, 1959.

MacShane, Frank. *The Life and Work of Ford Madox Ford.* New York: Horizon Press, 1965.

McAlmon, Robert. *Being Geniuses Together.* London: Secker & Warburg, 1938.

McAlmon and the Lost Generation: A Self-Portrait. Edited with a commentary by Robert E. Knoll. Lincoln: University of Nebraska Press, 1962.

Poli, Bernard. *Ford Madox Ford and the Transatlantic Review.* Syracuse: Syracuse University Press, 1967.

Putnam, Samuel. *Paris Was Our Mistress: Memoirs of a Lost and Found Generation.* New York: Viking, 1947.

Rascoe, Burton. *We Were Interrupted.* Garden City, N.Y.: Doubleday, 1947.

Ross, Lillian. *Portrait of Hemingway.* New York: Simon and Schuster, 1961.

Schorer, Mark. *Sinclair Lewis: An American Life.* New York: McGraw-Hill, 1961.

Stearns, Harold. "Apologia of an Expatriate," *Scribner's Magazine* (March 1929), pp. 338–341.

The Street I Know. New York: Lee Furman, 1935.

Strout, Cushing. *The American Image of the Old World.* New York: Harper & Row, 1963.

This Quarter (Spring 1925–December 1932).

Transatlantic Review (January–December 1924).

Transition (April 1927–Spring 1938).

Wilson, Edmund. *The Shores of Light: A Literary Chronicle of the Twenties and Thirties.* New York: Farrar, Straus and Young, 1952.

Young, Philip. *Ernest Hemingway: A Reconsideration.* University Park: Pennsylvania State Press, 1966.

V. VIRGIL THOMSON

Antheil, George. *Bad Boy of Music.* Garden City, N.Y.: Doubleday, 1945.

Collaer, Paul. *A History of Modern Music.* Translated from the French by Sally Abeles. Cleveland: World Publishing Company, 1961.

Copland, Aaron. *Our New Music.* New York: McGraw-Hill, 1941.

Copland on Music. Garden City, N.Y.: Doubleday, 1960.

Damrosch, Walter. *My Musical Life.* New York: Scribner's, 1923.

Dictionary of Modern Ballet. Translated from the French by John Montague and Peggie Cochrane. New York: Tudor Publishing Company, 1959.

Goss, Madeleine. *Modern Music Makers: Contemporary American Composers.* New York: Dutton, 1952.

Harris, Roy. "What the Library of Congress Means to American Composers," *Musical Courier* (May 19, 1934), pp. 6, 21.

"Perspective at Forty," *Magazine of Art* (November 1939), pp. 638–639, 667–671.

Hoover, Kathleen, and John Cage. *Virgil Thomson: His Life and Music.* New York: Thomas Yoseloff, 1959.

Imbs, Bravig. *Confessions of Another Young Man.* New York: Henkle-Yewdale House, 1936.

Joyce, James. *Letters of James Joyce.* Edited by Stuart Gilbert. New York: Viking, 1957.

Pound, Ezra. *Antheil and the Treatise on Harmony with Supplementary Notes by Ezra Pound.* Chicago: Covici, 1927.

Stein, Gertrude. *Operas and Plays.* Paris: Plain Edition, 1932.

Four Saints in Three Acts: An Opera To Be Sung. Introduction by Carl Van Vechten. New York: Random House, 1934.

Everybody's Autobiography. New York. Random House, 1937.

Stravinsky, Igor. *Stravinsky: An Autobiography.* New York: Simon and Schuster, 1936.

Thomson, Virgil. *The State of Music.* New York: Morrow, 1939.

The Musical Scene. New York: Knopf, 1945.

The Art of Judging Music. New York: Knopf, 1948.

Music Right and Left. New York: Holt, 1951

Preface and Notes to Gertrude Stein, *Bee Time Vine and Other Pieces [1913–1917].* New Haven: Yale University Press, 1953.

Virgil Thomson. New York: Knopf, 1966.

VI. HENRY MILLER

Americans Abroad: An Anthology. Edited by Peter Neagoe. The Hague: Servire Press, 1932.

Céline, Louis-Ferdinand. *Voyage au Bout de la Nuit.* Paris: Denoël et Steele, 1932. *Journey to the End of the Night.* Translated by John H. P. Marks. New York: New Directions, 1934.

Cendrars, Blaise. "*Un Ecrivain Américain Nous Est Né*," in *Henry Miller and the Critics.* Carbondale, Ill.: Southern Illinois University Press, 1963.

Durrell, Lawrence and Henry Miller. *A Private Correspondence.* Edited by George Wickes, New York: Dutton, 1963.

Fraenkel, Michael. "The Genesis of the *Tropic of Cancer*," in *The Happy Rock: A Book About Henry Miller.* Berkeley, Calif.: Bern Porter, 1945.

Miller, Henry. *Tropic of Cancer.* Paris: Obelisk Press, 1934.

Aller Retour New York. Paris: Obelisk Press, 1935.

Black Spring. Paris: Obelisk Press, 1936.

Money and How It Gets That Way. Paris: Booster Publications, 1938.

Max and the White Phagocytes. Paris: Obelisk Press, 1938.

Tropic of Capricorn. Paris: Obelisk Press, 1939.

The Wisdom of the Heart. New York: New Directions, 1941.

Henry Miller Miscellanea. San Mateo, Calif.: Bern Porter, 1945.

Remember to Remember. New York: New Directions, 1947.

The Books in My Life. New York: New Directions, 1952.

Quiet Days in Clichy. Photographs by Brassaï. Paris: Olympia Press, 1956.

The Time of the Assassins: A Study of Rimbaud. New York: New Directions, 1956.

Big Sur and the Oranges of Hieronymus Bosch. New York: New Directions, 1957.

The Henry Miller Reader. Edited by Lawrence Durrell. New York: New Directions, 1959.

Henry Miller Letters to Anaïs Nin. Edited by Gunther Stuhlmann. New York: Putnam, 1965.

Moore, Thomas H. *Bibliography of Henry Miller*. Minneapolis: Henry Miller Literary Society, 1961.

Nin, Anaïs. *House of Incest*. Paris: Siana Editions, 1936.

The Diary of Anaïs Nin, 1931–1934. Edited with an introduction by Gunther Stuhlmann. New York: Swallow Press and Harcourt, Brace & World, 1966.

Osborn, Richard G. "No. 2 Rue Auguste Bartholdi," in *The Happy Rock: A Book About Henry Miller*. Berkeley, Calif.: Bern Porter, 1945.

Perlès, Alfred. *My Friend, Henry Miller*. London: Neville Spearman, 1955.

Widmer, Kingsley. *Henry Miller*. New York: Twayne, 1963.

Index